Hedge Funds in Emerging Markets

Hedge Funds are among the most innovative and controversial of financial market institutions. Largely exempt from regulation and shrouded in secrecy, they are credited as having improved efficiency and adding liquidity to financial markets, but also having severely destabilised markets following the Asian financial crisis and the near-collapse of Long-Term Capital Management.

De Brouwer presents a nuanced and balanced account to what is becoming an increasingly politicised and hysterical discussion of the subject. Part I explains the workings of hedge funds. Part II focuses on the activities of macro hedge funds and proprietary trading desks in east Asia in 1997 and 1998, with case-study material from Hong Kong, Indonesia, Malaysia, Singapore, Australia and New Zealand. Part III of the book looks at the future of hedge funds, their role for institutional investors, and policy proposals to limit their destabilising effects.

GORDON DE BROUWER is Professor of Economics at the Australian National University, having previously worked at the Reserve Bank of Australia. He is the author of numerous books and journal articles, including *Financial Integration in East Asia* (CUP 1999). He is widely regarded as one of the leading young economists in international economics.

Hedge Funds in Emerging Markets

Gordon de Brouwer

Australian National University

CAMBRIDGE UNIVERSITY PRESS
Cambridge, New York, Melbourne, Madrid, Cape Town, Singapore,
São Paulo, Delhi, Dubai, Tokyo, Mexico City

Cambridge University Press
The Edinburgh Building, Cambridge CB2 8RU, UK

Published in the United States of America by Cambridge University Press, New York

www.cambridge.org
Information on this title: www.cambridge.org/9780521168670

First published 2001
First paperback edition 2010

A catalogue record for this publication is available from the British Library

ISBN 978-0-521-80233-8 Hardback
ISBN 978-0-521-16867-0 Paperback

Contents

Figures

Tables

Preface

My interest in hedge funds in emerging markets was sparked by my involvement in the Study Group on Market Dynamics, which reported to the Financial Stability Forum Working Group on Highly Leveraged Institutions, in 1999. At the time I was Chief Manager, International Markets and Relations, at the Reserve Bank of Australia, a position I left when I became Professor of Economics at the Australian National University in January 2000.

Much of the information used in this book was collected at that time, in visits to Auckland, Hong Kong, Johannesburg, Kuala Lumpur, New York, Singapore, Sydney and Wellington. A lot of important information was also gathered after that, in visits as an academic to Bangkok, Singapore and Tokyo and in subsequent conversations with market participants and officials.

It is important to stress at the outset that I have not used confidential information collected while I was a central bank official or discussed official meetings in this book. I have consulted widely with officials from relevant national and international authorities about the material presented here, and I am confident that I have not breached any commercial or official confidence. This is not intended to implicate these people; not everyone I consulted necessarily agrees with my analysis and views.

I am deeply indebted to many people for their advice, assistance, information and support in writing this book. It could never have been written but for the willingness of hundreds of market participants and officials to talk, often frankly, about the activities of hedge funds, banks and securities companies in financial markets in 1997 and 1998.

I am grateful in the first instance to my former colleagues at the Reserve Bank of Australia, especially Ric Battelino, Stephen Grenville, Philip Lowe, Bob Rankin and Mike Sinclair. I am deeply indebted to the other members of the FSF Study Group on Market Dynamics, Charles Adams (International Monetary Fund, convenor), Hervé Ferhani

(Banque de France), Dino Kos (Federal Reserve Bank of New York), Julia Leung (Hong Kong Monetary Authority), Robert McCauley (Bank for International Settlements, Hong Kong Representative Office), Anthony Richards (International Monetary Fund), Nouriel Roubini (US Treasury, now New York University), Andrew Sykes (Financial Services Authority, UK) and Iwao Toriumi (Bank of Japan).

I am also grateful to Ashwin Rattan and the staff at Cambridge University Press for their support and professionalism, and to Malhar Nabar for excellent research assistance in writing Chapter 8. I received helpful comments from fellow academics, especially Peter Drysdale, Ross Garnaut, Adrian Pagan and David Vines.

I am most deeply grateful to Michael Sparks and Jakob Spink for their support and endurance during the months I spent travelling collecting the information used in this book and the months writing it up. This book is dedicated to them.

1 The issues

"Stick to the boat, Pip, or by Lord, I won't pick you up if you jump; mind that. We can't afford to lose whales by the likes of you; a whale would sell for thirty times what you would, Pip, in Alabama. Bear that in mind, and don't jump any more." Hereby, perhaps Stubb indirectly hinted, that though man loved his fellow, yet man is a money-making animal, which propensity too often interferes with his benevolence.

Moby Dick by Herman Melville, Chapter 93

Hedge funds are private collective investment vehicles for the very rich and, more recently, entities like university endowments, pension funds and insurance companies. They are designed to make money – and the more of it the better – which they do by taking positions on perceived price discrepancies in financial markets, although they have widely varying appetites for risk. They are institutions that tightly guard their privacy, which, combined with the fact that they are largely exempt from regulation, means that very little is known about them. Along with other institutions that sometimes engage in activities similar to them – like the proprietary trading desks of banks and securities companies – they are also called 'highly leveraged institutions' (HLIs), although this term can be misleading since they vary substantially in their use of credit. They are managed by some of the brightest and most creative people in the finance industry.

The first hedge fund was established in 1949 and they now number in the thousands. The growth of the hedge-fund sector has closely followed the liberalisation, development and internationalisation of financial markets, since this process has given rise to a system of large, flexible-price asset markets which provide the opportunity to bet on price changes. Such speculation provides two key benefits. First, it enables households and firms to shift financial risk to other entities which want to hold that risk. An exporter who wants to eliminate the risk that the currency will appreciate before he receives his foreign-exchange receipts, for example, can sell that foreign exchange now for delivery at some time in the future. A process of intermediation follows whereby banks trade the foreign-

1

exchange risk until someone who wants the exposure – typically a speculator – can get it. The second advantage of speculation is that it provides depth and innovation to markets and may shift financial prices to their fundamental or fair value over time.

Hedge funds are an integral part of this process, and their development and growth goes hand in hand with the development and growth of large, internationalised flexible-price financial markets. They are widely regarded by market participants and regulators alike as among the most innovative of institutions in financial markets, and are widely credited with improving efficiency in, and adding liquidity to, the gamut of financial markets. They tend to lead the development of techniques and products in financial markets, and are widely seen as 'The Future'. Given that diversity and innovation in the financial sector are necessary for supporting both the development of business and long-term saving, institutions like hedge funds are one of the many important components underpinning sustainable economic growth.

But there are concerns that, under certain conditions, highly leveraged institutions can cause material damage to financial systems and financial markets, with potentially serious adverse economic impact. As shown by the near-collapse of Long-Term Capital Management (LTCM) in the United States in September 1998, some highly leveraged institutions have the potential to generate systemic risks in financial markets and systems (President's Working Group on Financial Markets 1999). As shown by elements of the east Asian financial crisis, some highly leveraged institutions also have the potential at times to destabilise financial markets and cause overshooting of key financial prices, like exchange rates and stock prices, and economic dislocation (FSF Working Group on Highly Leveraged Institutions 2000).

There is a wide range of views about hedge funds and other HLIs. The debate about them has become intensely politicised, which has conditioned policy responses in both developed and industrialised countries, and in east Asia and the United States, and led to the debate becoming highly polarised. There are those, on the one hand, who think that the benefits provided by hedge funds far outweigh any costs they may impose, and indeed dispute that hedge funds can cause serious systemic risk or damage to the integrity of financial markets at all.[1] Proponents of this view are inclined to say that speculation is necessarily stabilising. There are those, on the other hand, who think that hedge funds are a seriously destructive force in financial markets, and blame them for

---

[1] For example, see Baily, Farrell and Lund (2000).

undermining the rule of law and wreaking the havoc of the east Asian financial crisis.[2] Proponents of this view are inclined to say that speculation is necessarily destabilising.

The aim of this book is to provide some balance, nuance and middle ground in the debate. While hedge funds have become an essential feature of financial markets, and can make a substantial and important contribution to the continuing development of the financial sector and economic growth, they can also create vulnerabilities of which market practitioners and policy-makers alike need to be aware and to which they need to respond.

This book does not focus on systemic risk issues because they have been well covered elsewhere. The near-collapse of LTCM following the Russian debt default caused severe dislocation in US and emerging-market bond markets, and led to the Federal Reserve organising a creditor bail-out of LTCM and easing US monetary policy to accommodate the financial shock affecting the US financial markets. LTCM had extraordinarily large and concentrated positions in financial markets, made possible by virtually unlimited lending by its banks. Its positions were designed to exploit price discrepancies in a range of financial markets, but the size and leverage of these positions made the strategy vulnerable to shocks, as the Russian debt default revealed. This episode has shown the importance of proper counterparty risk management by banks and of proper risk assessment, especially of market and liquidity risks, by highly leveraged institutions. These have been the subject of considerable international policy discussion and action.[3]

What the book focuses on, rather, are the possible adverse effects some HLIs can have on market integrity, as shown by the experience in some east Asian financial markets in 1997 and 1998. This is controversial. To argue that HLIs can, under certain circumstances, materially undermine market integrity is not to argue that they were the cause of the crisis. The east Asian financial crisis was a complex phenomenon – its trigger was the deterioration in the Thai current-account deficit and pressure on the fixed exchange rate, but the severity of the crisis was exacerbated by large unhedged short-term borrowing in foreign currencies, weak banking and financial systems, policy errors by national governments and interna-

---

[2] This seems to be the view of the Malaysian Prime Minister, Mahathir Mohamad. He is quoted in Baily, Farrell and Lund (2000) as saying in January 1998: 'All these countries have spent 40 years trying to build up their economies and a moron like Soros comes along with a lot of money to speculate and ruin things.'

[3] See, for example, the reports by the President's Working Group on Financial Markets (1999), the Counterparty Risk Management Policy Group (1999, 2000), and the FSF Working Group on HLIs (2000).

tional organisations, excessive risk affinity followed by excessive risk aversion by international investors, and bouts of destabilising speculation by either residents or non-residents or sometimes both.[4] Nor is it to argue that hedge funds should be excluded from financial markets; they are a key source of liquidity and innovation, and, indeed, one argument of this book is that policy-makers do their countries a disservice if they think that the lesson from the crisis is that they should exclude speculators from their markets.

But the crisis has shown the possibility that, under certain conditions, some HLIs can damage the integrity of financial markets – that is, the fair and efficient formation of financial prices. This is evident in two respects. The first is that large and concentrated positions may have an undue and possibly destabilising influence on price dynamics in financial markets. Rapid adjustment of large positions can have a substantial impact on market prices, especially at times when liquidity in markets is thin. The effect can also be more subtle, with the presence of large players affecting decision making by other market participants, either encouraging them to mimic what they think the large players are doing, or to drop out of the market and hence not take contrary positions. This has the potential to generate overshooting in asset prices. These effects certainly occurred at times in east Asian financial markets in 1997 and 1998, and may or may not have been the intention of particular large players.

The second issue related to market integrity is that some macro hedge funds and proprietary trading desks of banks and securities firms appear to have engaged in highly aggressive trading tactics in east Asia in 1997 and 1998, designed explicitly to shift prices in a manner which helped the profitability of their positions. A number of incidents of this sort occurred in financial markets in Australia, Hong Kong, Malaysia and South Africa during 1998 (FSF Working Group on HLIs 2000). This marked a structural shift from such players being price-takers in markets, and adversely affected market efficiency.

These are serious issues but international policy cooperation in dealing with vulnerabilities to market integrity has not been forthcoming. This is partly because views about the seriousness of the issues differ between countries. There is a tendency, for example, for the authorities in major countries to downplay the impact of hedge funds on financial prices, perhaps reflecting their own experience that no market participant or set of participants is able to significantly affect markets as

---

[4] See, for example, Grenville (1998), Krugman (1998), Radelet and Sachs (1998) and de Brouwer (1999a).

deep and liquid as their own. This view should have been seriously challenged by the extraordinary fall in the dollar/yen exchange rate in October 1998, when the rate moved 15 per cent in 30 hours, and 25 per cent in a month, when hedge funds were forced to liquidate positions. This showed that liquidity, even in one of the world's largest foreign-exchange markets, is highly elastic, and that, in conditions of variable liquidity, large price changes can occur, either incidentally or by design. The reluctance of major countries to address issues of market integrity also lies partly in the perception that their interests may not be served by policy action. In particular, they appear to be concerned that measures to protect market integrity could adversely affect the operation of institutions based in, or operating from, their jurisdiction.

Structure of the book

This book has three parts. The first is background. Chapter 2 provides an explanation of what hedge funds are, and summarises published material on their performance. Hedge funds tend to be defined by regulators in terms of their legal structure or organisation, while they tend to be defined by market participants in terms of the strategy they use in financial markets. This provides two interesting 'cuts' at understanding hedge funds and what they do, and it shows just how heterogeneous hedge funds are. The strategies of macro hedge funds, which have been the funds of most relevance to the region in the past, are examined in relative detail.

The second part of the book, encompassing Chapters 3 to 8, focuses on the activities of macro hedge funds and proprietary trading desks in east Asia in 1997 and 1998. Chapter 3 provides an overview of some of the issues and reviews the events in east Asian financial markets in 1997 and 1998. It draws on the work of two major international reports.

The first is the study published by the IMF in 1998, which includes staff research into the structure and operation of hedge funds and an assessment of their activities in east Asia in 1997. Led by Barry Eichengreen and Donald Mathieson, the study has become a basic reference on hedge funds, and is often cited in support of the view that highly leveraged institutions pose no threat to financial stability or market integrity. While it contains much valuable analysis and insight, it has been overtaken by events and crucial aspects of the analysis now need reassessment.

The second is that published by the Financial Stability Forum (FSF) in 2000, which examined the issue of highly leveraged institutions in 1999, drawing mostly on the experience of financial markets in 1998.[5] The FSF Working Group on HLIs (2000) reported on the policy issues raised by the near-collapse of LTCM and the events in the financial markets of mid-sized economies in 1998.[6] It argued strongly for policy action on the systemic risks posed by HLIs but was mixed in its assessment of policy action on risks to market integrity. Nevertheless, it provides valuable detail about events in regional financial markets, and it sets out the basic issues of the effects of large and concentrated positions and highly aggressive action in already unsettled financial markets.

Chapters 4–6 examine in relative detail the experience of particular countries, or groups of countries, in the region. Chapter 4 examines the experience of Hong Kong, Chapter 5 examines the experience of Indonesia, Malaysia and Singapore, and Chapter 6 looks at what happened in Australia and New Zealand. These case studies offer a range of insights into the many diverse market activities and strategies of hedge funds, proprietary trading desks and other players, and show how private decision making is affected by recent experience and the policy environment. These chapters are structured in a similar way: after the economic context has been set, the price action in financial markets and the role of highly leveraged institutions are described, analysed and assessed. The cases studies draw on published material and interviews with officials and traders at relevant financial institutions, who, to preserve their anonymity, are referred to generally as 'market participants'.

Chapter 7 seeks to interpret the events in east Asian financial markets in terms of the insights provided by the academic literature on financial markets. Herding, market manipulation and multiple equilibria were all key features of east Asian financial markets in 1997 and 1998, and this chapter goes through key models for each of these topics. Three important policy insights flow from this exposition. First, while economists have conventionally argued that speculation is stabilising, it can in fact be destabilising and cause asset prices to deviate in both the short and medium term from their fundamental value.

Second, a crucial aspect for herding and multiple equilibria to occur in many models is an information asymmetry between players, with some participants having better information than others. This dovetails with

---

[5] The Financial Stability Forum comprises the finance ministers, central bank governors and securities exchange regulators of the G-7 nations (Canada, France, Germany, Italy, Japan, the United Kingdom and the United States), as well as central bank governors of Australia, Hong Kong, the Netherlands and Singapore.

[6] The Working Group established a Study Group on Market Dynamics to report to it. The Study Group examined financial markets in Australia, Hong Kong, Malaysia, New Zealand, Singapore and South Africa. Its report is Annex E of the Working Group report.

the experience of 1997 and 1998. The large macro hedge funds were widely regarded at the time as having the best analysis and understanding of the regions' economies and financial markets, with, in particular, an unrivalled understanding of the changing patterns of liquidity in markets. They also had information that everyone else wanted to know but could only guess at – knowledge of their own strategies and positions in markets. This was information that everyone in markets regarded as essential to predicting the immediate outlook for asset prices, especially exchange rates, and made them the focus for all other players, including the proprietary trading desks of banks.

Third, the literature on manipulation in financial markets has focused on stock prices and tended to ignore action-based and word-based manipulation because these have effectively been regulated out of existence in stock markets. But both these forms of manipulation are rife in foreign-exchange markets. If such attempts to influence prices are unacceptable in stock markets, surely they are also unacceptable in foreign-exchange markets.

Chapter 8 follows up on the issue of the size of HLI positions in east Asian markets in 1997 and 1998. A number of papers have argued that hedge fund positions can be inferred from aggregate returns data for individual funds, and have then concluded that these positions were either small or uncorrelated with changes in regional asset prices. This chapter argues that these assessments are premature and invalid. Not only do many of the estimates not make sense, but the method is fundamentally flawed on a number of counts. In particular, the reliability of the method is tested by using it to infer positions from an artificial portfolio where the true positions are known. The inferred positions differ substantially from the actual positions: they are misleading with respect to the magnitude, sign and the timing of the true positions, and they give false signals about changes in the true position. The implication is that there is no substitute for the facts.

The third part of the book looks forward. Chapter 9 argues that hedge funds have become integral and important institutions in financial markets and are here to stay. Hedge funds are becoming more important to other institutional investors, like pension funds and insurance companies, which are seeking diversified returns. They are also vital to banks, not just in the direct business they provide, but also because they are increasingly important to banks' asset management operations, which, among other things, provide seed capital to new funds. While the macro hedge fund sector declined somewhat in 2000, it is primed to return – and probably strongly – once the sector has finished restructuring.

Chapter 9 also examines some key policy proposals. It argues for a clear break between thinking about what happened in regional financial markets in 1997 and 1998 and thinking about how to deal with what happened. Policies geared to solve the problems of the past may just create a new set of problems, and policies directed at particular categories of institutions are likely to lead to the creation of categories of other, unregulated institutions and may distract focus from other potential instabilities. In short, policies need to be directed at limiting the activity of destabilising speculation, and not necessarily be focused on institutions like hedge funds.

If east Asia is to develop its regional financial markets fully, it needs to involve hedge funds. And for east Asia to obtain the full benefits of international openness, it needs to be integrated financially with the rest of the world. But the events of recent years have shown that speculation in financial markets can be destabilising and costly to people's well-being. Experience and academic insight indicate that destabilising speculation is more likely to occur when there is some vulnerability in the economic or policy structure, which is precisely the time when stabilising forces are needed.

The chapter assesses four policy proposals to limit destabilising speculation: greater disclosure of positions by unregulated entities, more stringent margining requirements for borrowers, a code of conduct for market participants, and some regulation of foreign-exchange transactions conducted through electronic broking. It argues that, if adopted, these proposals are better pursued through indirect rather than direct means. That is, regulation is probably more effective and less easy to evade if it works through already regulated entities, like banks, than by a new set of restrictions on largely unregulated entities.

These proposals are modest and will certainly not prevent all future crises, but they are a step forward. They are not, however, on the agenda of policy-makers. Without recognition by the major countries of the damage to market integrity that some HLIs can cause, and without international policy coordination to address them, countries in east Asia and elsewhere will adopt the risk-averse strategy of limiting financial integration and looking inwards, for national and perhaps regional solutions. A shift to autarky and insular regionalism is ultimately not in the long-term economic and strategic interests of the major countries, nor, indeed, of benefit to the global community.

2   What is a hedge fund?

This chapter sets out definitions of hedge funds in terms of their legal structure and in terms of the strategies they pursue. It reviews evidence on the number and size of hedge funds, as well as their performance as investment vehicles.

The term 'hedge fund' was first coined in 1949 to describe a private investment partnership set up by Alfred Winslow Jones which 'hedged' the risk in its operations by buying what it perceived to be undervalued stocks and 'short selling' (Box 1) what it perceived to be overvalued stocks, with the combination varying over time as Jones' assessment of market conditions changed.[1]

Box 1: *Short-selling*

Short-selling is the sale of an asset, such as a bond, equity or foreign currency, that the vendor does not own. The vendor first borrows the asset from another party, with the promise of repaying it back at some future time, and then sells it. If the price of the asset has fallen by the time the vendor is due to repay it to the lender, then he can buy it back in the market for less than he initially sold it. The profit is the selling price less the buying price and the cost of borrowing the asset.

This strategy effectively enabled Jones to secure good returns whether the market fell or rose. The use of gearing or leverage (Box 2) was also a crucial element in his strategy – it is implicit in the use of short-selling since this involves borrowing an asset in order to sell it. This combination of strategic, active management of sometimes leveraged positions by private partnerships in financial markets is the hallmark characteristic of a hedge fund. Since then, the number of hedge funds and the assets under their management have expanded rapidly, albeit not always uniformly.

Because they cover such a wide range of institutions and strategies, there is no standard definition of a hedge fund. There is also no legal

---

[1] See Caldwell (1995) and Chadha and Jansen (1998) for a history of hedge funds.

definition. Indeed, to a large extent, hedge funds are defined by what they are not, rather than what they are – they are collective investment groups or vehicles but they are not regulated institutional entities along the lines of mutual funds or pension funds. Accordingly, Sharma (1998) defines hedge funds as limited partnerships exempt from certain laws.

There are two main ways to describe hedge funds – either in terms of their legal structure or organisation, or in terms of their trading strategy in financial markets.

Box 2: *Leverage*

A fund can acquire assets either by using its own capital or by using borrowed funds. Leverage commonly refers to the use of debt to acquire assets. Leverage is usually expressed in terms of a ratio of assets to capital. For example, a ratio of 3 (that is, 3 to 1) means that one dollar of capital supports three dollars of assets, implying that the fund has two dollars of debt for each dollar of capital. This definition of leverage is called on-balance-sheet leverage, since assets, capital and debt (or liabilities) are all balance-sheet items – in a simplified balance sheet, assets are equal to capital and other liabilities. Hedge-fund data providers typically use the on-balance-sheet definition of leverage.

Leverage can also arise through off-balance-sheet transactions, such as short positions, repurchase agreements, and derivatives contracts. In a short sale, for example, a fund does not have an asset and corresponding liability on its balance sheet – it has borrowed the asset and then sold it – but it does have an exposure or a position which is 'off balance sheet'. It is a contingent liability in the sense that it is a future, not current, liability. This definition of leverage is called economic leverage and is a measure of risk. A fund may have little or no on-balance-sheet leverage but may have substantial economic leverage associated with its off-balance-sheet exposures. The amount of economic leverage obtained by a fund depends on the willingness of financial intermediaries to provide the credit underlying the off-balance-sheet transactions, the cost of leveraging, and the risk appetite of the fund itself. No comprehensive information about hedge funds' economic leverage is available.

Leverage can be important for a number of reasons. On-balance-sheet leverage allows a fund to boost its assets, and economic leverage enables a fund to boost its positions or exposures in financial markets. This can add depth and liquidity to a market. But it can also make these markets more vulnerable to sharp price movements when positions shift, and it can make positions vulnerable to changes in the credit intermediation process (Counterparty Risk Management Policy Group 2000). These vulnerabilities have the potential to adversely affect the stability of the whole financial system (President's Working Group on Financial Markets 1999).

Defining hedge funds by organisation

Some, particularly regulators, define hedge funds in terms of their *legal structure* or *organisation*. The President's Working Group on Financial Markets (1999: 1), for example, defined a hedge fund as 'any pooled investment vehicle that is privately organised, administered by professional investment managers, and not widely available to the public'.

Typically, hedge funds are limited partnerships or limited liability companies, they trade in financial instruments, they are not permitted to solicit funds from the public, and they are exempt from investor protection and (some) disclosure legislation. The minimum investment in a hedge fund ranges between $100,000 to $5 million, with $1 million common. As limited partnerships, managers also own capital in their fund, at least equal to the fund's minimum investment requirements. The main investors in hedge funds to date have been wealthy individuals or families and, to a lesser degree, university endowments and foundations. As discussed in Chapter 9, institutional investors are also investing in hedge funds.

Hedge funds charge high fees – 'incentive' fees of between 15 to 20 per cent on realised trading profits and 1 per cent annual management fees are standard. If a fund makes losses, not only do the fund's managers not receive the incentive fee, but they are not usually paid the incentive fee on later earnings until losses have been made up – so-called high watermark provisions. Some funds charge up-front entry fees as well. Investments in hedge funds are usually locked in for a specified period, or withdrawals are subject to advance notification, with three months being the most common. Individual investors in hedge funds in the United States number in the tens of thousands.

Most hedge funds use leverage, but the degree of leverage can vary enormously between hedge funds and between types of hedge fund (OECD 1999). The President's Working Group on Financial Markets (1999) reckons that most hedge funds have on-balance-sheet leverage ratios of less than two, suggesting that hedge funds support their asset base with a broadly even mix of capital and debt. Estimates by private data providers tend to be similar (Chadha and Jansen 1998). There is, however, substantial variation between hedge funds, with a dozen or so large hedge funds leveraging their capital more than 10 times. At September 1998, the highest ratio for on-balance-sheet leverage by a large fund was 37, although higher ratios have been reported at other times, up to 71 at the end of 1997 (President's Working Group on Financial Markets 1999). General estimates of economic leverage are not available.

This contrasts starkly with US mutual funds. Like hedge funds, they are also pooled investment vehicles. But, unlike hedge funds, US mutual funds are registered with the US Securities and Exchange Commission (SEC) and are incorporated under state law as corporations or business trusts. They are subject to a wide range of federal legislative restrictions on their activities and organisation. The management of mutual funds is subject to a board structure, at least 60 per cent of which must be from outside the mutual fund, ensuring that they are externally managed. Mutual fund managers are employees, not co-owners, of the funds.

Mutual funds' fee structure is also regulated. The minimum investment is usually $1,000 but can be lower, and investors are free to withdraw their funds at any time at a specified market price.[2] About 83 million Americans have investments in mutual funds (ICI 1997, 1998, 2000).

Mutual funds are not highly leveraged: in practice, a mutual fund's debts are not allowed to exceed one-third of its total assets, effectively limiting their on-balance-sheet leverage (President's Working Group on Financial Markets 1999). Short selling or repo transactions by mutual funds is constrained,[3] and their use of derivatives is strictly monitored and controlled by the SEC, which effectively constrains their economic leverage (Box 2).[4]

The differences that exist between hedge funds and mutual funds did not arise by accident. Hedge funds in the United States, for example, are structured specifically so that they satisfy one or more of the exclusions from regulation and disclosure required by the various pieces of legislation that cover the operation of collective investment vehicles.

The regulatory framework in the United States

While hedge funds are located in most main financial centres, their management is heavily concentrated in the United States. In order to minimise their tax liabilities, a substantial proportion of hedge funds are domiciled outside the United States, in offshore tax havens. Based on MAR/Hedge data, for example, about half of all hedge funds are registered in the United States and about half offshore, mainly in the Caribbean – the British Virgin Islands, Cayman Islands and the Bahamas (Chadha and

---

[2] This is only the case for 'open-end' investment companies, which are required to redeem their shares at any time upon shareholder request. Open-end funds, which are the bulk of funds, are required on redemption to pay a shareholder a price based on the net asset value of the fund's investment portfolio within seven days of receiving a request for redemption. 'Closed-end' investment companies do not redeem their shares and are usually listed on the stock exchange. Shareholders in closed-end mutual funds must sell their shares in the open market if they want to dispose of them (ICI 1997).

[3] The Investment Company Act (1940) limits investment funds (like mutual funds) issuing what are called 'senior securities', that is, bonds, notes, debentures or obligations which have priority over the distribution of assets or payment of dividends. Short sales and reverse repos are regarded as senior securities (President's Working Group on Financial Markets 1999, Appendix A).

[4] See Chapter 3.

Jansen 1998). In terms of funds under management, about two-thirds of funds are domiciled offshore. But even if funds are domiciled offshore, the vast majority of hedge fund managers live in the United States, and in the greater New York area in particular. They are also very active in US financial markets, which are the world's largest.

Given this, the discussion of the legal status of hedge funds mainly focuses on US law and practice. Hedge funds are structured to circumvent five key US federal laws – the Securities Act (1933), the Securities Exchange Act (1934), the Investment Company Act (1940), the Investment Advisers Act (1940), and the Commodity Exchange Act (1974).[5]

The Securities Act (1933) requires entities which issue securities – for example, shares – to be registered and to make extensive disclosure through their prospectuses. Section 4(2) of the Act, however, exempts entities which offer securities to investors by 'private placement' – that is, not by public advertisement or appeal.

Rule 506 of Regulation D of the Securities Act explains this further. A private placement can be made to an unlimited number of so-called accredited investors but only to thirty-five or fewer non-accredited investors. An accredited investor is defined as savings and loan associations, broker dealers, employee investment plans with total assets in excess of $5 million, private business-development companies, organisations, corporations, trusts or partnerships with total assets over $5 million, persons with individual net worth (or joint with a spouse) of $1 million, or persons with individual income over $200,000 (or joint income with a spouse of $300,000).

The Securities Act affects hedge funds in three ways: it substantially reduces disclosure requirements on them; it prohibits them from advertising directly; and it restricts investment in them to the very rich. It is worth noting that hedge funds still have to provide investors with all material information about their securities, which they do so in an offering memorandum. But there is no requirement to provide this information publicly or to provide detail on investment strategies or positions.

The Securities Exchange Act (1934) regulates brokers and dealers,[6] and requires them to be become members of registered national securities

---

[5] This material is sourced mainly from the report of the President's Working Group on Financial Markets (1999), ICI (1997, 1999) and Sharma (1998).

[6] A broker is a person paid to act as agent in making a contract, a person who executes someone else's trading orders on the trading floor of an exchange, or a person who deals with customers and their orders in commission house offices. A dealer is a financial intermediary that makes a market in a financial instrument and so participates as principal in the financial transaction (Eichengreen et al. 1998).

exchanges or associations. They have to keep detailed information about their financial dealings and customer transactions. However, hedge funds are generally considered to be traders rather than brokers or dealers and so are exempt from registration. This is because hedge funds trade only on their own account rather than on behalf of other entities, and they do not carry on a public securities business. Dealers deal directly with public investors and quote market prices to customers.

The Investment Company Act (1940) requires investment companies to have an independent board of directors which exercises control over investment strategies and operations. A board is independent if at least 60 per cent of its members are external. Investment companies also face controls or prohibitions over certain types of transactions, such as those with affiliate businesses, and the extent to which they can use leverage and derivatives, all of which can have a substantial impact on their investment strategies. Mutual funds, for example, are investment companies.

Hedge funds are exempted from the operation of the Act.[7] The rationale is clear – the law is involved to protect investors from exploitation, but very high-worth individuals who choose to invest in risky ventures are well placed to make their own investment choices and defend their own interests.

The exemptions to the Investment Company Act have changed over time. Before 1997, Section 3(c)(1) of the Act exempted funds from investment-company status if they had less than 100 beneficial owners and did not offer their securities to the public. The National Securities Markets Improvement Act (1996) has modified the exemption to also cover funds that sell their securities to 'qualified investors' and do not make public offerings of their securities. A qualified purchaser is defined as a person or family company with investments of at least $5 million, certain trusts, and institutional investors with assets over $25 million. By limiting investors to high-worth individuals and trusts, like university endowments, hedge funds have avoided investment-company status. These restrictions are binding, in the sense that the law looks through arrangements which are set up for the purpose of avoiding the intent of the legislation.

The Investment Advisers Act (1940) also seeks to protect shareholders in collective investment vehicles by regulating the activities of the adviser. It restricts the ability of registered advisers to receive performance-based compensation and imposes some disclosure requirements. Collective investment vehicles are exempted, however, if the adviser does not solicit

---

[7] This is similar to other countries, for example, Germany, Japan, the United Kingdom and Australia.

business and it does not have more than fifteen clients. Anti-fraud provisions still apply.

Hedge funds are, however, still subject to two other sets of legislation. Most hedge funds are subject to regulation under the Commodity Exchange Act (1974) since they are either commodity pool operators (CPOs) or large traders in exchange-traded futures markets.[8] According to Section 1(a) of the Act, a commodity pool is defined broadly as any entity that solicits or accepts funds for investment purposes and uses them to take positions in futures contracts or commodity options. The Act requires funds to be registered, to report information about risks, historical performance, fees, business background, and conflicts of interest to the Commodity Futures Trading Commission (CFTC), provide monthly reports to investors and annual reports to the CFTC, and maintain records for possible inspection by the CFTC and US Department of Justice.

The CFTC also requires daily reporting of large positions, and monitors selected hedge funds. With respect to large traders, the CFTC has extensive inspection powers and rules to limit the speculative positions of market participants.

There are no general exemptions to the Commodity Exchange Act, but some exemptions apply for CPOs with sophisticated investors – called qualified eligible participants – in this case registered securities professionals or accredited investors under the Securities Act (1933). Offshore funds are subject to CFTC registration but CPOs registered in the United States can obtain relief from reporting if they are organised and operated outside the United States, no participant is a US citizen, no US sources commit capital, and the pool is not marketed in the United States.

Hedge funds are also subject to requirements relating to the general oversight of financial market integrity by US government bodies. These include the collection of data on large positions in US Treasury bonds by

---

[8] There are three types of investment vehicles, or 'managed futures', for investors who want to participate indirectly in commodity markets or in the trading of futures, forwards and options contracts on both physical commodities and financial instruments: commodity trading advisors (CTAs), commodity pools (CPOs), and public commodity funds (Edwards and Liew 1999). CTAs manage an investor's funds on an individual basis, directed at the investor's particular risk preferences. CPOs pool investors' funds into a common portfolio with particular characteristics. Commodity pools usually have high minimum investment requirements and are generally only available to high-net-worth individuals and institutional investors. Public commodity funds are like conventional stock or mutual funds, except that they deal in derivatives rather than spot stocks and bonds. They are available to low-capital investors, like mutual funds. Fees by managed futures funds are high – median admin fee of 2–3 per cent, and incentive fees of 20 per cent. According to MAR/Hedge, at the end of 1999 there were 2,194 managed futures funds and 1,456 hedge funds.

the New York Federal Reserve Bank under the Government Securities Act, in registered securities (namely equities) to the Securities and Exchange Commission under the Securities Exchange Act, and in major foreign currencies to the New York Federal Reserve Bank on behalf of the US Treasury. Hedge funds are also subject to margin requirements imposed by various regulatory bodies and industry groups.

There have also been some changes to supervisory and regulatory arrangements concerning hedge funds in the United States, following the near collapse of Long-Term Capital Management and seizure of US financial markets in the December quarter of 1998.

In its report, the President's Working Group on Financial Markets (1999: viii), which comprised the US Treasury, Federal Reserve, SEC and CFTC, was concerned that 'excessive leverage can greatly magnify the negative effects of any event or series of events on the financial system as a whole'. The Working Group argued that excessive leverage can occur with a range of institutions and not just hedge funds, and it focused on addressing its concern by suggesting ways to improve risk-management and credit-assessment practices at banks and other credit providers. These were designed to improve market discipline.

The President's Working Group made a number of recommendations, including, among others:

- Greater public disclosure and reporting by hedge funds, including quarterly, rather than annual, reporting by large hedge funds which report as CPOs to the CFTC and finding a mechanism for hedge funds which are not CPOs to report on a similar basis. The reports would include measures of market risk (for example, value-at-risk or VaR results) but not positions or proprietary information.
- Public disclosure by financial institutions of material financial exposures to hedge funds. These would be reported to the SEC which would release aggregated exposure by sector, such as commercial banks, investment banks, insurance companies, and hedge funds.
- Expanding the authority of regulators over the unregulated affiliates of broker-dealers and futures commission merchants. This would provide regulators with a more comprehensive understanding of market developments, including concentration and size of positions in financial markets.
- Aligning capital adequacy requirements to the actual risks taken by financial institutions. In particular, the capital needed to support a credit exposure for a derivatives transaction should be the same as, rather than half, that which applies to a commercial loan to the same counterparty.

- Improving counterparty risk-management practices within the private sector to better manage economic leverage. This includes improving the risk assessment and monitoring systems of lenders and the internal control systems of hedge funds. One key feature in risk assessment is incorporating changing market liquidity in VaR models.

The first few of these recommendations require legislative change, and this process is under way in Congress (FSF Working Group on Highly Leveraged Institutions 2000). In terms of the first recommendation listed above, greater public reporting of non-CPO hedge funds has been restricted to large hedge funds of systemic importance. The Hedge Funds Disclosure Act 2000 (Baker Bill) requires quarterly disclosure of risk taking and leverage by large hedge funds, namely those with more than $1 billion in capital or groups of funds with more than $3 billion in assets. The Derivatives Reform Act (Markey-Dorgan Bill) enables the SEC to obtain quarterly disclosure statements from non-bank over-the-counter derivatives dealers and to issue large trader reporting rules so that it can monitor and report on the activities of hedge funds. Both bills were referred to House or Senate Committees in either late 1999 or early 2000, and have not yet been enacted. The FSF Working Group on HLIs (2000) endorsed the recommendations of the President's Working Group, and has called on other jurisdictions, including offshore financial centres, to ensure complementary disclosure by major hedge funds in their markets.

The fifth recommendation does not require action by Congress. Improved counterparty risk management has been encouraged by both the official and private sectors. Under the auspices of the Multidisciplinary Working Group on Enhanced Disclosure,[9] the official sector has set out a template for improved reporting of credit and market risks between credit providers and users. It measures the distribution and concentration of price risk, market-liquidity risk, cash or funding risk, and credit risk, as well as on- and off-balance-sheet leverage. The template is being trialed by participants in the foreign-exchange market. The tentative assessment seems to be that it is too complex and difficult, and that the exercise has not proved successful. The private sector has also been active in improving counterparty risk management (Counterparty Risk Management Policy Group 1999; Group of Hedge Fund Managers 2000). According to the FSF Working Group on HLIs (2000), many

---

[9] This is an international committee jointly sponsored by the Basle Committee on Bank Supervision (of the Bank for International Settlements), the International Organisation of Securities Commissions (IOSCO), the International Association of Insurance Supervisors (IAIS), and the G-10 Committee on the Global Financial System (CGFS).

credit providers and hedge funds still fall short of best practice in risk management.

The regulatory framework outside the United States

Provisions similar to those which apply in the United States also apply in other major countries (Cottier 1997; Sharma 1998). Cottier (1997) provides detail on other jurisdictions. The general rationale is to protect unsophisticated or small investors, but to allow sophisticated investors choice over their investments.

In the United Kingdom, for example, the Financial Services Act 1986 distinguishes between authorised trusts and collective investment vehicles and unregulated schemes. The latter cannot be advertised but they are not subject to the same rules about disclosure, investments, pricing and management. 'Experienced investors' are allowed to invest in unregulated schemes (Sharma 1998).

Defining hedge funds by strategy

Others, particularly market participants and investors, define hedge funds by the *strategies* they use in markets. All hedge funds share a basic strategy – to maximise absolute returns in all market conditions. To quote Goldman Sachs and FRM (2000: 21):

The term 'hedge fund' is historically rooted and has evolved over time to include a multitude of skill-based investment strategies with a broad range of risk and return objectives. The common element among these strategies is the use of investment and risk management skills to seek positive returns regardless of market direction.

In short, hedge funds are collective investment vehicles designed to make as much money as possible out of their investments. This provides the underlying rationale for their fee structures – zero return means virtually no fees, and the higher the return, the higher the fee.

This is a key defining behavioural difference with regulated collective investment vehicles, like mutual funds, and regulated asset management vehicles, like pension funds or superannuation funds. Regulated investment entities focus much more on assessing their performance relative to market benchmarks and the performance of their peers. Hedge funds, on the other hand, do not aim at reproducing market benchmark rates of return. They aim at positive returns in all market environments. They are, however, generally sensitive to risk, and seek to maximise risk-adjusted returns, by seeking high returns and low variability.

Figure 2.1 shows returns for the Van Global Hedge Fund Index, the Morningstar Average Equity Mutual Fund Index, and the MSCI World Equity Index (Van Hedge website).[10] The compound average returns from 1988 to 1998 were 17 per cent, 14.5 per cent and 24.2 per cent respectively. Adjusting for variability in returns, the risk-adjusted-return ratios (Sharpe ratios) were 1.6, 0.7 and 0.4 respectively. The market view is that over the past decade at least, hedge funds on average have out-performed other types of collective investment vehicle and standard benchmarks.

To achieve their aim of absolute return, hedge funds themselves may adopt a range of strategies in financial markets. This provides a way to distinguish between different hedge funds. Data providers and analysts use different ways to broadly categorise hedge fund strategies (Table 2.1). Van Hedge, for example, identifies eighteen hedge fund styles, MAR/ Hedge identifies eight, Goldman Sachs and FRM (2000) identifies four, and Kodres (1998) identifies two. All of them identify many more sub-categories.

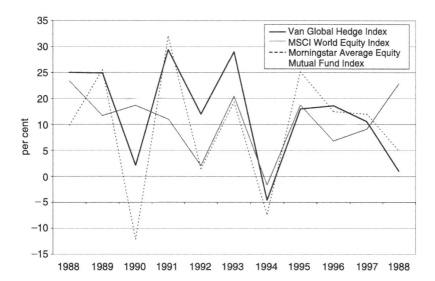

Figure 2.1 Hedge fund and mutual fund returns

[10] See *http://www.vanhedge.com/glchart.htm* and *http://www.venhedge.com/hedge.htm*.

Table 2.1. *Classification of hedge funds*

Kodres hedge fund types	Goldman Sachs and FRM hedge fund strategies	number	MarHedge hedge fund styles	number	assets bn	Van Hedge hedge fund strategies	number
1. arbitrage-type	1. market neutral/relative value	160	1. market neutral	231	$25.6	1. market neutral – arbitrage	414
						2. market neutral – securities hedging	332
	2. long/short	255	2. short sellers	17	$0.9	3. short selling	93
			3. long only leveraged	n/a	–	4. value	1114
			4. sector	75	$4.6	5. health care	
						6. technology	
						7. media/communications	
						8. financial services	
	3. event-driven	110	5. event driven	106	$13.1	9. distressed assets	152
						10. special situations/event driven	385
	4. tactical trading	243	6. global	34	$5.7	11. aggressive growth	653
			– international				
	– systematic		– regional emerging	85	$4.5	12. emerging market	542
	– discretionary		– regional established	245	$34.5	13. market timing	192
						14. opportunistic	641
						15. income	204
						16. several strategies	134
2. macro	– global macro		7. global macro	58	$24.9	17. macro	163
			8. fund of funds	231	$25.6	18. fund of funds	805
Total		768		1082	$139.4		5830

Notes: numbers are at end 1998 for Goldman Sachs and FRM, and Van Hedge, numbers at end 1999 for MarHedge; sources are Kodres (1998), Goldman Sachs and Financial Risk Management (2000), MarHedge website http:\\www.marhedge.com\benchmarks\useterms.htm, Van Hedge website http:\\www.vanhedge.com\disstyle.htm

Kodres (1998) is a useful starting point. She argues that there are two main types of hedge fund: macro funds, which attempt to achieve profit from perceived discrepancies in macroeconomic policies, and other hedge funds which pursue arbitrage-type strategies. Data providers tend to go into substantial detail about arbitrage-type strategies. Consider these two types in turn.

Macro hedge funds

Macro funds tend to use a 'top down' approach in constructing their positions. They assess a country's macroeconomy, financial markets and policymaking process, as well as the impact of international conditions on that country, to determine if there are fundamental imbalances which are likely to result in substantial movement in financial asset prices, like exchange rates, stock prices, bond yields and short-term interest rates. If such movements are likely, and if the country's asset markets are large and liquid enough, then macro funds will structure their positions in financial markets accordingly.

For example, if they think that there have been major advances in technology and its impact on the economy, then they would buy stocks – that is, go 'long' in stocks – that they think will rise in price, in this case technology stocks. If they think that the rise in technology stocks has been excessive and the market is overbought, then they will sell these stocks short, that is, they will borrow the stocks and then sell them. Indeed, macro hedge funds have been active in the US stock market in the past several years, on both sides of the market, with varying success.

If they judge that a country's exchange rate, say, is out of line with its economic fundamentals – that is, variables like real exchange rates, net exports and current account deficits, inconsistencies between the exchange rate and interest rates, reserves, relative inflation, and stability of the domestic financial system – and should be devalued, then they would bet that the exchange rate will be devalued. In this case, they would go short the currency, that is, borrow it in the currency-swap market and then sell it in the spot foreign-exchange market in the expectation that they will be able to buy it back profitably at a much cheaper rate after it is devalued. For example, macro hedge funds shorted the baht ahead of its devaluation in July 1997.

In all cases, the macro hedge funds continually monitor conditions and the behaviour of other participants in financial markets, including other hedge funds. This is crucial. Even if economic conditions or policy suggest a misalignment with 'fundamentals', financial markets need to be deep and liquid enough first for a position to be established and then for it to be closed with profit. Liquidity in markets refers to the willingness of participants to enter the market and buy or sell. The more buyers and sellers willing to enter the market, the more liquid it is.

If a hedge fund reckons that the price of a financial asset will fall, for example, it will establish a short position. Typically it will borrow the asset and then sell it in the spot market in the expectation that by the time it repays the asset, the price will have fallen and it can buy it back in the spot market at a decent profit. It is a two-staged process – sell high and then buy cheap. For this strategy to be successful, the bulk of the selling leg of the transaction has to be done with minimum effect on price. The fund wants to establish its short position when the price of the asset is high, but if it sells too much, and too fast, then it may push the price down in the market. Similarly, the fund wants to reverse, 'close out' or 'cover' its short position when the price is low, but if it is to buy the asset back at a low price, it wants to do so without pushing up the price.

If liquidity in a market were always constant, then selling would put downward pressure, and buying would put upward pressure, on the asset price, making it difficult for a fund to make profit. But liquidity is elastic – it can vary substantially within a trading day, and over days, weeks and even months, as market sentiment and the number and type of active participants in a market change. By monitoring flows and participants in markets, a fund can see if it can match its needs with what is available in the markets. If there are big flows in and out of a market at times, and a fund knows this, then it will match changes in its positions to take advantage of these flows. By continually monitoring markets, macro hedge funds have expert knowledge on patterns of liquidity and know how much buying or selling they can do in a particular market without substantially affecting price.

If prices in a particular financial market are fixed, as in a fixed-exchange-rate regime, then the problem of how changes in positions affect price may be less serious for a macro hedge fund. If the authorities fix the exchange rate, establishing or closing out a short position does not affect the price. Moreover, when a currency is fixed and the monetary authority does not ration the amount of currency that it will provide at that parity, then a macro hedge fund – or any other speculator for that matter – is guaranteed unlimited liquidity. If the current parity is viewed as unsustainable, then, so long as there is no problem in obtaining local currency funds or rationing of foreign exchange, there is no major risk of loss of liquidity for the speculator.

For this reason, fixed-exchange-rate regimes are more attractive to macro hedge funds than flexible-exchange-rate regimes.[11] This also explains why macro hedge funds' positions tend to be larger in fixed-exchange-rate regimes than in flexible-exchange-rate regimes – as discussed in Chapter 3, this is one reason why macro hedge funds' positions in the baht were larger than their positions in other currencies in the region.

Macro hedge funds use a variety of techniques and instruments to establish their positions, with the particular technique and instrument depending somewhat on the market itself. Macro hedge funds are active in foreign-exchange, money, bond and equity markets, in either exchange-traded or over-the-counter markets. They also use the full spectrum of instruments, ranging from spot, forward, swap and futures markets, to highly complex derivatives. Take foreign-exchange markets as an example.

In foreign-exchange markets, the standard way to establish a position is through a combination of the swap and spot markets. The spot market is the wholesale market for a currency relative to another (typically the US dollar), with settlement due in two days. The swap market is simply a wholesale market for borrowing a particular currency: one party borrows a currency from another party for a period of time, typically ranging anywhere from overnight to a year, at the going market rate of interest. The parties in the swap market are typically financial institutions, like banks and securities companies, but corporate treasuries are also active. Macro hedge funds do not deal in these markets directly but trade through financial intermediaries, like banks and securities companies. These intermediaries provide trading, brokerage and analytical services to hedge fund clients.

A short position in a currency, such as the baht for example, is established by borrowing baht in the swap market at the prevailing rate of interest, and then selling those baht funds in the spot market for US dollars (see Box 3). The US dollar funds can then be invested in other financial assets, denominated in US dollars or otherwise. The position is 'closed' by reversing the trade – the US dollar funds are converted back to baht and the baht repaid to the initial lender.

A fund can also use an 'outright forward' to establish a position in a currency market. For example, if a fund wanted to establish a short position in a currency, it could simply sell the currency forward, typically at frequencies like one, three, six and twelve months ahead. This means that the fund has an obligation to sell the currency at a specified rate (determined by the interest differential) at a specified time in the future,

---

[11] For this reason, fixed-exchange-rate regimes are fundamentally vulnerable.

although the forward can generally be extended or 'rolled over'. If the currency depreciates in the meantime, then the fund can buy the currency in the spot market at a relatively low price and sell it according to the forward contract at a relatively high price. Forward markets tend to be smaller and less liquid than spot and swap markets, and so speculators use them less.

Box 3: *An example – shorting the baht*

Suppose the baht is currently 30 baht to the dollar, baht can be borrowed in the three-month swap market at an annual interest rate of 10 per cent, and annualised three-month US interest rates are 6 per cent. The cost of holding the position is the baht–dollar interest differential, which in this case is 4 per cent. Through a bank or securities company, a fund borrows 30 billion baht in the swap market and then sells the funds in the spot foreign-exchange market for $1 billion – it has a short position of $1 billion. If the authorities subsequently devalue the baht 25 per cent, from 30 to 40 baht, then the fund only needs $750 million to repay the 30 billion baht it owes plus $18.75 million to pay the interest of 750 million baht. Adding the $15 million in interest it earns on a three-month US security, it makes $246.25 million from the short position. This represents an annual compounded earnings rate of 141 per cent on the investment.

More technically, a short currency position can be established and funded using a foreign currency swap in the following manner (RBA 1998: 14):

Day 1: Sell baht for US dollars in the spot market for delivery in the spot market, due on Day 3.

Day 2: Undertake a currency swap, with the first leg involving the purchase of baht and sale of US dollars (delivery due Day 3), and the second leg the sale of baht and the purchase of US dollars at some future date.

Day 3: Undertake settlement: receive baht from swap counterparty and deliver them to the spot counterparty (implying zero net flow), and receive US dollars from spot counterparty and deliver them to swap counterparty (zero net flow).

Through these transactions, the hedge fund has a forward commitment which requires neither capital nor funding. The cost of the swap is the interest differential between baht and US interest rates.

Some macro hedge funds also use complex derivatives such as options in forming their positions. The use of derivatives depends on two factors. The first is the preference of the fund itself. Some macro hedge funds do not use complex derivatives but only use instruments in spot, swap, futures and forward markets. This makes for easier risk management, and perhaps for greater anonymity in mid-sized financial markets where options activity is less. The second is the size and liquidity of the instruments. Being able to smoothly exit a position is crucial to macro hedge funds, and options markets tend to be less liquid than spot, swap, forward and futures markets. The smaller or less liquid a derivatives market is, the less likely is a macro hedge fund to use it.

Macro hedge funds tend to be among the most highly leveraged of the hedge funds. Using MAR/Hedge data, Chadha and Jansen (1998) report that on-balance-sheet leverage seems to be highest for macro funds – about a third of funds which report leverage have leverage ratios greater than 3 to 1, that is, one dollar of capital supports three dollars of assets. Market estimates of on-balance-sheet leverage ratios for macro hedge funds tend to range between 4 and 10 (FSF Working Group on HLIs 2000).

Large macro hedge funds are also able to obtain substantial economic leverage. In order to obtain the funds, a borrower is typically required to put up collateral. For a small hedge fund with no credit history with a bank, this could be the full amount of the loan. By posting full collateral, such a fund is only able to use its own capital to establish a position and cannot leverage its capital at all. For medium-sized hedge funds with some history and reputation, the funds would be provided at a margin, with the percentage of required collateral ranging anywhere from a few per cent up to 20 per cent of the borrowed amount. In this case, funds are able to leverage their capital, and substantially so if the margin requirement is only a few percentage points. The margin enables the bank to cover daily mark-to-market exposures associated with a hedge fund's position.

For a half dozen or so of the large macro hedge funds, however, no collateral is required and a hedge fund can establish a position without using any of its own capital. In this case, leverage with respect to that position is infinite, although the fund's overall leverage is not. If these funds' positions move into loss, margining requirements are only applied when they reach a certain loss threshold (FSF Working Group on HLIs 2000).

Until mid-2000, macro funds were the biggest type of hedge fund in terms of assets under management. At the end of 1999, they accounted for less than 6 per cent of hedge funds in the MAR/Hedge database but about 22 per cent of assets under management (see Table 2.1). Their average size at this time was $429 million, compared to $122 million for global funds. But the distribution of macro hedge funds is highly positively skewed and highly concentrated: at the end of 1997, the eight largest macro funds ranged from US$1 billion to US$6 billion under management, representing over 80 per cent of the sector (Chadha and Jansen 1998).[12] The management groups were at times substantially

---

[12] They are also more likely to be domiciled offshore (in terms of funds under management, 5 per cent domiciled in the US compared to 29 per cent for hedge funds in general in 1997) and they have the highest offshore domicile status of all types of funds.

larger. At the end of 1998, for example, Julian Robertson's Tiger Management Group had $15.1 billion of assets under management, and Soros Fund Management had $14 billion of assets under management. The next largest macro hedge fund was Moore Global Investment with $4 billion of assets.

In the first half of 2000, the macro hedge funds underwent substantial downsizing following the effective closure of the two largest macro hedge funds. Julian Robertson's Tiger Fund Management, which had about $6.5 billion of assets under management, closed down in March 2000 after sustaining substantial losses in the US stock market. In May 2000, following substantial losses from long positions in US technology stocks, George Soros substantially downsized his flagship Quantum fund, which had $8.5 billion of assets under management. He renamed the fund the Quantum Endowment Fund and announced that it would do a mix of 'macro' business and long/short strategies. The implications of this for future directions and for policy are assessed in Chapter 9.

Arbitrage-type strategies

The underlying logic of an arbitrage-type strategy is to take advantage of price discrepancies in two financial instruments. Hedge funds are not engaged in arbitrage activity in the true meaning of the word. The text book definition of arbitrage is that it is a set of risk-free transactions by which a market participant can lock 'in a profit by simultaneously entering ... two or more markets' (Hull 2000: 14).

For example, an arbitrage opportunity arises when a stock listed on two exchanges trades at a different price in each: a trader can make a risk-free profit by buying the stock in the cheap market and simultaneously selling it in the expensive market. Similar arbitrage opportunities arise, for instance, from the differences between interest differentials and foreign-exchange forward premiums or discounts. Arbitrage takes advantage of short-term market inefficiencies, and, in the process, eliminates them.

This is *not* an accurate description of what hedge funds do. They are speculators, not arbitragers.[13] What they do is try to profit from what appear to be mispricings or misalignments between sets of prices of financial instruments based on historical or expected relationships. These relationships may be based on sophisticated analytical models,

---

[13] To quote Edwards (1999: 189) 'It is hard to imagine a greater misnomer than "hedge fund", since hedge funds typically do just the opposite of what their name implies: they speculate.'

observed patterns of correlations, or, more loosely, on an expectation that the prices will respond to some event in a similar manner.

Based on expected patterns of pricing, an arbitrage-type hedge fund will buy the asset that appears undervalued and simultaneously sell the asset that appears overvalued. An asset is undervalued if its price is below its expected price, and is overvalued if its price is above its expected price. It is a great misnomer to refer to this as arbitrage because that term implies that the activity is essentially risk free, which, as the US experience with Long-Term Capital Management in the December quarter of 1998 showed, is clearly not even close to being true at times. It is, however, now standard to classify the approach as an 'arbitrage-type' strategy, and this practice will be followed even though it is misleading.[14]

Arbitrage-type hedge funds are active in many financial markets and in many instruments. Goldman Sachs and Financial Management Services (2000) identify four main types of arbitrage-type activity. These are not a tight set of definitions: hedge funds are involved in financial markets in many different ways, sometimes with myriad strategies, and so these characterisations are not always exact for any particular fund. There is also typically a broad spectrum of risk and return within each group reflecting the different risk proclivities of fund managers and risk appetites of investors. With this caution in mind, consider the four types of fund in turn.

The first is *market-neutral* or *relative-value* funds. These types of funds do not focus on the general direction of markets as much as try to identify and exploit expected pricing disparities between related financial instruments or sets of financial instruments with similar pricing characteristics. To the extent that they attempt to lock out or neutralise market risk, these funds employ a classic 'hedge' fund strategy, but they differ from the original Jones strategy in that they are largely based on technical rather than fundamental analysis.

They are active in many financial markets, most notably in fixed income, stocks, convertible bonds, mortgage-backed securities and derivatives. They also include funds which focus on price anomalies driven by government intervention, policy changes or forced selling. Van Hedge calls these arbitrage-type market-neutral funds. Market-neutral funds also include funds that construct portfolios consisting of a basket of long positions and a basket of short positions based on observed statistical patterns of asset prices. This balance reduces overall market risk of

---

[14] *The Economist* (17 October 1998) calls it 'expectations arbitrage' since positions are based on historical relationships between financial prices.

the portfolio but offers the prospect of relatively high returns. Van Hedge calls these securities-hedging market-neutral funds.

One popular relative-value trade is profiting from differentials between cash (or 'spot') and futures prices in bond, currency and equity markets. Funds will establish positions in markets to take advantage of wedges that emerge between the prices of futures that are due for delivery at a nearby date and the prices of the underlying securities that trade in the cash or spot market. Kodres (1998) reports that hedge funds are very active players in these markets. Funds also assess pricing discrepancies between prices in the spot market and in other derivatives markets, as well as between the various derivatives prices offered by banks and other financial institutions.

Other strategies include establishing positions to take advantage of price differences between bonds of similar maturity, between bonds with virtually identical maturity but different benchmark status (that is, on-the-run versus off-the-run securities), between various mortgage-backed instruments based on US Treasury bonds, or between convertible bonds (that is, bonds which are convertible into equities). These plays are progressively more speculative in nature.

Market-neutral funds are active in both spot and derivatives markets, and, almost by definition, they make extensive use of derivatives of all degrees of complexity. Given this, it is not surprising that they are also among the most highly leveraged of the hedge funds – based on MAR/Hedge estimates of on-balance-sheet leverage, borrowing is more than two times the value of capital for about a third of these funds (Chadha and Jansen 1998). This group also included Long-Term Capital Management, although LTCM's leverage was extremely high – with capital of $4 billion and assets of $125 billion, it had a leverage ratio of about 33 – and unrepresentative of leverage by hedge funds.

These funds also use a wide range of models and techniques, with varying technical complexity, to identify possible price discrepancies in markets (Goldman Sachs and FRM 2000). They probably also include more of the 'rocket-science' type hedge funds. Based on the numbers in Table 2.1, market-neutral funds account for about a quarter of all hedge funds.[15] According to Eichengreen, et al. (1998), market-neutral funds comprise about 25 per cent of funds and 20 per cent of assets under management.

The second type is *long/short* funds which invest mainly in equity markets, but also in fixed-interest markets, combining short sales with

---

[15] These figures, and succeeding ones, exclude fund of funds. Fund of funds are explained later in the chapter.

long investments to reduce, but not eliminate, market exposure. These funds can take positions along the whole risk–return spectrum and try to distinguish their performance from that of the asset class as a whole.

Equity long/short funds manage long and short portfolios of equities, with biases either to be long, short or neutral in a market. These funds focus on stock selection rather than market timing – that is, whether a particular stock is a good buy or not based on its fundamentals, rather than whether the market as a whole is rising or falling. Managers tend to focus on a particular type of stock, like small-cap stocks, or particular sectors, like financial companies, technology, energy, health care, or media and software.

In the environment of rising stock markets of the late 1990s, 'long' funds have focused on equities which are strongly positively correlated with the rises in the market but only weakly correlated with falls in the market, which enables them to make substantial returns. 'Short' funds look for overvalued securities. The 'no-bias' fund follows the original Jones model, establishing relatively market-neutral positions based on fundamental assessments of the strength of stocks. They are different from the long/short relative-value funds in the first group of funds, which construct portfolios based largely on quantitative modelling.

The numbers of long/short funds tend to differ between data providers. They account for a third of the hedge funds in the database used by Goldman Sachs and Financial Risk Management (2000), and about a quarter of funds in the much larger Van Hedge database. These funds also seem to be among the least leveraged of the hedge funds. As reported in Chadha and Jansen (1998), according to MAR/Hedge data, their on-balance-sheet leverage is well below that of the average hedge fund. Goldman Sachs and FRM (2000) report that many of these funds use little or no debt in establishing their positions in financial markets.

The third type are *event-driven* funds. They are active in fixed interest and equity markets, and base their strategies on the actual or anticipated occurrence of a particular event, such as a merger, bankruptcy announcement or corporate reorganisation. This is a risky strategy. Not only may the event not occur, but, even if it does, it is unusual for a fund to know the timing. Goldman Sachs and FRM (2000) argue that successful event-driven funds need to conduct high-quality intensive research, and to have solid transaction experience and disciplined risk management.

There are four main types of event-driven funds. The first is distressed-securities funds which invest in the debt or equity of troubled firms in the expectation that they are mispriced because of illiquidity, forced selling, or uncertainty. The second is merger-arbitrage funds which speculate on the spread between the current market prices of firms and the expected prices of those firms after they have merged – this spread measures the risk that the transaction will not be completed or will be finalised on different conditions. The third is special-situations funds which focus on possible price effects of corporate reconstruction and restructuring, or on exploiting differences in the prices of securities of the same issuer. The fourth is private-placement-arbitrage funds which invest short term in firms which need immediate capital through the use of special debt instruments which are convertible to equity. These instruments are not well traded and are subject to default risk.

From Table 2.1, as recorded by the major data providers, event-driven funds account for between 10 to 15 per cent of hedge funds and assets under management. According to Chadha and Jansen (1998), their on-balance-sheet leverage is average for hedge funds in general: 60 per cent of reporting funds are leveraged at less than 3 to 1 (that is, one dollar of capital supports three dollars of assets). Some event-driven funds are not leveraged at all – Goldman Sachs and FRM (2000) report that distressed-securities funds tend to be unleveraged.

The fourth arbitrage-type funds are *tactical-trading* funds, which speculate on the direction of market prices of currencies, commodities and equities and bonds on spot or futures markets. While the time profile of these investments can vary substantially, positions can be reversed quickly as economic and financial markets circumstances change. Goldman Sachs and FRM (2000) includes systematic traders, discretionary traders and global macro traders in this category. The main data providers classify these types of funds as 'global', with focus on international, emerging and established markets. Following Kodres (1998) and the main data providers like MAR/Hedge and Van Hedge, global macro traders are treated separately in this book, because they are so large, employ a macroeconomic-oriented top–down analytical approach, and act opportunistically in any financial market which offers sufficient liquidity.

Goldman Sachs and FRM (2000) define systematic traders as those funds which rely exclusively on model-based technical systems to dictate the size and timing of their positions. These funds follow trends in markets, recognising the importance of feedback and herding in the short-run price dynamics of financial markets. The use of stop-loss programs and portfolio diversification across a number of uncorrelated markets are both important in limiting funds' exposure to losses from discrete changes in trend. Discretionary traders use many of the same techniques as systematic traders, but allow the managers of the fund a judgmental override with respect to size and timing of positions. They may also combine the technical analysis with analysis of economic and financial fundamentals.

The Goldman Sachs and FRM (2000) definition of tactical traders appears to include what MAR/Hedge calls 'global' hedge funds, which comprise international, regional emerging, and regional established funds. International global funds invest in non-US financial markets and use a bottom–up analytical approach – that is, they tend to be 'stock pickers'. Emerging regional global funds focus on specific emerging- market regions and tend to take outright unleveraged positions in stock markets. Established regional global funds focus on opportunities in Europe, Japan and the United States.

According to Goldman Sachs and FRM (2000), tactical trading funds (excluding macro funds) account for about a quarter of hedge fund managers. According to MAR/Hedge and Van Hedge, they account for over 40 per cent of funds and assets under management (excluding fund of funds). Reported on-balance-sheet leverage varies somewhat between these funds, and it is lower than the average for hedge funds – 70 per cent of reporting global funds have on-balance-sheet leverage of 3 to 1 or less (Chadha and Jansen 1998).

Numbers and size of hedge funds

The fact that hedge funds lie largely outside the regulatory framework means that few data on them are collected, and that little in fact is known – as opposed to believed or surmised – about them. There are no official sources of data, although there are a number of private-sector companies which collect and analyse data on hedge funds. Some of the most well-known of these are MAR/Hedge, Van Hedge, Tass and Financial Risk Management (FRM). While these data providers provide a lot of valuable information free to the public, most of the disaggregated data is provided – not unreasonably – for a fee, often several thousands of dollars a year.[16]

In constructing their databases on hedge funds, however, data providers are in a difficult position in the sense that they have to rely on self-reporting by funds. This is problematic. In the first place, there may be substantial non-reporting bias in these databases. Funds which want to remain anonymous can. And funds which do not want to answer a particular question do not. This is most obvious in relation to estimates of the leverage of hedge funds. Chadha and Jansen (1998), for example, analyse the leverage of hedge funds using MAR/Hedge data, but more than half of hedge funds in the sample – and 80 per cent of macro hedge

---

[16] Their website addresses are: *http:\\marhedge.com*, *http:\\vanhedge.com*, *http:\\www. tassman.com*.

funds – do not report their figures. This matters because strong inferences tend to be made on what is fundamentally fragile data.

Hedge funds also apply their own, rather than common, definitions of key variables of interest. For example, there is no common definition of leverage, which is an important characteristic of hedge funds. There is also no validation or due diligence performed on the data. There is, however, substantial information on hedge-fund returns, and this tends to be of better quality. This is also the information that is of most interest to the clients of the data providers, since they are prospective investors in hedge funds.

The lack of data means that there is even considerable uncertainty about the number of hedge funds and the size of their assets. Before going through various estimates of the numbers, there is an important distinction to be made between hedge-fund managers and hedge funds. It is not unusual for one hedge-fund manager to manage a number of funds, and so the number of hedge funds may substantially exceed the number of hedge-fund managers. Soros Fund Management, for example, managed seven funds at its peak. Some data providers talk about numbers of hedge-fund managers (for example, Goldman Sachs and FRM) while others talk about numbers of hedge funds. They are not the same thing and the former are smaller in number than the latter.

The number of funds varies by data provider. Goldman Sachs and FRM (1998; 2000), for example, estimate that there are 1,300 hedge-fund management groups which operate over 3,500 hedge funds. They estimate total capital of these funds to be about $200 billion, with total assets of about $400 billion. They use data on 768 fund managers in their analysis. Van Hedge estimates that there were 5,830 hedge funds at the end of 1998, with $311 billion of assets under management. MAR/Hedge had 1,082 hedge funds in its database at the end of 1999, with $139 billion of assets under management.[17] The President's Working Group on Financial Markets (1999) estimates that there were 2,500 to 3,500 hedge funds in mid 1998, managing capital of between $200 to $300 billion and assets of $800 billion to $1 trillion. Obviously, there is a wide range in estimates.

What is clear is that the number of hedge funds has risen steadily over time. According to Chadha and Jansen (1998), the number of hedge funds rose from one in 1949 – Alfred Winslow Jones' fund – to 140 in 1968. Figures 2.2 and 2.3 show estimates of hedge fund numbers and assets under management for the past decade from the MAR/Hedge

---

[17] See 'Number of Hedge Funds Increases for Tenth Consecutive Year' at *http://www.van hedge.com/size.htm*, and Mar Hedge website.

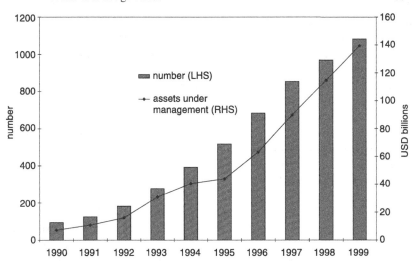

Figure 2.2 Hedge funds – MAR/Hedge

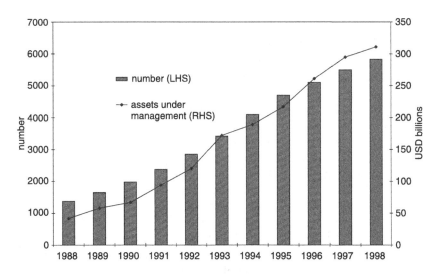

Figure 2.3 Hedge funds – Van Hedge

and Van Hedge databases respectively. While the absolute numbers vary somewhat, the figures tell the same story – the number of hedge funds and assets under their management have grown spectacularly over the past decade.

Based on the Van Hedge numbers at least, the growth rate appears to have slowed down somewhat. The slower growth rate in 1998 appears to be due to the myriad difficulties of hedge funds in emerging markets and US markets, especially fixed-interest markets, in 1998. The figures for 1999 appear to be relatively strong, and this has been attributed to four factors. It is partly due to the sustained strength in US and world stock markets, and partly due to a rebound from a slow 1998 and relief at no major regulatory changes in the United States. Van Hedge (1999) has also argued that lower leverage has helped some hedge funds, especially those pursuing market-neutral strategies, to achieve better performance because it has lowered volatility in some financial markets and enabled these funds to more nimbly shift positions without affecting price.

There is also a wide range in the size of hedge funds. Based on CPO filings with the CFTC, the President's Working Group on Financial Markets (1999) reckons that there are only a few dozen hedge funds with capital over $1 billion, and only a half dozen that exceed $5 billion. While the largest hedge fund had $12 billion in capital, the capital size of a management group can be double this when funds in the same management 'stable' or 'family' are added together.

Performance of hedge funds

Most of the literature and analysis of hedge funds focuses on assessing their performance. This is not surprising since the bulk of interest in hedge funds is by rich individuals and endowments which want to invest funds for a high return (and are willing to pay for information). Accordingly, considerable information is available about the returns on assets and risk of investing in hedge funds. Table 2.2 provides a summary of some key indicators over the past five years or so for the three data providers listed in Table 2.1.

The first group of columns set out returns on assets, standard deviation and Sharpe ratio by fund strategy from Goldman Sachs and FRM (2000). The standard deviation is a standardised measure of the variability of returns. The Sharpe ratio is a measure of return relative to risk – calculated as the actual return less the risk-free rate (US Treasury bills), divided by the standard deviation of returns. The higher the number, the better the return relative to the risk of an investment strategy.

Table 2.2. Hedge fund performance

Goldman Sachs and Financial Risk Mgmt, 1994–98

Strategy	Return (%)	std dev (%)	Sharpe ratio
Market neutral	11.9	2.3	2.9
Long/short	15.2	7.3	1.4
Event driven	12.7	4.6	1.6
Tactical trading	17.0	9.3	1.3
S&P	24.1	13.9	1.4
World index	12.9	13.0	0.7
Bond index	7.3	4.1	0.5

MAR/Hedge, 1995–99

Style	Return (%)
Market neutral	12.3
Short sellers	−2.7
Long only	n/a
Sector	n/a
Event driven	14.4
Global internat.	14.8
Global emerg.	13.6
Global est.	23.8
Global macro	12.6
Funds of funds	12.8
S&P	28.6
World index	18.1

Van Hedge, 1995–99

Strategy	Return (%)	Risk of loss (%)
Neutral – arbitrage	15.0	5.7
Neutral – securities	18.3	14.8
Distressed assets	12.3	11.5
Special situations	22.6	8.5
Short selling	−10.3	57.5
Value	24.1	13.6
Growth	33.8	14.4
Emerging market	7.5	42.6
Market timing	24.0	15.7
Opportunistic	26.4	10.7
Income	6.6	9.4
Several strategies	19.9	6.3
Macro	19.2	24.2
Fund of funds	16.1	11.3
S&P	28.6	—
World index	18.1	—

Notes: returns are annualised and compounded except for the MAR/Hedge figures which are the average of annual median rates of return; the Sharpe ratio is the return less the US Treasury Bill rate divided by the standard deviation; the Van Hedge risk of loss is the M2 (Method 2) Van Ratio; the world index is the FTSE world index for Goldman Sachs and FRM and the Morgan Stanley Capital International Index for MAR/Hedge and Van Hedge, and the bond index is the Lehman Brothers Aggregate Bond Index. See Table 2.1 for sources.

Over the period 1994 to 1999, the four aggregate categories all posted positive returns, with tactical funds posting the highest. These funds, however, also had the greatest variability in returns, and produced the lowest risk-adjusted returns of the four categories of funds. While market-neutral funds had the lowest cumulative returns, they had the lowest variability and highest risk-adjusted returns of the four fund types.

The next two sets of columns provide information on more detailed returns from MAR/Hedge and Van Hedge. Van Hedge provide a number of proprietary measures of risk, and the one shown here is the risk of a loss occurring to the particular type of hedge fund in a particular period. Only short sellers as a group suffered cumulative losses from 1995 to 1999, a period of rising stock prices, and they had the greatest probability of loss. Emerging market and macro hedge funds had the next highest risk of loss.

Clearly, these performance indicators depend on the particular period examined (Fung and Hsieh 1997; Brown, Goetzman and Ibbotson 1999). On an absolute or risk-adjusted basis, for example, market-neutral funds performed worse, and tactical trading funds better, than other types of funds in 1998 (Goldman Sachs and FRM 2000). Returns can also be very volatile, even year to year. Emerging regional global funds, for example, performed strongly in 1996 and 1997, with annual median returns of 32 and 18 per cent respectively, performed very poorly during the market turmoil in 1998, with negative median returns of 31 per cent, and performed with distinction in 1999 with median returns of 51 per cent. 1998 was a bad year for most funds, especially market-neutral funds (returns of 2.6 per cent and a Sharpe ratio of −0.5), but not so bad for tactical trading funds (returns of 15 per cent and a Sharpe ratio of 1.5).

One striking feature of hedge fund returns in the past several years is that they appear to have performed less well than key benchmarks like US and world stock price indices. In the Goldman Sachs and FRM database over 1994 to 1999, for example, only 7 per cent of funds – and no market-neutral fund – outperformed the S&P, and only 47 per cent of funds outperformed the world stock market index.

This should not be overstated. In the first place, by historical standards, the returns on stock markets in the late 1990s were extraordinarily high, and are unlikely to be repeated. Using MAR/Hedge data, Chadha and Jansen (1998) report that most classes of hedge funds outperformed the S&P 500 during the first half of the 1990s, ahead of the major rally in stock prices. Funds also did much better in other markets – for example, 82 per cent of funds outperformed bond market benchmarks. Moreover, the volatility in stock prices has been high, and risk-adjusted measures, like the Sharpe ratio, suggest that risk-adjusted returns from investing in hedge funds are generally higher than for standard benchmark indices (Agarwal and Naik 1999). Ackermann, McEnally and Ravenscraft (1999) report that while hedge funds do not consistently outperform market benchmarks in absolute returns, they do outperform mutual funds on a risk-adjusted return basis, that is, their average Sharpe ratios are consistently higher.

An important feature of hedge fund returns is that they are not highly correlated with each other or with market benchmarks (President's Working Group on Financial Markets 1999). Table 2.3 reproduces correlations from Goldman Sachs and FRM (2000), and Table 2.4 reproduces correlations from Van Hedge.

There are two interesting results. First, hedge-fund returns over the past half decade have been correlated with US and world equity markets, but far from perfectly, especially for tactical-trading funds (like macro funds). Hedge fund returns are noticeably uncorrelated with bond-market indices. In general, hedge funds are less correlated than mutual funds with market benchmarks (Fung and Hsieh 1997; Schneeweis and Spurgin 1998; FSF Working Group on HLIs, Annex D, 2000). This implies that there are advantages to stock and bond investors in diversifying into hedge funds. Hedge fund returns also appear to be less correlated with market downturns, especially in currency markets (Martin 2000), which suggests that they provide a means for investors to limit downside risks.

Second, while there are pockets of high correlation between particular types of funds, correlations between fund types in general have not been very high. In recent years, returns have been most highly correlated between funds which have taken long positions in equity markets, and they have been least correlated with tactical trading funds. Correlations are lowest for macro funds, distressed securities funds and emerging market funds. This implies that investors in hedge funds can diversify their risk by investing in a range of hedge funds (Edwards and Liew 1999; Goldman Sachs and FRM 2000). The correlations between individual hedge funds, even those which pursue the same strategy, are lower than the correlations between individual mutual funds (FSF Working Group on HLIs 2000 Annex D).

The gains from diversification of investing in a variety of hedge funds was in fact the main impetus for the development of what are called fund of funds. These are simply hedge funds which invest in other hedge funds. As shown in Table 2.1, fund of funds account for about 20 per cent of all hedge funds, in terms of both numbers and assets under management. They tend to provide more stable returns than for most hedge fund

Table 2.3. *Correlation of returns*
Goldman Sachs and FRM database, 1994 to 1998

	Market neutral	Long/short	Event driven	Tactical trading	S&P 500	World index	Bond index
Market neutral	1.00				0.38	0.41	0.20
Long/short	0.62	1.00			0.77	0.73	0.11
Event driven	0.72	0.85	1.00		0.70	0.68	0.07
Tactical trading	−0.04	0.07	−0.07	1.00	0.10	0.07	0.29

Source: Goldman Sachs and FRM (2000).

Table 2.4. Correlation of returns
Van Hedge database, 1995 to 1999

	AG	DS	EM	FF	IN	MA	NA	NS	MT	OP	SV	SH	SS	VA	SP	WS	WB
AG	1.00																
DS	0.36	1.00															
EM	0.49	0.45	1.00														
FF	0.52	0.44	0.56	1.00													
IN	0.43	0.30	0.52	0.59	1.00												
MA	0.34	0.44	0.47	0.58	0.63	1.00											
NA	0.32	0.64	0.46	0.50	0.35	0.40	1.00										
NS	0.61	0.47	0.50	0.67	0.52	0.49	0.50	1.00									
MT	0.71	0.30	0.27	0.31	0.33	0.36	0.31	0.50	1.00								
OP	0.81	0.53	0.58	0.62	0.54	0.64	0.45	0.68	0.65	1.00							
SV	0.82	0.68	0.57	0.64	0.49	0.50	0.57	0.73	0.59	0.86	1.00						
SH	-0.90	-0.31	-0.48	-0.38	-0.33	-0.19	-0.25	-0.53	-0.54	-0.70	-0.72	1.00					
SS	0.65	0.84	0.53	0.62	0.46	0.45	0.57	0.65	0.44	0.70	0.85	-0.63	1.00				
VA	0.92	0.49	0.60	0.63	0.49	0.42	0.45	0.67	0.65	0.87	0.89	-0.86	0.78	1.00			
SP	0.83	0.21	0.43	0.44	0.40	0.25	0.36	0.43	0.60	0.65	0.66	-0.77	0.55	0.83	1.00		
WS	0.68	0.24	0.44	0.37	0.42	0.30	0.23	0.28	0.46	0.49	0.55	-0.65	0.53	0.73	0.83	1.00	
WB	0.17	-0.01	-0.14	0.15	0.41	0.28	0.07	-0.05	0.17	0.20	0.09	0.00	0.06	0.10	0.27	0.19	1.00

Notes: AG is aggressive growth, DS is distressed securities, EM is emerging markets, FF is fund of funds, IN is income, MA is macro, NA is market-neutral arbitrage, NS is market-neutral securities hedging, MT is market timing, OP is opportunistic, SV is several strategies, SH is short selling, SS is special situations, VA is value, SP is the S&P 500, WS is the MSCI world equity index, WB is the Lehman Brothers aggregate bond index.

Source is Van Hedge website, *http:\\www.vanhedge.com\style.htm*.

categories, both on an absolute return basis and a risk-adjusted return basis. According to Van Hedge, the only fund types to provide higher risk-adjusted returns from 1988 to 1998 were the market-neutral, market timing and opportunistic funds, all of which benefited from the sustained rally in the US stock market in the latter part of the 1990s.[18]

Superior performance by hedge funds appears generally to be related to the nature of their investment activity, rather than the skills of fund managers. After taking type of strategy into account, Fung and Hsieh (1997), for example, find that there is no persistence in fund returns, which suggests that funds' returns are not related to the ability of the manager. Goldman Sachs and FRM (2000) report that investment experience is also not related to performance: in fact, they find that, in their sample, newer funds performed better than well-established hedge funds. Van Hedge argues that size is related to performance – the bigger the fund, the higher are its returns.[19]

---

[18] See *http://www.vanhedge.com/glchart.htm* for compounded returns, standard deviations, and Sharpe ratios of global hedge funds, including fund of funds.

[19] *http://www.vanhedge.com/quantit.htm*

3   Hedge funds in east Asia

Policymakers, practitioners and academics alike hold diverse and strong views about the role of speculators in the east Asian financial crisis, and about the role of hedge funds and proprietary trading desks in particular. The views range along a spectrum, where the two ends are that speculators played no independent role in the crisis and that speculators were the causes of the crisis, turning what should have been a modest adjustment of the baht into a fully fledged regional crisis with serious economic and social consequences.

While there is a lack of uniformity in views within countries and regions, it is probably fair to say that most of the critics of the role of hedge funds and other HLIs are based in east Asia and Europe, rather than in the United States where most of the hedge funds and proprietary trading desks are located and where the links with government, the financial markets and academia are strongest.

The controversy about hedge funds has led to two major international studies on their role in financial markets. The first was the IMF study, *Hedge Funds and Financial Market Dynamics*, led by Barry Eichengreen and Donald Mathieson, which was published in May 1998. The study examined many features of hedge funds and other highly leveraged institutions, including their role in east Asian financial markets in 1997. It collected and analysed a wide range of material on hedge funds, which was a difficult task given that so little information is in fact known and available about hedge funds.

Eichengreen, *et al.* (1998) argued that hedge funds are essentially a benign force in financial markets, and that it is misguided to blame them for the 1997 financial crisis. With respect to the events of 1997, it formed two main conclusions. The first was that hedge funds are too small to have mattered:

While hedge funds are large in absolute terms, they are dwarfed by other institutional investors (banks, pension funds, mutual funds), some of whom engage in many of the same activities as hedge funds. This points against the conclusion that hedge funds play a singular role in precipitating crises.   (1)

The second is that hedge funds were only one of many players and came late to the action in east Asia:

Hedge funds did have large positions against the Thai baht in the summer of 1997 [that is, mid 1997], but so did other investors, and most hedge funds were relatively late to take those positions. That is, they were at the rear, not the front, of the financial 'herd'. And there is scant evidence that hedge funds had equally large positions against other Asian currencies.   (1)

It also noted that proprietary trading desks engaged in many of the same activities as hedge funds, emphasising the point that hedge funds are just one of many players in markets. For this reason, most commentators talk about highly leveraged institutions, rather than just hedge funds. The IMF study also argued that hedge funds, especially macro hedge funds, are not highly leveraged.

The second major international report was written by the FSF Working Group on Highly Leveraged Institutions and published in March 2000.[1] It addressed issues raised by the near-collapse of Long-Term Capital Management in September 1998 and the instabilities in financial markets in east Asia and emerging markets in 1998, with particular focus on Australia, Hong Kong, Malaysia, New Zealand, Singapore and South Africa. On the latter issue of market dynamics, the Working Group noted:

Even in the absence of HLI activity, there would certainly have been considerable market pressure in these economies because of vulnerabilities in their economic structures or financial systems or the size of external shocks they faced. In unsettled and fragile conditions, large and concentrated HLI positions have the potential materially to influence market dynamics. Although the Working Group was concerned about some of the practices of HLIs identified in the six case studies, it was not able to reach a firm conclusion on their scale and the implications for market integrity.   (1–2)

While its assessment is cautious, reflecting the views of the United States, the report of the FSF Working Group on HLIs (2000) marks a distinct shift from the 1998 IMF report. It recognises that by virtue of their large concentrated positions and highly aggressive trading tactics, hedge funds and proprietary trading desks have the potential to materially destabilise financial markets which have some vulnerability. The potential of HLIs to destabilise financial markets lies not just in the size and concentration of positions, which in their own right can over-

---

[1] The full report is available at the FSF website: http://www.fsforum.org.

whelm a market, but also in the effect perceptions of such positions can have on the position-taking of other market participants, who either mimic large players' positions or drop out of the market altogether. This can be exacerbated by highly aggressive trading tactics.

It is hardly surprising that a shift in thinking about the possibility of speculators being an *independent* source of pressure in financial markets occurred in 1998. There was broad consensus that the baht was modestly overvalued in early 1997, even if the extent of the fall and its effect on other regional currencies was unexpected and, to many economists, unwarranted. But the continuing fragility in financial prices and the ferocity of the selling pressures in east Asian and South African asset markets in the first nine months of 1998, as well as the turmoil in US and emerging bond markets after the Russian debt default and near-collapse of LTCM in the last four months of 1998, shook the confidence of many in the self-stabilising forces in financial markets.

The events of 1998 have changed the perceptions of many about the importance of financial market dynamics and it is important to understand why this has occurred. Taking this as the starting point, this chapter seeks to do two things. It first examines some of the key elements of the activities of highly leveraged institutions in east Asian financial markets in 1997 and 1998, focusing particularly on market events in Australia, Hong Kong, Indonesia, Malaysia, New Zealand and Singapore. It is based on the work of the Study Group on Market Dynamics, which reported to the FSF Working Group on HLIs (2000),[2] and on the author's interviews with officials and market participants in 2000. Because of the need to maintain confidentiality, these sources cannot be specified and are generically referred to as 'market participants'.[3]

With the benefit of hindsight, it then revisits the findings of the 1998 IMF report on hedge funds. The Fund study assessed the impact of hedge funds by comparing the size of hedge funds to other institutional investors, whereas it is more relevant to compare their positions to those of other market participants, the size of the market in which they had their positions and the strength of their reputation and influence on other market participants at the time. It also argues that there is simply not enough data to draw strong conclusions about the magnitude and timing of hedge fund positions in east Asia, particularly Thailand, in 1997. It

---

[2] The Study Group's report is included as Annex E in the main report.
[3] The next three chapters in this book discuss market developments in Hong Kong (Chapter 4), Indonesia, Malaysia and Singapore (Chapter 5), and Australia and New Zealand (Chapter 6) in relative detail.

notes that key participants in the market say that macro hedge funds' baht positions were large, highly concentrated and established ahead of many others. Furthermore, while proprietary trading desks can be very aggressive and can collectively have large positions in financial markets, they often tend to follow macro hedge funds rather than lead them. It also argues that the Fund's assessment of financial market developments in 1997 was influenced by a set of non-economic factors.

Highly leveraged institutions in Asia

Hedge funds, especially the macro hedge funds, had substantial experience in east Asia before the financial crisis. Like many other financial institutions, they had large short positions in the yen from the mid-1990s in what was called the yen carry trade. While in practice the yen carry trade took a variety of forms, in essence it entailed borrowing at very low interest rates in yen and investing the proceeds in higher yielding assets, either US Treasury bonds or emerging market financial assets, to earn a positive spread or 'carry' (Eichengreen, et al. 1998). Market participants in Tokyo and New York reckon that the yen carry trade reached $200–300 billion by mid 1998, with at least half of these positions held by hedge funds. Positions of individual macro hedge funds were large and are believed to have reached as high as $20–25 billion.

The macro hedge funds, more than any other type of highly leveraged institution, were also active and knowledgeable about the rest of east Asia, including Australia and New Zealand. Traders and analysts in the region speak fulsomely of the regional knowledge and expertise of macro hedge fund analysts and traders at this time. This expertise and familiarity with the region went back a long way, either because some funds had been active in regional markets since the early 1990s or because a number of key people in the funds were born in the region or have close connections with it.

The macro hedge funds had long positions in 1996 in many of the east Asian economies with liquid markets, before closing these out and establishing short positions at the end of 1996 and in 1997. They have been both long and short in these markets at various times: the view that they are always on the sell side of a market is a misleading caricature. Highly leveraged institutions were but one set of players in east Asian financial markets in 1997 and 1998. Institutional investors, exporters and importers, multinationals, local banks and central banks were also active (FSF Working Group on HLIs 2000). But in many instances, it was the HLIs – and generally the macro hedge funds – that were the key players in these markets.

While position size varies by market and economy, in many instances, hedge funds had large and concentrated positions. The FSF Working Group on HLIs (2000) reports that market participants reckon that by mid-1998 HLI short positions reached $10 billion and $7 billion in the HK dollar and stock market respectively, $9 billion in the ringgit, $2 billion in the Singapore dollar, $10 billion in the Australian dollar, and $9 billion in the NZ dollar, implying a total of at least $47 billion. These positions were held mostly by hedge funds, and, of these, almost exclusively the macro hedge funds.

The dominant position of the macro hedge funds in regional markets is shown by the positions data from the Hong Kong Securities and Futures Commission contained in the report of the FSF Working Group on HLIs (2000), shown in Figure 3.1. These are the only 'hard' data available on hedge fund positions in east Asia in 1998. The FSF Working Group on HLIs (2000) reports that four hedge funds, three of which market participants identify as macro hedge funds, held around half of the net open interest in the Hang Seng Futures Index in mid 1998, and that one macro hedge fund accounted for a third of all positions, which is a degree of concentration that would be illegal on US exchanges.

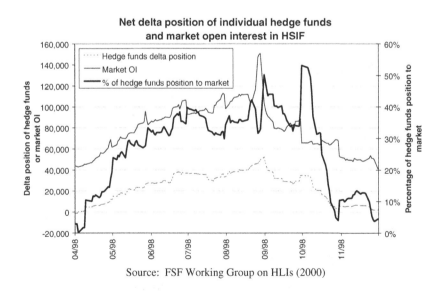

Source: FSF Working Group on HLIs (2000)

Figure 3.1 Net delta position of individual hedge funds and market open interest in HSIF

The data provide three insights into the behaviour of macro hedge funds, all of which tend to lead to exaggerated price movement. First, a speculator needs to be confident of his bet, and macro hedge funds will only establish big positions if they think that the story supports it. In some cases, an asset price correction seems inevitable – the story is obvious – and the hedge fund puts the position on early. This is the way the macro hedge funds talk about Thailand at the end of 1996 and early in 1997, and it is the same for New Zealand in 1997 (see Chapter 5). But in other cases, the story is only convincing after some price action has occurred and a trend is emerging. In the case of Hong Kong, the short positions were only established after the Hang Seng Index had already fallen over 35 per cent. To make these positions profitable, further substantial price falls were necessary.

Second, the HSI position-taking by the two main macro hedge funds involved was positively but imperfectly correlated (FSF Working Group on HLIs 2000). These hedge funds moved their positions in a similar way throughout all of 1998, both in the way they established and then reversed their positions. At the minimum, it shows that the big players can think and act alike, which compounds the price effect. Indeed, if herding increases with the size of the large player – say, because reputation or the expected price effect is greater – then the effect of the group may be bigger than the sum of the effects of the single parts.

Similarity in position-taking does not necessarily mean that hedge funds collude. While traders and analysts of different macro hedge funds regularly talk and socialise with each other, the macro hedge funds are also highly competitive and have very different corporate cultures, making it most unlikely that they explicitly collude in markets. This is probably right as a general proposition but it is not necessarily so in all cases: the FSF Working Group on HLIs (2000: 105) noted that its study group heard several reports of explicit collusion between hedge funds.

Similarity in position-taking by a couple of macro hedge funds in the HSI should also not obscure the fact that macro hedge funds do at times adopt different strategies and tactics in markets. Macro hedge funds are a diverse group. Some macro funds, for example, are inclined to hold positions for months, while others are inclined to regularly trade or 'churn' positions, taking advantage of price variability to try and enhance their profits.

The third aspect of hedge fund behaviour revealed by the HSI data from Hong Kong is their sheer aggressiveness in the market. The positions of the two main players increased sharply after the HKMA started its intervention on 14 August. Market participants reckon that the hedge funds' short positions in Hang Seng Index futures increased by about

$HK5 billion during the intervention episode. The general increase in hedge funds' short positions was also associated with widely reported criticisms of the HKMA's intervention by some hedge funds.

A noticeable feature of markets in 1998 was that, as positions became more profitable, hedge funds would increase them and their borrowing from banks and securities companies (FSF Working Group on HLIs 2000). In practice, the short positions of the major hedge funds in east Asian financial markets were not backed by any of their own capital and were infinitely leveraged. This meant that there was no effective external constraint on position-taking in these markets, and that the positions were vulnerable to changes in credit conditions, as ultimately occurred in October 1998 when US financial markets seized up.

While the price action in east Asian financial markets was generally driven by a range of market participants, in many cases it was focused on the macro hedge funds. The main exception was Indonesia, where the price falls in late 1997 and 1998 were associated with domestic capital flight. In general, the banks and securities companies followed – often aggressively – what they thought the hedge funds were doing, although in particular cases they may have been the initiators of some price action, such as the 'correlation plays' on the ringgit and rupiah, and the ringgit and the Malaysian stock market (see Chapter 5). As observed by the FSF Working Group on HLIs (2000: 105), the fact that hedge funds execute and finance their transactions through banks and securities firms creates an important 'structural opportunity' for prop desks to follow the positions and flows of the hedge funds, 'notwithstanding hedge fund efforts to distribute orders to prevent copy-cat trading'.

In some instances, the price action generated by speculative selling was compounded by other activity, or the lack of it, in the market. In New Zealand, for example, exporters had over-hedged, and importers had under-hedged, and so exporters were not buying, and importers were actively selling, as the NZ dollar started depreciating. Similarly, in Malaysia, domestic companies with foreign-currency payment streams sold ringgit to hedge against anticipated currency weakness.

One of the remarkable characteristics of the macro hedge funds in the 1990s was their attention to, and mastery of, liquidity conditions in financial markets: it is no use shorting a currency if the depreciation that makes the position profitable is offset by an appreciation associated with buying the currency to close out the short position. Understanding financial flows and what triggers them is crucial to being able to establish and reverse large positions with large profit, as investors require. The macro hedge funds always pay close attention to large predictable flows in markets. This means understanding the state of hedging by importers and exporters, incipient investment flows by domestic and international institutions, and the reaction function of other banks and the central bank (since intervention to support a fixed or weak currency can be a source of liquidity to close a short position). Liquidity overall in Asia in 1998 was also damaged by the withdrawal of Japanese banks, coincident with weakness in the Japanese banking system (de Brouwer 1999b), and this increased the susceptibility of regional markets to the effects of swings in large positions.

The way to make profits from a short position is to sell quietly without making prices fall. This means selling into other players' buying. After prices have fallen, the key is to close the position by buying without forcing prices up. This means buying into other players' selling. If prices do not fall after the short positions have been established, the speculator has an incentive to encourage prices to fall by some 'noisy' or aggressive selling. Similarly, if the speculator wants to close out its short position but there is not the volume of selling in the market to support this without pushing prices up, it has an incentive to encourage selling by some 'noisy' or aggressive selling. If the speculator is credible and other participants want to follow its trades, then copy-cat trading by others in the markets increases the effectiveness of the 'noisy' selling; such feedback effects mean that the speculator only has to sell a relatively small amount noisily.

This is essentially what market participants say occurred in east Asia in 1998. Everyone trading and investing in financial markets in 1997 and 1998 wanted to know what the macro hedge funds' positions were. The only ones who knew this for sure were the funds themselves, although the financial institutions which did their transactions for them had some insight. The hedge funds had a clear informational advantage over all other players: they knew their strategy and positions. Knowing the positions of the macro hedge funds was important for two reasons: traders thought that the flows were so big that they would influence the path of prices, and the funds had such a strong reputation that traders wanted to play the same bet. The macro funds' reputations remained strong despite their well-reported losses on the rupiah in late 1997 and early 1998 because these were seen as bad luck rather than a bad call.

Most market participants say that some macro hedge funds and other HLIs do more than just respond to liquidity flows in markets; if they can, they try to generate flows which either make their positions more profitable or allow them to exit their positions without generating price movement adverse to the profit of their positions. While this entails buying into the selling of other participants, it defies common sense to describe this as a stabilising action, as is done by Fung and Hsieh (1999).

There are at least three circumstances where market participants say that HLIs tried to force price changes in 1998. The first was the double play in Hong Kong, whereby short positions were initially established in the equity market followed by aggressive sales in the foreign-exchange market or money market which pushed up interest rates and pushed down equity prices. The macro hedge funds were large active participants in both markets (FSF Working Group on HLIs 2000), although it does not follow that all funds used this strategy. The second was in Malaysia, where market participants say that hedge funds and other HLIs made use of the fact that domestic corporates were prone to sell the ringgit on talk of hedge fund selling. The third was the activity of some hedge funds and banks in the Australian dollar market in June, designed to substantially reduce liquidity in the market and depreciate the currency.

These cases were associated with unusually aggressive trading tactics, like rapid selling, posting large sell orders with many banks and securities companies, unusually heavy trading in quiet times, and, in Hong Kong, placing false quotes on the electronic trading system. Market participants also mention an increase in rumours and published analysis of financial institutions which had previously not been active in the market. The increase in rumours is hard to evaluate. On the one hand, there were more newsworthy stories about the region at the time, and just because someone expresses a negative view it is hardly evidence that they are trying to push on a market. On the other hand, the market was more sensitive to talk in 1998 because of the heightened uncertainty of the time. Traders knew this and would certainly have used this to make money if they could.

Aggressive tactics were evident to different degrees in east Asian markets. They were least evident in New Zealand and Singapore. In New Zealand, this was probably because aggressive activity by hedge funds would undermine access to liquidity, since there are so few market makers in the currency and access to 'best' prices depends on maintaining good relations with them. Moreover, the hedge funds' short NZ dollar positions were established relatively early and were already highly profitable; they did not need any pushing. In Singapore, tight and effective capital controls were the mainstay in limiting speculation. The inability to access swap funding for short currency positions was also the main reason why market participants say that hedge funds were not involved in Korea or Taiwan.

Aggressive tactics in Australia, Hong Kong and Malaysia were necessary to generate price action. In all three cases, the speculative short positions were established *after* a price trend had been established in financial markets. To put on a position, hedge fund traders have to be convinced that there is a story. They were quick to pick this up in Thailand in 1997, even though they thought that the 'baht event' was just a one-off national event. The short positions that were established in 1998 were largely done after some momentum was in place, and they were associated with overshooting of financial prices, as discussed above. To ensure profit, this meant that the HLIs had to act more aggressively in markets to push prices further.

These markets were also among the most liquid in the region, and offered the opportunity to speculate not only on domestic developments but also on regional developments and emerging market risk. This meant that not only were intra-market dynamics important, but so too were cross market dynamics and effects. Falls in one market generated falls in another, and the market used these correlations as trading rules. The outstanding correlation in 1998 was that of the yen with the convertible currencies in the region (FSF Working Group on HLIs 2000). Traders also identified and used other correlations.

The experience of Indonesia provides additional insight into the activities and effects of hedge funds. It is an example of hedge funds being on the buy side of the market. The view that hedge funds only sell is an ignorant one: they can be on both sides of the market. But the losses incurred by hedge funds' long positions in Indonesia at the end of 1997 and start of 1998 had two important effects on their later behaviour. It made them hungry for profits: they had to make up for the losses to investors. And it made them wary of the upside: it left them with the view that east Asian markets were more vulnerable and susceptible to falls than they were to rallies. Both of these factors influenced their decision making in 1998.

There were many features to the market dynamics that occurred in east Asia in 1997 and 1998, but hedge funds and, to a lesser extent, proprietary trading desks played a significant role in much of what occurred. From the point of view of market integrity, there is nothing at all wrong in principle with speculation. It can be a necessary part of the mechanics of relative price adjustment in and between economies.

But there is a further dimension to this. The events in east Asia in 1997 and 1998 show that large speculators in mid-sized markets can pose a twofold threat to market integrity. In the first place, perceptions that large players are active can affect the position-taking of other participants, either encouraging them to establish similar positions – a classic case of herding – or to refrain from taking a contrary position and stand aside from the market altogether. In either case, liquidity in the market is adversely affected and price movement becomes more disorderly and exaggerated. Overshooting may have serious economic consequences if it triggers the shift to a different equilibrium or invokes a policy response. Second, knowing this effect, some large players may make use of it to bring about price adjustment. In this case, the speculator is not just making a bet, but using his influence in the market to improve the odds of a favourable outcome. The macro hedge funds have been involved in the region for a number of years but only the 1997–98 episode is talked about by market participants as an example of some funds attempting to force changes in markets.

The 1998 IMF study on hedge funds

The 1998 IMF study on hedge funds provides a wide ranging, seminal analysis of hedge funds and their activities in financial markets, and it is widely quoted as a major authoritative source on hedge funds and emerging markets.[4] But while there is much of merit and a wealth of information in the IMF study, the analysis and methodology used to assess the impact of hedge funds on emerging markets in 1997 can now be seen to contain a number of serious flaws.

Relative institutional size

The first weakness of the 1998 IMF study is one of its two key findings: that hedge funds and other highly leveraged institutions could not have had an impact on Asian financial markets in 1997 because the size of their capital is small relative to other institutions, like banks, pension funds, mutual funds, which are active in financial markets.

More specifically, Eichengreen, *et al.* (1998) report that assets under management by all hedge funds totalled $110 billion at the end of 1997, while those of institutional investors – mutual funds and pension funds – around the world total more than $20 trillion. That is, hedge funds account for less than half of one per cent of investment funds under management.[5] More recently, Baily, Farrell and Lund (2000) use the same argument and have updated the figures. They say that pension funds, mutual funds and insurance companies hold nearly $25 trillion in assets worldwide, whereas hedge funds hold only about 4 per cent of

---

[4] See, for example, the Presidents Working Group (1998), Barth and Zhang (1999) and the FSF Working Group on HLIs (2000).

[5] Eichengreen, *et al.* (1998) quote the MAR/Hedge database. MAR/Hedge note that their figures do not include all hedge funds, implying that the true figure is bigger.

that, about $800 billion to $1 trillion. They also regard this as *prima facie* evidence that hedge funds can have little impact on markets.

The argument is misleading. In the first place, it is necessary to compare like with like. If the issue is whether hedge funds have been a key force in some emerging markets, it is necessary to compare their assets and positions to other investors in those markets. The vast bulk of assets under management by pension funds, mutual funds and insurance companies are in US and European markets. It does not make a lot of sense to argue that hedge funds cannot impact on emerging markets because institutional investors dominate equity and bond markets in the United States.

Emerging-market assets are a very small proportion of mutual funds' and pension funds' total assets. At the end of 1999, for example, US mutual funds had total assets of $6,846 billion, but only $22 billion in emerging markets, or around 0.3 per cent of total assets.[6] These are concentrated in equities, whereas most of the activity of hedge funds and other HLIs in 1997 and 1998 was in the foreign-exchange market. When hedge funds were active in the equity market, as in Hong Kong, the 'hard data' in fact show that their positions dominated those of all other market participants (FSF Working Group on HLIs 2000).

The relative exposure of mutual and pension funds to Asian emerging markets is even smaller. According to Barth and Zhang (1999), for example, hedge funds' global assets were only $1\frac{1}{2}$ per cent of US and UK pension funds' global assets in 1996 – $91 billion compared to $5,501 billion – but the assets of hedge funds with an Asian exposure were almost three times that of pension funds with an Asian exposure – $13 billion compared to $5 billion. They reckon that mutual funds had total assets of $1,726 billion, but mutual funds with an Asian exposure were substantially smaller, with assets of $85 billion. Using TASS data, Barth and Zhang (1999) show that 25 per cent of hedge funds had an 'Asia focus' by mid-1997, up from 4 per cent a decade earlier.

Furthermore, it is not just the size of an institution's position in a market that matters to price dynamics, it is also the way in which those positions are established, how regularly they are changed or restructured, and the degree of leverage underlying them.

Data on various institutions' positions are not available, but it is widely accepted by financial-market participants that hedge funds are more likely to change their positions sharply than are either pension funds or mutual funds (Barth and Zhang 1999; FSF Working Group

---

[6] See Investment Company Institute (ICI), the national association of the American mutual-fund industry, at *http://www.ici.org*.

on HLIs 2000). Since pension and mutual funds generally follow bench-marks (rather than seek to maximise absolute returns) and since their investment in emerging markets is motivated by diversification, they tend to focus less on very short-term asset management. They do not change their portfolios substantially in the short term. Barth and Zhang (1999) quote anecdotal evidence, for example, that pension funds typically allocate funds in emerging markets on a five- to ten-year horizon and they argue that mutual funds also have captive commitments in emerging markets. They tend to adjust their positions in response to changes in market benchmarks, and so implicitly typically follow rather than lead market developments.

In relation to mutual funds at least, this is evident in Figures 3.2 and 3.3. Figure 3.2 shows mutual funds' assets in emerging markets and Figure 3.3 shows changes in assets adjusted for valuation effects. While asset values in emerging east Asia deteriorated substantially during the crisis, actual outflows by mutual funds were relatively small and assets in emerging markets were largely maintained. The change in assets was primarily a valuation effect.

Post and Millar (1998) show that mutual funds only became net sellers of Asian equities in November 1997, well after the crisis had begun in Thailand and spread to other parts of east Asia. And even then, their

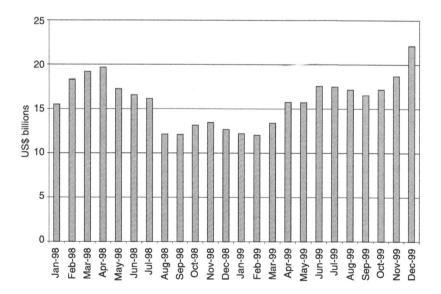

Figure 3.2 Mutual funds total assets in emerging markets

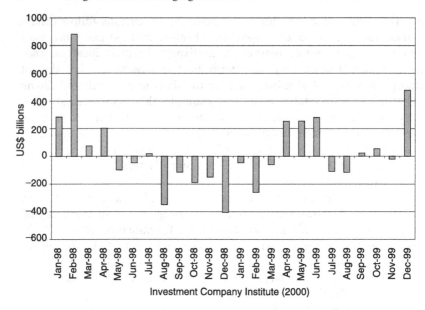

Investment Company Institute (2000)

Figure 3.3 Mutual funds total assets in emerging markets net new cash flow

sales were very modest and short lived: emerging market funds only sold $36 million in November 1997 – equivalent to 1 per cent of their assets. This appears to have been motivated by shareholder cash withdrawals at the time. This is why Barth and Zhang (1999: 198) conclude that 'pension plans and mutual funds are stabilizing forces in emerging markets'.[7]

Because mutual funds do not appear to have been aggressive sellers of stocks during the crisis, it is probably right to say that they were also not big outright sellers of local currencies, although this depends in particular circumstances on the degree to which funds hedged their long exposures in emerging markets. The fact that US mutual funds are strongly restricted in their use of derivatives (see below) suggests that hedging was minimal, but this assessment is tentative.

As discussed in Chapter 2, hedge funds adopt many different trading strategies, with some continually managing and changing positions in

---

[7] Their claim is probably exaggerated in the sense that benchmarking requires pension and mutual funds to sell assets that have falling prices, which tends to add to the momentum (Nofsinger and Sias 1999). These sorts of predictable flows are exactly the ones that the macro hedge funds search out, to enable them to establish or reverse positions without generating offsetting price movement, as discussed above and in Chapter 2.

financial markets, and others continually monitoring their positions but holding them for a relatively long time. While mutual funds and pension funds retained substantial assets in emerging markets, including Asia, during the region's turmoil, the positions of hedge funds and proprietary trading desks were rapidly closed. Eichengreen, *et al.* (1998) note that almost all HLIs quickly took profit and closed out their short positions in the baht after it was devalued in July 1997, and the FSF Working Group on HLIs (2000) found the same for hedge funds' short positions in other emerging markets in 1998. Motivated by the pursuit of absolute returns, hedge funds continually monitor their positions in markets and can change them rapidly as asset prices or expectations change.

Mutual funds face greater internal decision-making constraints. At hedge funds, the decision is made by the general partner or portfolio manager and can be implemented immediately. Chadha and Jansen (1998: 35) note that this 'leaner institutional structure increases the ability of hedge funds to move quickly'.

Hedge funds tend to be substantially more leveraged than mutual funds, pension funds and insurance companies, which face strict limits on the amount of leverage they can use. In the United States, the Investment Company Act (1940) denies mutual funds a high degree of leverage by limiting their issuance of 'senior' securities – that is, bonds, notes, debentures or obligations which have priority over the distribution of assets or payment of dividends. In practice this means that a mutual fund's debts cannot exceed one-third of its total assets (President's Working Group on Financial Markets 1999: A-1). The use of reverse repos and short sales may involve the issuance of senior securities and so contravenes the Investment Company Act, limiting the access of mutual funds to key instruments in establishing short positions.

Use of derivatives does not necessarily involve balance-sheet leverage but may involve economic leverage. Mutual funds are allowed to use derivatives, but face constraints in practice. For example, use of derivatives has to be stated in the mutual fund's prospectus. According to the President's Working Group on Financial Markets (1999: A-1), the SEC 'has also emphasised the importance of mutual fund managers directors in the oversight of fund derivative instruments, risk management, internal controls, and disclosure, in order to ensure that mutual fund assets are properly valued.' That is, the SEC exercises moral suasion over mutual funds in their use of derivatives.

The capacity of hedge funds to acquire greater leverage can affect market dynamics. For a given position in a market, the higher the leverage supporting the position, the more difficult it becomes to maintain that position, the more it moves into loss and margin calls are made for more collateral. This means that highly leveraged positions can need to be unwound rapidly when they move into loss, with a potentially large impact on market prices, as the US experience with the near-collapse of LTCM in September 1998 showed. By being less leveraged, mutual and pension funds are less subject to forced unwinding of positions as credit conditions change (FSF Working Group on HLIs 2000).

These differences between hedge funds and mutual and pension funds was recognised by the President's Working Group on Financial Markets (1999: 2):

Although individually and as an industry, hedge funds represent a relatively small segment of the market, their impact is greatly magnified by their highly active trading strategies and by the leverage obtained through their use of repurchase agreements and derivative contracts. . . . [H]edge funds often use leverage aggressively.

The report further notes that hedge funds are not conventional buy-and-hold investors:

The propensity of hedge funds to alter market positions quickly distinguishes them from pension funds and bank personal trusts. Mutual funds, however, are similar to hedge funds in that they can quickly liquidate portfolios, but because of cost, tax, and other considerations, they may be less likely to shift their market positions often.   (A-2)

This is not just an official view. To quote one market participant (Stolz 1998: 17):

Although they represent a tiny minority of the investor base, hedge funds punch above their weight . . . By virtue of their ownership structure, unregulated nature and wide trading mandate, hedge funds play a disproportionately high role in providing short-term liquidity and price formation.

Hedge funds and the baht

The second main finding of the 1998 IMF study was that hedge funds did not play a leading role in the dynamics of financial markets in 1997, especially in the baht market. This was a premature and hasty judgment. In the first place, available information about hedge funds' positions is, in reality, scant and largely second-hand; assessments are necessarily judgmental. In the absence of actual positions data, not enough is known about the positions, trading strategies and market activities of highly leveraged institutions to make categorical statements that hedge funds played no substantial role in the dynamics of the baht foreign exchange market in 1997. Moreover, the evidence on hedge funds' positions in the baht and their influence on financial-market dynamics that is available is considerably more ambiguous and controvertible than asserted by the 1998 IMF study.

Based on interviews, Eichengreen, *et al.* (1998) estimate that hedge funds directly had about US$7 billion of the Bank of Thailand's $28 billion forward book. Eichengreen and Mathieson (17) add that hedge funds may have sold baht forward through offshore counterparties, onshore foreign banks and onshore domestic banks, noting that there 'is no way of breaking the magnitude of these transactions.' They argue (18) that although some hedge funds sold some long-dated forward contracts on the baht in February 1997, 'the bulk of hedge funds' forward sales to the Bank of Thailand appears to have occurred only in May at the tail end of the process'.

The issues of scale and timing of positions are important ones, and the IMF's assessment is not consistent with the views and experience of many key players in the baht market, either in terms of the scale of hedge funds' positions or their timing.

Take the scale of hedge funds' positions. Key domestic and international participants in the baht foreign exchange market at the time estimate that hedge funds' aggregate short baht positions were in the range of $10–15 billion, which is between a third to half of the Bank of Thailand's forward book, rather than a quarter. While many hedge funds were active in the market, these positions appear to have been concentrated, with, for example, (at least) two macro hedge funds each said to have had short baht positions of between $3–4 billion. The individual positions of the proprietary trading desks of banks and securities companies also seem to have been smaller than those of the big hedge funds – probably, at most, $1 billion – and probably smaller in aggregate than the sum of hedge funds' positions. The picture that emerges from talking with these market participants is similar to that told in the 1998 country studies in the FSF Working Group on HLIs (2000): a substantial agglomeration of short positions held by the proprietary trading desks, centred on large concentrated short positions held by macro hedge funds.

Consider, also, the timing of the positions. While there was a flurry of market activity in April and May 1997, most market participants say that hedge funds started establishing short positions in late 1996, and that the big positions were mostly in place by February 1997.[8] There certainly was increased across-the-board activity in April and May, but it appears to have been dominated by a lot of smaller players trying to get some of the

---

[8] One participant said that his fund was surprised by the IMF's assessment that macro hedge funds were relatively late in establishing short baht positions, noting that they 'couldn't believe that they bought the story'.

action, although market participants do say that there was also increased activity by some of the large macro hedge funds at this time. It is misleading to say that the bulk of baht short sales by hedge funds were at the tail end of the process.

Hedge funds and proprietary trading desks

The 1998 IMF study tends to regard hedge funds and the proprietary trading desks of banks, securities companies and insurance companies as identical. To be sure, 'prop desks' are active in the same markets as hedge funds and adopt many of the same trading strategies and practices, but that does not mean that they are necessarily the same in all respects. Indeed, the crucial distinction between the two categories of HLI in east Asia in 1997 and 1998 was that the macro hedge funds tended to be the focus for much, but not all, of the positioning by the proprietary trading desks. While it is impossible to know the counterfactual, this suggests that had macro hedge fund positioning been smaller, the overall stresses on regional financial markets may have been less.

Market participants speak of four important differences between hedge funds and prop desks, with implications for pricing dynamics in markets. The first is that, at least with respect to the financial markets examined in this book, individual macro hedge funds' positions have probably been substantially larger than those of individual prop desks. According to a wide range of market participants, individual prop desk positions in these markets rarely exceeded $1 billion, while individual hedge fund's positions reached as much as $4 billion. Moreover, market participants in general reckon that the sum of hedge funds' positions generally exceeded the sum of prop-desk positions. Either individually or collectively, hedge funds probably have had bigger positions than proprietary trading desks.

The principal reason for this is that prop desks generally face lower position limits than hedge funds, and this is because prop-desk traders at banks, securities companies and insurance companies are subject to the broader franchise interest of their institution. Banks, for example, are involved in a wide range of business activities and are generally not willing to sacrifice their global interests, even for potentially large risky gains from one division of their business. This is reinforced by quarterly reporting to shareholders. This will, of course, vary by institution. Particular US and European investment banks, for example, are perceived as having a greater appetite for risk. At a hedge fund, however, position limits are higher; the trading desk of a hedge fund is more likely to be the franchise.

The size of positions can have an important impact on market dynamics. In the first place, assuming everything else is given, simple supply and demand analysis indicates that the effect on market prices will be greater the bigger the position. In general, there is a strong empirical link between volume and price movement (Karpoff 1987; Stickel and Verrechia 1993).

But there is another more subtle impact on market dynamics: the effect of large players on position-taking by other players. This can take a number of forms. It can be that other players try to place directionally similar positions in the same market, in which case perceptions and beliefs about the large player's positions can give rise to herding. Or it can be that perceptions and beliefs about the large player's positions have a chilling effect on other players taking the alternative position in a market, for fear of being on the wrong side of the momentum in the market. In either case, the one-sidedness in the market is increased and the price movement is greater than it would otherwise have been. The effect on position-taking is more important the stronger the reputation of the large player.

Market participants tend to talk about macro hedge funds, not prop desks, as being the key players in financial markets, because they tend to be the institutions with the big positions and, at least until the end of 1998, the ones with the extraordinarily powerful reputations of omniscience and omnipotence in financial markets. Many participants in financial markets try to discern the positions of hedge funds with a view to trying to understand likely flows and price trends in their market. Indeed, trading desks, including prop desks, are one of these groups and it is a key reason why they seek and value hedge fund business.

Hedge funds rarely trade directly in a market in their own name but execute their trades through the trading desks of banks and securities companies, so that it is the name of the bank or security company that appears in the market.[9] This gives the trading desk valuable information from which it actively tries to discern the aggregate position of the hedge fund client. In the past couple of years, this has become a more complex game, since hedge funds trade with a range (say a dozen or so) banks and securities companies, and they both buy and sell through banks and securities companies to confuse the market and hide their positions. This makes it harder, but not impossible, for banks and others to front-run or mimic positioning by hedge funds.

The second difference between hedge funds and prop desks is that hedge funds tend to be able to hold a loss-making position for longer

---

[9] This can be even more complicated because some intermediaries acting for hedge funds will in turn use other intermediaries to act for it in the market. This is more likely to occur when a particular institution becomes identified with a particular hedge fund.

than prop desks can. Both hedge funds and prop desks mark their positions to market on a daily basis but a hedge fund is able to hold a loss-making position for longer because its traders generally have greater autonomy. This relates in part to the fact that the trading desk at a hedge fund is generally more important to the hedge fund than the prop desk is to a bank or securities company. But it is also because a hedge fund is able to 'lock in' capital for fixed periods, even up to several years, and so can reduce short-term pressures from investors. Some hedge funds have lock-in periods of several years, which enable them to hold positions for a relatively long time. This is not the case with prop desks.

The effect on pricing dynamics is unclear. On the one hand, the ability of hedge funds to take longer-term positions in markets adds to the depth of those markets and hence improves market efficiency. This means that hedge funds taking a longer-term perspective, focusing on fundamental valuations at a time when prices are away from fair value, add to price stability. For example, a fund selling when a market is overbought or buying when a market is oversold stabilises market prices. This capacity to take a longer term view is all the more striking because hedge funds are predominantly American-owned or managed, and the caricature of US institutions is that that they are excessively focused on the near term. Hedge funds that take long-term positions are an important exception to that view.

On the other hand, a hedge fund's greater capacity to hold a loss-making position may also mean that it is more willing to hold a bigger position than it otherwise would, which is plausible since the fund is less subject to the vagaries of the market. If this is so, then the covering or closing of loss-making positions will be associated with larger price movements than otherwise.

The third difference between hedge funds and prop desks is that the degree of leverage is different. Chadha and Jansen (1998: 36) argue that banks in fact have higher leverage than hedge funds. This is the case with *on-balance-sheet* leverage. Using MAR/Hedge data, they argue that the typical hedge fund has two dollars of debt for every dollar of equity, and the typical global macro hedge fund has three dollars of debt for every dollar of equity. They compare this to a bank with an 8 per cent capital adequacy ratio, which, by implication has more than 12 dollars of debt for every dollar of equity.

That is right as far as it goes, but it ignores economic leverage (see Box 2 in Chapter 2). Through the use of derivatives and swaps, the *off-balance-sheet* or economic leverage of hedge funds can be much higher than for banks and securities companies. As discussed above, hedge funds' positions in emerging financial markets in 1997 and 1998 appear to have been individually and collectively larger than those of the banks and securities companies. These positions were also highly leveraged. The macro hedge funds invest in a variety of markets and instruments and have diversified asset structures. Market participants reckon that on-balance-sheet leverage ratio for many of the large macro hedge funds is around 3 to 4 and that their aggregate off-balance-sheet leverage – total positions relative to capital – is typically a similar level but on occasion is much higher. The FSF Working Group on HLIs (2000: Annex III of Annex E, p. 139) noted that, taking account of off-balance-sheet positions, 'leverage used by the largest hedge funds could be of the order of 10:1 or 15:1 as a peak'.

If investors are constrained in their access to credit, then lower leverage may indicate that position-taking is limited and constrained in some manner. If the IMF's view in 1998 were right, lower leverage at hedge funds would imply that they were externally constrained in position-taking; the system itself would be imposing a discipline on position-taking. This was not the case for the large hedge funds in 1997 and 1998 (before the near-collapse of LTCM in September).

The economic leverage of the big hedge funds with respect to individual positions could at times be infinite (FSF Working Group on HLI 2000 Chapter 2 and Annex III of Annex E). When these hedge funds established short currency positions in east Asia in 1997 and 1998, their banks did not require them to put up any of their own capital as collateral. Furthermore, if these funds' positions moved into loss, margining requirements only came into effect *after* the losses had reached a certain threshold. Banks have limits on overall exposures to individual funds, but market participants reckon that during this period, none of the major macro hedge funds reached these limits, even with positions in individual markets of several billion dollars. Essentially, the large macro hedge funds faced no external constraint on position-taking in emerging markets in 1997 and 1998. This was not the case for the prop desks at banks and securities firms, which were constrained by the need to meet capital adequacy standards.

The fourth difference between hedge funds and prop desks that market participants mention is that the constraints on the use of aggressive trading practices may be moderately weaker for hedge funds than it is for prop desks. It is important not to over-generalise this difference, and it should not be construed as implying that prop desk traders are not aggressive or that all hedge funds are more aggressive than prop desks.

Market practitioners give two reasons why hedge funds may be less constrained in how aggressively they operate in a market. The main one is that while traders at hedge funds and prop desks are both motivated by the pursuit of absolute returns, prop desk traders are constrained by the broader interests of the franchise. A hedge fund is more inclined than a bank's prop desk to regard a set of positions in a country – especially a mid-sized or emerging market far away from the United States – as a one-shot game. A bank or securities company, by way of contrast, is more likely to see that set of positions within the context of its overall set of activities in a country.

More specifically, banks and securities companies are usually intent on preserving their reputation and not damaging other corporate and government relationships if they are engaged in a range of business activities in a country. If a trader at a bank uses unacceptably aggressive trading practices, then traders at other banks will tend to penalise that trader or bank, especially in relatively small markets, like New Zealand (see Chapter 6). Moreover, banks which engage in market practices which are viewed as unacceptable by the monetary authorities tend to find that they lose access to official business – like advisory services, underwriting bonds or privatisations, or counterparty business in financial markets – even if temporarily. The market discipline on aggressive behaviour is greater for banks and securities firms than hedge funds.

The other reason market participants say that hedge fund traders are less constrained is that their personalities are different: they reckon that hedge fund traders are more idiosyncratic, individualistic and risk-loving than prop-desk traders. Most hedge fund traders started in banks or securities companies and often leave and set up their own hedge fund because they want more autonomy and a greater share of trading profits.[10]

Chadha and Jansen (1998: 34) argue against this popular market conception of the difference between traders. They say that hedge-fund traders are more risk averse than prop-desk traders because, as managers of the fund, they lose their capital and reputation if the hedge fund fails. If a prop-desk trader makes losses, he loses his job not his capital. This sounds right in theory but is not necessarily the case in practice. Consider the fortune of John Meriwether, the chief trader of LTCM. Dunbar (2000) reports that while Meriwether's capital in LTCM fell precipitously, he still had a proprietary interest in the bailed-out LTCM worth millions of dollars and he was able to keep his personal wealth intact, coincidentally transferring assets to his wife at the end of

---

[10] Stolz (1998: 17), a market participant, notes that hedge funds are able to recruit the brightest and best from the proprietary trading desks of investment banks.

August 1998. He was also able to return to the hedge fund business in June 1999, less than a year after the bail-out organised by the Fed.[11]

Reviews of the 1998 IMF study   The 1998 IMF study has been influential and widely and approvingly quoted. The President's Working Group on Financial Markets (1999: A-7–8), for example, quoted it as an authority that the hedge funds 'were not the dominant players' in the 1997 east Asian financial crisis and 'were at the rear of the herd rather than in the lead'. *The Economist* magazine has done the same (6–13 June 1998).

This has been followed by other authors. Fung and Hsieh (1999) argued in support of the IMF study and inferred positions from hedge fund returns data. But, as shown in Chapter 8, the method they use is flawed. More recently, Baily, Farrell and Lund (2000) argued in the prestigious US policy journal *Foreign Affairs* that blaming hedge funds for the east Asian crisis is wrong.[12] To support this, they revisit the arguments of Eichengreen, *et al.* (1998) that hedge funds are small relative to other institutions, that hedge funds are the same as proprietary trading desks, that hedge funds were late to the action in the baht and that hedge funds are not typically highly leveraged. The problem is that, as argued in this chapter, these points are either not relevant, are exaggerated or are plain wrong.

Baily, Farrell and Lund (2000: 99) also argue that hedge funds 'were not the prime cause of the volatility of global capital flows. In fact, the hot money in the recent crises came mostly from bank lending, not from hedge funds or other non-bank investments such as pension and mutual funds'. This argument has initial appeal. It is certainly true that bank lending was the most volatile component of capital flight in the east Asian financial crisis and was a crucial element in the instabilities that arose (Grenville 1998; de Brouwer 1999b), and it is the reason why the debate about private-sector involvement in the prevention and resolution of financial crises continues.[13] But it is simplistic to say that this means that hedge funds had no role: the crisis was a complex phenomenon and it is not necessary to reduce it to one problem.

The exchange-rate falls of 1997 preceded the bank outflows, and the unstable financial-market dynamics and collapse of regional asset prices

---

[11] See the *Wall Street Journal*, 7 July 1999.
[12] *Foreign Affairs* billed their article as 'Absolving Hedge Funds' and the editors showed a picture of George Soros with the line, 'Innocent, after all'.
[13] See, for example, the summary of the discussion by the IMF Executive Board on this issue in Public Information Notice (PIN) No. 00/80.

were key factors in stimulating bank outflows. Correcting changes in cross-border assets for exchange-rate changes, BIS data show that bank cross-border outflows from Thailand did not begin until the June quarter of 1997 at a trickle of $300 million (Table 3.1).

The real bank outflows occurred in the September quarter – after the first round of currency devaluations – when bank outflows totalled $10.5 billion, and continued in successive quarters, with $7.2 billion in December 1997 and $8.5 billion in March 1998. The BIS figures indicate that bank outflows were not in the March quarter of 1997 as Baily, Farrell and Lund argue, but in the September quarter of 1997, after the hedge-fund positions had been closed. Indeed, bank inflows to Thailand were strong throughout all of 1996 – according to BIS data, the bank inflows into Thailand in the four quarters of 1996 totalled $8.9 billion, $4.1 billion, $1 billion and $1.1 billion respectively – even as short positions were being established against the baht.

The political economy of the IMF study

The 1998 IMF study concluded that hedge funds were not material to what happened in east Asian financial markets in 1997. While this assessment reflects the Fund's interpretation of the arguments and facts, that interpretation itself reflects its view of the world and the political circumstances that existed at the time.

Economics is a subtle discipline and there is a mix of views about the role of institutions in financial markets, and about the links between financial markets and economic growth. In economists' minds there are two sides to the argument that the dynamics of financial markets can matter. Consider each side of the argument in turn.

On the one hand, there are four reasons to think that financial dynamics should not really matter all that much. In the first place, asset-price adjustment should not be thought of as 'a problem' because it occurs for economic reasons. It is a matter of looking through the veil of the dynamics of financial markets to identify the underlying economic determinants of the asset-price adjustment. There are also important stabilising mechanisms in financial markets which should smooth liquidity in markets and prevent overshooting from occurring: if a market were really oversold, for example, rational speculators would enter the market – hence providing liquidity – and buy – hence preventing deviations from fair value.

With this in mind, economists tend to explain the depreciation of the baht in July 1997, for example, as the result of the interaction of expectations and a large and growing current-account deficit, emerging domestic inflation pressures flowing from excess demand and 'structural bottle-

Table 3.1. *Changes in banks' unconsolidated assets in Asia, US$ billion*

	1997				1998				Outstandings
	March	June	September	December	March	June	September	December	December 98
Indonesia	1.8	2.8	3.3	-2.1	-5.0	-3.9	-2.1	-1.6	50.5
Korea	4.3	4.8	-1.9	-11.5	-16.4	-4.2	-4.6	-4.9	74.6
Malaysia	5.3	1.8	0.2	-3.7	-2.8	-1.5	-1.1	-0.7	23.2
Philippines	1.6	1.9	-0.8	0.5	-0.8	0.8	-2.0	1.7	16.3
Thailand	0.5	-0.3	-10.5	-7.2	-8.5	-5.3	-4.8	-5.4	56.6
Affected-5	**13.5**	**11.0**	**-9.7**	**-24.0**	**-33.5**	**-14.1**	**-14.6**	**-10.9**	**221.2**
China	2.4	4.2	5.2	-0.3	0.3	-3.3	-6.2	1.0	82.7
Taiwan	1.9	0.5	-0.3	-2.3	-0.4	0.3	-1.3	2.0	23.2
Total	**17.8**	**16.3**	**-4.8**	**-26.6**	**-33.6**	**-17.1**	**-22.1**	**-7.9**	**327.1**

Source: BIS International Banking and Financial Market Developments. Exchange-rate adjusted.

necks', and a time-varying risk premium. Similarly, the events in east Asian financial markets in 1998 are also seen as the outcome of position-taking based on deteriorating economic fundamentals (Corsetti, Pesenti and Roubini 1998).

Second, the fact that the process of adjustment is not smooth is hardly surprising. Asset markets, like foreign exchange, stock, or bond markets, are forward looking and react to what is expected to occur rather than what has already happened, and so they adjust rapidly and sometimes unevenly – or 'jump' – as expectations or information about the future change (Dornbusch 1976). Such adjustment is not something to be especially concerned about; it is simply part of the process of flexible-price asset markets.

Third, focusing on the role of any particular institution or set of institutions in the mechanics of asset price adjustment can be a distraction from the substantive issue: changing economic fundamentals. The individual speculators are just part of the sweep of the invisible hand, and criticising them is akin to shooting the messenger. Moreover, speculative crises and bubbles will always occur, even if the institutions doing the speculating change, and so focusing on one particular set of institutions is futile. Hedge funds in the 1990s were the Belgian dentists of the 1980s and the gnomes of Zurich in the 1970s. In the 2000s, it will just be some other exotic investor group affecting markets.

Finally, even if particular institutions do have an effect on market dynamics in the short run, the effect is likely to be negligible or non-existent for any meaningful period of time. Shocks or disturbances may occur but they are just noise and tend to be offset by some other disturbance. Even if the effects of shocks do turn out to be longer lasting on the odd occasion, a market-based system is still far more likely to provide better outcomes in general than a government-directed or tightly regulated one.

On the other hand, there are four reasons to think that dynamics in financial markets should matter. First, the crucial assumption that markets are efficient does not really hold in practice (Summers 1986; Shleifer and Summers 1990; Krugman 1993; Shleifer 2000). To paraphrase Cutler, Poterba and Summers (1990a, b): the efficient-markets hypothesis is a good place to start but it is not the end of the story. There is substantial evidence of overshooting, not least the stock price bubble of 1987 and the appreciation of the US dollar in 1985.[14] Overshooting is also evident in the tendency for returns on all types

---

[14] See the *Journal of Economic Perspectives* symposium on bubbles, in volume 4, number 2, 1990.

of assets to show strong positive autocorrelation in the short term but negative correlation in the longer term, which is indicative of short-term overshooting and longer-term correction to fundamental value (Cutler, Poterba and Summers 1990a, b). Liquidity in financial markets is elastic, and actions, information or trading that affect the willingness of other participants to trade can affect liquidity and price formation in a market (see Chapter 7).

Second, models of fundamentals for almost all asset prices have weak explanatory and predictive power, notably exchange rates (Meese and Rogoff 1983), and it is difficult even for traders and investors in financial assets to base their decisions on fundamentals. Traders and others tend to rely heavily on technical rules, like charting, which can give rise to substantial and sustained deviations from fair value (Frankel and Froot 1988; Froot and Thaler 1990). In this context, market dynamics can be relevant to economic and financial outcomes when the willingness of market participants to sell and buy depends on the perceived presence of large players who can affect momentum in the market and the profitability of particular strategies (De Long, et al. 1990a, b), especially in mid-sized markets. An important upshot of these analyses is that Friedman's (1953) presumption that speculation is always stabilising is not in fact a general proposition.

Third, there is a strong empirical literature which argues that the asset-price movements in 1997 and 1998 in east Asia and elsewhere went well beyond the adjustment predicted by mainstream models of asset prices. The sign of the adjustment may have been right, but the movements were unambiguously excessive.

Furman and Stiglitz (1998), for example, use a variety of models to estimate the degree of over-valuation of regional real exchange rates, reproduced in Table 3.2. These suggest that at June 1997, the rupiah was overvalued by at most 6 per cent, the baht by at most 11 per cent, the ringgit by at most 12 per cent, and the Singapore dollar by at most 20 per cent. The actual movements were, of course, in reverse order to this ranking. Barrell, et al. (1999) estimate fundamental equilibrium exchange rates (FEERs) for Korea, Singapore, Taiwan and Thailand from 1982 to 1996, which provided good fit and showed minimal misalignment ahead of the crisis.

Finally, financial-market dynamics has been shown in a variety of recent models to be potentially important to the occurrence of multiple equilibria in economies (see Dooley and Walsh 1999 for a survey). The implication of these models is that the economic effects of financial 'shocks' can be relatively long-lived or even permanent. Similarly, even

Table 3.2. *Measures of real exchange rate misalignment*
Percentage deviation from equilibrium value, positive is overvaluation

	PPP-1 model Jan–June 1997	PPP-2 model May 1997	PPP-3 model 1996	Monetary model May 1997
Indonesia	6	−5	−16	0
Korea	−5	9	1	−12
Malaysia	12	8	−41	2
Philippines	37	19	−16	−24
Singapore	20	−6	−18	35
Taiwan	−2	−3	—	8
Thailand	11	7	−18	2

Notes: PPP-1 model is the percentage difference between the real exchange-rate average for 1989–91 and that for the period January to June 1997. PPP-2 model is based on Chinn's (1998) estimate of PPP exchange rates from 1975 to 1996. PPP-3 model is the percentage difference between the actual real exchange rate in 1996 and the predicted value based on fitted values from a regression of the real exchange rate on per capita GDP measured in PPP dollars. The actual real exchange rate is the World Bank's calculation of the ratio of the PPP rate to the dollar exchange rate. The monetary model is based on Chinn's (1998) monetary model.
Source: Furman and Stiglitz (1998).

if the argument that the effects of large traders and manipulation are just noise in asset markets is right, the literature on random walks indicates that the effects of noise and shocks can be substantial – they may be noise but they can have a big and permanent effect on the path of prices if they are drawn from the far tails of the distribution.

These are two sets of arguments on whether financial market dynamics matter, and people and institutions clearly differ in their assessment. The IMF, for example, along with the US Treasury and Federal Reserve, appear to be inclined to the first set of arguments, and this influenced how the IMF and the key economic policy institutions in the United States assessed the events in east Asian financial markets in 1997 and 1998. Most other policy-makers in the east Asian region would be inclined to a mix of the two sets of arguments on the importance of financial market dynamics.

Most economists would probably see elements of truth in both these sets of arguments, and opt for a compromise view. Indeed, the rejection in the 1998 IMF report of the argument that on particular occasions some hedge funds could create a market failure was not a necessary outcome of the intellectual traditions of the Fund. It had, after all, set a strong precedent in its published assessments of the ERM crisis about the actual and potential importance of hedge funds in financial markets.[15] The debate about hedge funds since 1997 has been affected by other, non-economic factors.

There are probably three political-economy factors which influenced the view of the IMF in 1998, and also of the US Treasury and the Federal Reserve, that HLIs did not substantially adversely influence the market dynamics in east Asia in 1997 and 1998.

The first is concern that hedge funds were undeservedly being set up as scape-goats for the east Asian financial crisis, a crisis which they view as the outcome of bad policies with respect to exchange rates, governance, bank supervision, and corruption. From this point of view, to agree that some HLIs at times exacerbated instabilities in financial markets would give ground for the 'true culprits' to escape criticism and would be used to deflect arguments for economic and structural reform. There was also a sense in Washington that policymakers on the other side of the Pacific would make as much mileage as they could over any concession on destabilising speculation.

The second aspect of political economy was that the debate on the role of hedge funds became substantially more complicated after early 1998 – just at the time when the IMF report was being written – because it became intensely political. Some Asian politicians and commentators argued that speculation by hedge funds was a device to contain developing countries and an opportunity to imprint US-type markets and policies on the rest of the world. In January 1998, the Malaysian Prime Minister, Mahathir Mohamad, expressed this view in its most extreme form by associating hedge funds with a US–Jewish–Wall Street conspiracy to attack and subjugate Muslim and developing east Asia. Most commentators regard this rhetoric as an attempt to distract domestic attention from Mahathir's political conflict with his then-protégé now-nemesis, Anwar Ibrahim, who was widely highly regarded in Washington, D.C. But it raised the stakes in showing that the hedge funds were not responsible for the east Asian crisis.

These comments had the effect of making the IMF and US policy-makers more defensive about hedge funds and could not help but con-dition their response. The effect of Mahathir's claims was probably to make the IMF understate the possibility of market disruption by large

---

[15] The assessment of the 1998 Study is in sharp contrast to the IMF's 1992–93 International Capital Markets Reports, which conclude that macro hedge funds played a key role in the 1992 ERM crisis, although they skirt the issue of whether the outcome would have been any different had hedge funds not been involved.

players and overstate the positive effects they have on markets. This helps explain why the 1998 IMF study lacks nuance and reads like a defence of hedge funds, stating all the reasons why they are not a problem and all the ways that they enhance market efficiency. Even if aspects of Mahathir's claim that speculation in the ringgit was destabilising were right – as most market participants say (see Chapter 5) – this was lost in the broader political context.

The third political economy effect on the international debate about hedge funds is that countries are strongly disinclined to penalise profitable institutions which are based in, or operate from, their jurisdiction so long as they do not materially disrupt their own domestic financial markets. Countries have a natural vested interest in protecting their own. While most hedge funds are offshore legal entities, most managers of hedge funds are based in the United States, and in the greater New York area. These hedge funds, and the investment banks and securities companies that service them, have close working relations with the US Treasury and Federal Reserve which, for good reason, are highly valued by both market participants and the authorities alike. This has made US policy institutions less disposed to the criticism of HLIs made by foreigners; indeed the United States has been the most prominent supporter of hedge-fund activity in international markets. Given the close links between the IMF and US Treasury, this has influenced the IMF position.

The difficulty in separating official and market interests is a feature of many other countries, and not just of the United States. Some other HLIs, in particular some of the investment banks which run proprietary trading desks, are European, and some European governments, notably that of Germany, have been keen at times to protect the name and trading interests of banks that originate in their jurisdictions. It is also the case that financial centres in which HLIs are active have been supported by the authorities so long as they do not destabilise the local market. Singapore, for example, is a regional centre for foreign-exchange trading in east Asia, much of which is done by US and European investment banks. During the crisis, Singapore did not interfere in the trading of regional currencies other than its own, despite criticism from economies close to it, since such intervention could undermine its interests in advancing the status of Singapore as a regional financial centre.

The perception that it is necessary for the authorities to defend institutions based in, or operating from, a country's jurisdiction is not restricted to 1998. It was also a feature of the international debate about HLIs in 1999. The Financial Stability Forum, for example, dealt with two issues concerning hedge funds: counterparty risk management, as revealed by the near-collapse of LTCM, and market integrity, as revealed by the activities of some HLIs in regional and emerging markets. The issue of counterparty risk management was the crucial issue for the United States, because it posed a serious risk to the stability of *its* financial markets and institutions. Raising the issue of market dynamics only confused the issues and politics as they related to counterparty risk management, and may have added to pressures from Congress to directly regulate hedge funds. For this purpose, proposals to deal with market dynamics were shelved in favour of proposals to deal with counterparty risk management (FSF Working Group on HLIs 2000).

Conclusion

The east Asian financial crisis was a complex phenomenon. The trigger of the crisis was the deterioration in the Thai current-account deficit and pressure on its fixed exchange rate, but the severity of the crisis was exacerbated by excessive unhedged short-term borrowing in foreign currencies, weak banking and financial systems, policy errors by national governments and international organisations, excessive risk affinity followed by excessive risk aversion by international investors, and bouts of destabilising speculation by either residents or non-residents or sometimes both (Krugman 1998; Grenville 1998; Radelet and Sachs 1998; de Brouwer 1999a).

This chapter has sought to make two points. The first is that the macro hedge funds, and to a lesser extent the proprietary trading desks, at times generated instabilities in the price dynamics in regional financial markets in 1997 and 1998. This is not to say that hedge funds caused the crisis but it is to say that at times they were a material factor in the instabilities and asset-price overshooting that occurred. The next three chapters provide more detail and analysis for Hong Kong (Chapter 4), Indonesia, Malaysia and Singapore (Chapter 5), and Australia and New Zealand (Chapter 6).

The second is that some of the material published on HLIs, especially the 1998 IMF study on hedge funds and market dynamics, contains serious flaws. These are essentially that: the study focuses on the size of hedge funds' capital base relative to other financial firms, when what is relevant is the size and variability of institutions' positions in markets; it makes a hasty assessment about the size and timing of hedge funds' positions in east Asian, especially Thai, financial markets in 1997; and it oversimplifies the similarities and relative importance of hedge funds and proprietary trading desks in east Asian financial markets in 1997 and 1998. It is important to understand the IMF study in the context of the intellectual milieu and political pressures that existed at the time; the Fund's assessments were not based solely on the merit of the arguments before it.

4 Hong Kong

Hong Kong experienced some of the most dramatic action of all the financial markets in east Asia in 1997 and 1998, with short-term market interest rates rising on occasion to several hundred per cent, the stock market falling 60 per cent, the market subject to highly aggressive trading tactics by a range of participants, and talk of attacks on the currency peg, all culminating in an unprecedented $15 billion intervention by the authorities in the stock market in August 1998.

The gyrations in Hong Kong's financial markets were the consequence of a series of aggressive speculative attacks in late 1997 and 1998. These attacks appear to have been much more than simply market participants positioning to take advantage of expected changes in asset prices at a time of domestic and regional uncertainty. Rather, in a number of instances it appears that speculators – especially highly leveraged institutions, and some macro hedge funds in particular – had large positions and tried to force prices in equity, interest-rate and exchange-rate markets to move in a direction that put their positions in profit, but which also tended to force prices in these markets to overshoot. In some instances, highly leveraged players appear to have tried to take advantage of the negative correlation that developed between interest rates and stock prices to engineer stock-price falls by pushing on interest-rate markets. There is also talk of speculators trying to break the peg of the HK dollar with the US dollar. Whatever the case, the events in 1998 provide a fascinating study of the interaction between market players and the effect of concentrated position-taking and aggressive tactics on price dynamics.

This chapter first outlines the economic context of Hong Kong in 1997 and 1998, and traces through the market dynamics and the role of highly leveraged institutions in that. It provides an assessment of the dynamics.

The economic context

The economic context in which speculative pressures emerged in Hong Kong was mixed and ambiguous.

On the one hand, Hong Kong's economic structure and cycle were very different from those of many of the crisis economies. Its economy is renowned for flexibility and, at the onset of the crisis, was fundamentally sound. Unlike the crisis economies, it also had a strong banking sector. Risk-weighted capital ratios were around 20 per cent, and banks had low problem loans – they were about 2.8 per cent of total loans in 1997, only reaching about 3 per cent by mid-1998 and about 5 per cent by the end of 1998.

On the other hand, the economy had a number of vulnerabilities in 1998. Hong Kong's real exchange rate was widely seen as overvalued (see Figure 4.1), particularly in the face of depreciating regional currencies. The fixed exchange rate system forced adjustment to the domestic economy, compounding the negative effects on growth of the regional economic recession (see Figure 4.2). Asset prices, including property prices and stock prices, were at historical highs and widely regarded as overvalued and ripe for a fall (see Figure 4.3).

The exchange-rate system itself was seen by some as vulnerable, especially if the Chinese authorities devalued the renminbi. Others,

Figure 4.1 JP Morgan real effective exchange rate for Hong Kong

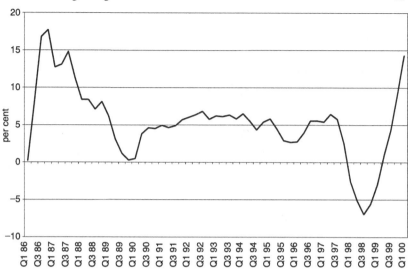

Figure 4.2 Annual GDP growth in Hong Kong

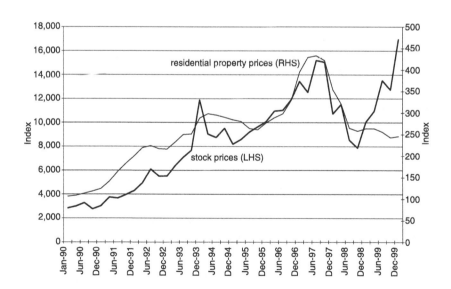

Figure 4.3 Asset prices in Hong Kong

however, did not think the peg would break. This was because they either did not think that China would devalue – the official renminbi rate had been devalued by 30 per cent in 1994 and was already depreciating in real terms because of deflation in China.[1] Or it was because they thought Hong Kong's $US90-odd billion of reserves – more than three times the domestic monetary base – would enable the authorities to defend the peg. There was also a view that China would use its resources in support of the HK dollar peg. Nonetheless, Hong Kong's deep economic links with China were thought to make it vulnerable to developments there, and particularly to concerns about recession in China.

Hong Kong was also vulnerable in one aspect of the operation of its currency-board system. By construction, sales of domestic currency (HK dollars) for the reserve currency (US dollars) tend to push up local money-market interest rates under a currency board. While this also tends to push up interest rates on loans, it is not long lived if the system is credible since the rise in rates makes domestic assets more attractive, inducing purchases of domestic currency and bringing interest rates back to around their initial level. The way this worked in practice at the time, market interest rates were highly sensitive to changes in the liquidity of interbank markets.

In Hong Kong, interbank clearing funds and reserve deposits are called the aggregate balance. Licensed banks in Hong Kong had access to liquidity assistance from the Hong Kong Monetary Authority (HKMA) through what was called the Liquidity Adjustment Facility (LAF) but at market-determined rates. A fall in banks' settlement funds could lead to a large rise in market interest rates. This changed in September 1998 when the government altered the currency-board arrangements: the HKMA replaced the LAF with a formal discount window and set the base rate for HKMA lending to banks at its own discretion (HKMA 1998).

It is also worth noting that Hong Kong has substantial liquid financial markets in assets ranging from equities, foreign exchange, corporate bonds and money markets. These markets are not controlled and are open. Put together, the size and openness of the markets provides market participants, locally and offshore, with an attractive means to hedge and speculate against both local and regional risks.

---

[1] According to JP Morgan figures available on its website, the renminbi real effective-exchange rate depreciated 5 per cent from January to May 1998. Over 1998, it depreciated 10 per cent.

Price dynamics in markets

Based on the survey evidence in Yam (1999) and FSF Working Group on HLIs (2000), the dynamics of financial markets in Hong Kong in 1998 unfolded in three stages. The first stage saw speculators establishing positions in currency and equity markets, the second stage saw heightened instability and susceptibility to large one-way movements in the market, and the third stage saw speculators exiting positions.

There are almost no 'hard' data available on hedge fund positions and activity in the financial markets examined in this book, and so inevitably there is heavy reliance on what specialists in the markets say – including the funds themselves, investment banks and monetary authorities. In the case of Hong Kong in particular, these perceptions are multidimensional. There are many players in Hong Kong's financial markets and they often follow complex and diverse strategies. Not all participants engage in the same trades, have the same strategy or are active in the same markets, and this means that any generalisation is a reduction of reality.

Establishing positions . . .

The positions of hedge funds and proprietary trading desks of investment banks and other financial institutions were established using offshore financial intermediaries, namely large US and European investment banks in Singapore, London or New York. They did not use local Hong Kong banks or the branches of the investment banks in Hong Kong. This is a general strategy of speculators because it keeps the transacting parties at arms length from the authorities.

. . . in equities . . .

There were two sequential steps in establishing market positions in Hong Kong in 1998. With respect to equity markets, hedge funds and other institutions established short positions in the cash or spot market, in the exchange-traded futures and options market, and in the over-the-counter (OTC) options market. In terms of the cash equity market, hedge funds and others sold Hong Kong stocks in both Hong Kong and elsewhere, principally in London. Five stocks, including HSBC, account for about 60 per cent of the index, and so an effective proxy for shorting the HSI is to short Hong Kong bank stocks. One macro hedge fund, for example, is reported to have sold short $US500 million of Hong Kong bank stock in London, which provides a good example of the macro hedge funds' savvy in regional markets.

Short sales in the cash market were highly leveraged. While the conventional margin for short sales in the cash market in Hong Kong is 50 per cent for retail investors, it is as low as 2 per cent for professional investors, implying leverage of 50 to 1. Market participants estimate that the shorting in the Hang Seng reached up to about 10 per cent of turnover in the spot market at the time, implying a value of up to $US1 billion. Hedge funds were a significant part of this activity.

In terms of the exchange-traded derivatives market for Hong Kong equities, hedge funds and others established large short leveraged positions in the Hang Seng Index futures and options. The gross open interest in the HSI futures more than doubled in the five months to the end of August 1998, to 103,101 contracts with a value of $US4.7 billion. It reached its peak in late August of 150,935 contracts, at a value of $US7 billion. The sharp increase in net open interest was associated with a rapid fall in stock prices (see Figure 4.4). The price effect was exacerbated by a sharp contraction in liquidity at the time: average daily turnover in August and September 1998 was as low as $HK4 billion when, for the same months a year earlier, daily turnover of $HK20 billion was not unusual (Tsang 1998).

Hedge funds, and the macro hedge funds in particular, were substantial holders of these short open positions. Figure 4.5 reproduces a chart from

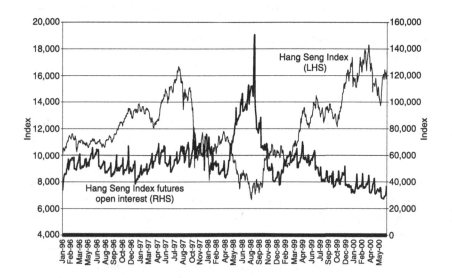

Figure 4.4 Hang Seng Index and net open interest

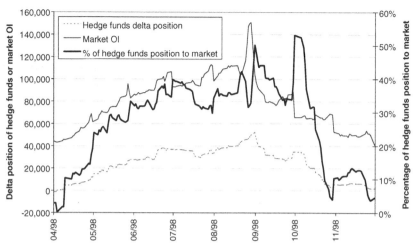

Figure 4.5 Net delta position of individual hedge funds and market open interest in HSIF

the report of the FSF Working Group on HLIs (2000) which shows the proportion of HSI futures positions held by identified hedge funds. Because they are based on exchange-traded markets, these are 'hard' data; they are in fact the only hard data publicly available on hedge fund positions in east Asian financial markets. Hedge funds accounted for all the doubling of short open positions in the HSI futures during May and June, giving them 40 per cent of the positions at that time. At times, hedge funds accounted for over half of the short positions.

As reported by the FSF Working Group on HLIs (2000), these positions were concentrated in four large hedge funds, which market participants identify as mostly large macro hedge funds. At the end of August, four hedge funds accounted for 50,500 contracts or 49 per cent of the total open interest. One hedge fund, which market participants identify as a large macro fund, accounted for 30 per cent of the open interest. (A position of this size would have been illegal in most exchanges, including in the United States.) These figures are the direct interest of the hedge funds: hedge funds may also have used the names of financial intermediaries who held their beneficial interest, and so total HSI futures positions may have been even larger. No estimates are available on indirect interests in the Hang Seng Index futures.

The short futures positions in the Hang Seng Index were highly leveraged. The margin requirement in HSI futures is 5 per cent. That is, a fund can establish a $1 billion position with only $50 million, implying leverage of 20 to 1.

Hedge funds and other speculators also bought put options on Hong Kong equities in 1998 in order to establish positions in the stock market. Open positions in the HSI options peaked at 76,986 contracts on 27 August 1998. Hedge funds' positions in exchange-traded options are included in the data shown in Figure 4.5.

Hedge funds were also active in OTC options markets. According to market sources, some of these positions took the form of purchases of put options embedded in structured notes sold through mostly US investment banks or securities companies to rich individuals in Hong Kong. These notes were arranged such that they paid an above-market yield if the price of a particular share remained above a set price. If the price fell below the set price, the investor's principal at maturity would be reduced in proportion to further price declines. As the market fell, investors sold shares in the Hang Seng Index to minimise – or hedge – losses from the put options they had sold, adding to downward momentum in the market.

Market participants say that this effect on price dynamics was understood by the speculators who bought the put options. The deal was attractive to Hong Kong based investors because it offered the prospect of high short-term gains, which appealed to the 'betting' mentality of the Hong Kong market participants. There are no market estimates of the size of hedge funds' positions in over-the-counter put options, but stock market positions in option-embedded notes could have been quite large, since an individual issue would be up to $US500 million.

Drawing all this together, hedge funds' short equity positions in Hong Kong are likely to have totalled at least $US7 billion and could possibly have been substantially higher. This is very large relative to average daily turnover at the time, which was about $US500 million.

It is clear that there was an unusually large amount of activity by non-residents in Hong Kong's financial markets in 1998. There was unprecedented activity by US and European investment banks and securities firms at this time who act on behalf of hedge funds, as well as on their own account. Many of the originating transactions came from offshore branches of these institutions. The sharp rise in offshore interest is also reflected in trade on futures exchanges. Overseas institutional investors comprised 26.3 per cent of market participants in the HSI futures market in 1998, up from 23.1 per cent in 1997. They also comprised 36 per cent of HSI options participants in 1998, up from 18.4 per cent in 1997.

. . . and in the HK dollar

With respect to currency positions, hedge funds and other participants had first to establish funding for their HK dollar short positions. Market participants report that the duration of swap funding lengthened considerably in the first half of 1998, from short term – that is, swaps with a daily to three-month duration – to more medium and long term – that is, three months to one to two years.

In Hong Kong's case, a large proportion of the funding for the short positions was obtained by swapping US dollars for HK dollars with international financial institutions (IFIs), like the World Bank, which issued large amounts of HK dollar debt in the first eight months of 1998. During this time, for example, IFIs launched seventy-two issues amounting to $HK36.7 billion or $US4.7 billion, most of which was in the one- to two-year range. Both the size of the HK dollar issuance by IFIs and its short-term structure were unusual – in the same period in the previous year, issuance was one-fourteenth the issuance in the first eight months of 1998, and was only for maturities over five years.

According to the FSF Working Group on HLIs (2000), market participants reckon that at the peak in August 1998, HLI short positions against the HK dollar may have amounted to over $US10 billion – over 6 per cent of GDP. The sale of HK dollars behind these short positions is reflected in a fall of about $US4–5 billion in the net foreign exchange assets of Hong Kong banks in the four months to August, and a run down in the monetary authority's foreign exchange reserves of $US4 billion in August. Some estimates of HLI positions were substantially larger, up to several tens of billions of US dollars.

Market participants indicate that two major hedge funds held about half of the short HK dollar positions. They also say that hedge fund positions were larger – both individually and in aggregate – than those of the dozen or so US and European investment banks that became active in the market at this time. Around two-thirds of these short positions were established in August 1998 in a period of rapid selling of the HK dollar.

There was also considerable activity in Hong Kong's money markets at the time. Trading in HIBOR (Hong Kong Interbank Offer Rate) rose substantially. Open interest in futures contracts steadily increased in 1998, peaking on 26 August 1998 at $HK36.6 billion ($US4.7 billion) (see Figure 4.6).

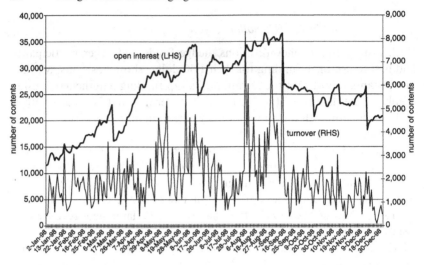

Figure 4.6 Three-month HIBOR futures open interest

Generating price action

As shown above, the bulk of the short positions in Hong Kong equities –
in the cash market, exchange-traded futures and options market, and
OTC options market – were established quietly during the March quarter
of 1998 as unfavourable political and economic events unfolded in the
region. Stock prices weakened, falling 25 per cent and taking the Hang
Seng Index to the 8,500 mark. In January 1998, the market had been
upset by the political crisis in Indonesia. In April and June, there were
heightened concerns about possible devaluation of the renminbi and problems in Indonesia. In July, these concerns deepened with bad domestic
economic news – Hong Kong GDP was revised downward and bank
earnings deteriorated.

The speculative dynamics became substantially more pronounced and
aggressive in August and September. Many market participants talk of
some players actively selling and trading in the foreign-exchange and
interest-rate markets in order to affect interest rates and forward
exchange rates. As discussed above, given the particular arrangements
of the currency board, local market interest rates were particularly susceptible to movements in the aggregate balances of banks – that is, the
sum of balances in commercial banks' clearing accounts and their reserve
accounts with the HKMA. Before the reforms of September 1998, average daily balances were about $HK2–3 billion, and market participants

reckon that total sales of, say, $HK4–8 billion ($US$\frac{1}{2}$–1 billion) could trigger sharp rises in interest rates. As seen in Figure 4.7, this is evident in the data in January, June and September 1998, which are the three periods of greatest speculative pressure in Hong Kong in 1998.

These were periods of concentrated selling of HK dollars. There is, of course, nothing at all inherently wrong in participants selling assets in a market. That is, after all, how asset prices move. But the selling was associated with heightened activity of three kinds which seems to have been designed to undermine the confidence of the market and magnify the effect of selling on market prices, possibly to make positions more profitable. None of these formally constitute illegal trading activity – which, because it is a criminal act, has an onerous burden of proof – but they are widely regarded by the authorities and most market participants as detrimental to the integrity of markets.

In the first place, there was a substantial increase in rumours in the market at this time – that the Hang Seng Index would fall to 4,000 (which would have been 75 per cent below its peak of mid-1997), that property prices were set to fall by a further 40 per cent after they had already fallen by that amount, that the peg was unsustainable, and that some local banks were set to fail. The view of the authorities and some participants in the market is that many of the rumours came from sources which had a strong interest in asset prices falling further. Some of the

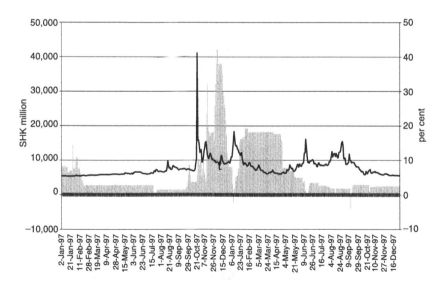

Figure 4.7 Aggregate balance and three-month interest rates

apocalyptic views also came from institutions which had never commented on Hong Kong before and had no established expertise on the region. It is difficult to evaluate claims about rumours. On the one hand, the use of rumours to try to affect market prices is standard practice in financial markets, especially in non-exchange-traded or OTC markets – it is called 'talking one's book'. Furthermore, Hong Kong, like some other markets, seems predisposed to rumours. It is also hard to identify just who is the source of rumours – if some traders and investors establish positions based on their perceptions of hedge fund positions, rumours from all sorts of sources will circulate about such positions. Moreover, given that the regional crisis was of world interest, it is not surprising that institutions which had not traded in, or commented on, the market before would do so.

But it does appear that there was an increase in rumour-mongering at the time, and that the market was particularly susceptible to rumours because of heightened uncertainty. Market participants point out that rumours seemed to increase at times of heavy selling in what were usually quiet trading times, like Friday evenings after Hong Kong had closed and ahead of New York opening.

There are also reports of spoofing on the electronic trading system (EBS). On a couple of occasions at critical points of market uncertainty, HK dollar quotes were placed in the electronic trading system which were outside the intervention bands of the HKMA, and which gave the impression that the HKMA was floating or devaluing the HK dollar. On each occasion, the quotations were removed but traders widely saw them as ruses by speculators to undermine confidence in Hong Kong's financial markets.

The third type of activity that occurred was trading in parts of the market that were more vulnerable to price movement, or trading in the market at quiet times. With respect to the former, foreign exchange can be traded in the interbank market – that is, banks trading between themselves – or in a broker market, such as through electronic broking. These markets have different characteristics. Large transactions, for example, tend to be taken to the interbank market first, and then to the broker market, to minimise disruption and effects on interest rates. In January, June and August 1998, however, large-volume trading shifted to the broker market away from the interbank market. This was understood by traders to be a tactic to obtain greater price effect from a trade. The broker market is more susceptible to rumours than the interbank market: traders in the broker market interact with prices on a screen, while interbank traders know each other and do their deals by phone.

There were also many reports of trading in the market at quiet times, especially late on Friday nights ahead of New York opening. This occurred a number of times in June and August, with a surge of selling in quiet times designed to have maximum impact on interest rates. Heavy selling of HK dollars was reported to have occurred on Fridays in August 1998. Market participants reckon, for example, that $US200 million was sold on 14 August and $US1.7 billion was sold on 21 August.

Just because a transaction, even a large one, occurs in a quiet trading period, it does not necessarily mean that the transaction is designed to force a price movement to the benefit of a speculator. Trading can occur in quiet times because someone needs to exchange a financial asset. Nor is it necessarily a 'bad thing' that transactions occur in quiet times: that is how market depth is expanded. But, that said, the scale of the sales and the fact that they occurred so frequently in quiet times suggest that some players were motivated to move prices rather than simply do transactions. It is also the typical modus operandi of large-scale speculators – as occurred also in Malaysia, Australia and South Africa – which suggests that these were actions designed to change prices.

The sharp rises in interest rates had two effects. One was that a rise in interest rates depreciated the forward rate of the HK dollar, given that the forward discount is simply the interest differential of Hong Kong with the United States. Large movements in the forward rate increased volatility and enabled traders to speculate on price movements. There was substantial churning of forward positions in the foreign-exchange market in 1997 and 1998, with most positions held only for a short time and seldom for more than a few months, although at least one large hedge fund is reported to have held its short currency position for a long time.

At this time, a market player, or group of players, who was willing to sell large amounts of HK dollars in the spot market – or whose sales would likely lead others to sell – could push up interest rates, depreciating the HK dollar forward rate. If that player had previously sold HK dollars forward, it would be able to cheaply buy HK dollars forward and close out the forward position at a profit. Given the psychology in the market at the time, suggestions of hedge fund selling or increased selling activity by offshore-based investment banks – who were the traders for the hedge funds – would readily lead to selling by other market participants. In this case, depending on the sentiment in the market at the time, a single speculator would not need to sell large amounts of HK dollars in the spot market on their own account to affect HK dollar interest rates; others would essentially do the job for them.

Two of the reasons that some market participants give for the concentrated selling on Fridays is that it was designed to test the HKMA's resolve to hold the peg, or to establish short positions ahead of the weekend since major policy changes typically are announced on weekends when international financial markets are closed. Speculators had many different views and it is unclear to what extent they actually expected the peg to break.

On the one hand, the key to generating a successful run on a currency board is to get locals to substitute foreign for local currency. This was monitored closely by hedge funds and others in Hong Kong but, as shown in Figure 4.8, HK dollar deposits continued to increase every month throughout 1998, indicating no substantial currency substitution by households or local businesses. The share of bank deposits denominated in domestic currency remained constant at about 57 per cent. There were also no bank runs. On the other hand, given the high degree of uncertainty at the time, some participants did think that the peg could break, especially if it was pushed at times. These participants did not have a good grasp of the determination of the authorities to hold the peg.

The other effect of interest rate rises was on the stock market. The Hong Kong index was regarded as particularly susceptible to interest-rate rises because of some key bank stocks – rising interest rates would

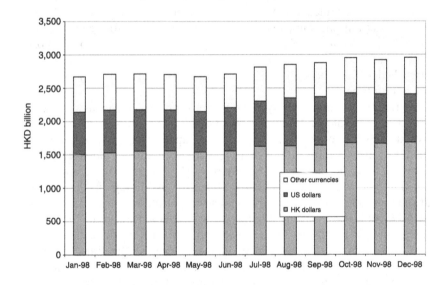

Figure 4.8 Deposits in Hong Kong by currency denomination

damage property values and the quality of banks' loan portfolio, unambiguously reducing the value of bank stocks. The negative correlation between interest rates and stock prices became most apparent during October 1997 when extremely sharp rises in interest rates had a big impact on Hong Kong stock prices (see Figure 4.9).

From 1990 to 2000, interest rates and stock prices were not significantly correlated – the correlation coefficient is −0.07. But in 1997 and 1998, they became significantly negatively correlated, with a correlation coefficient of −0.48. Similarly, a significant negative correlation between interest rates and stock prices developed in Malaysia at the same time. The correlation that emerged at this time provided some market participants with the idea of a 'double play' – short positions in the equity market could be made profitable by selling HK dollars and draining liquidity from the interbank market and pushing up interest rates.

Proving that a double play occurred is not straightforward. Without formal statements by market participants of their intentions, it cannot be shown to what extent players in Hong Kong financial markets had a double-play strategy in mind. Indeed, simultaneous short positions in equities and foreign exchange/interest rates are consistent with scenarios other than a double play. For example, a market participant who believed that financial prices would fall across the board would establish

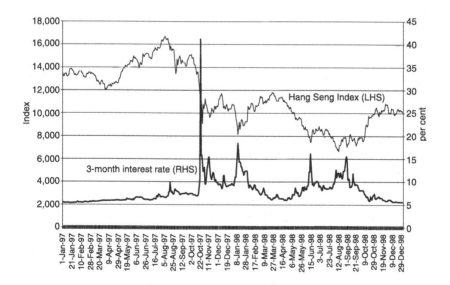

Figure 4.9 Hong Kong stock prices and interest rates

short positions in a range of financial assets. This strategy may be characterised as a general speculative play. But a market participant who believed this and realised that an operational link between stock prices and interest rates had developed may also sell aggressively in the HK dollar market in order to influence interest rates and hence the stock price.

Given the unusually high degree of activity designed to influence interest rates, as outlined above, it is impossible to believe that no-one at all had a double-play strategy in mind. By 1998, even if a speculator was not engaged in the double play, all speculators knew of the strategy. Market participants in a position to know the financial flows that occurred at the time uniformly say that some, but not all, hedge funds had joint short stock and exchange rate/interest rate positions and did indeed have such a strategy. Other players, especially the proprietary trading desks of some banks and securities firms, also had this strategy. The FSF Working Group on HLIs (2000: 117) reports the finding of its study group on market dynamics that 'some large HLIs had large short positions in both the equity and currency markets'.

Some market participants believe that the double play first occurred in Hong Kong in October 1997. Looking at Figure 4.9, this is certainly the most striking episode of sharp interest rate rises and stock-price falls. But there are a number of differences in the situation in mid-1998 that suggest that October 1997 was really the lesson for speculators to learn about the double play. In the first instance, there was not the same drain on the aggregate balance that occurred at the 'hot' times in 1998 (see Figure 4.7). More importantly, the short positions in the stock market were different.

The Securities and Futures Commission (SFC) of Hong Kong examined the positions and strategies of firms in Hang Seng Index derivatives in 1997, leading the HKSAR government to report that 'there was no basis for the allegation of intermediaries, local or international, manipulating the market through the futures market and that of correlation between currency speculators and futures market participants' (HKSARG 1998: 78). The SFC argued that the bulk of positions in 1997 was evenly spread and not concentrated in a few players. The positions were mostly established in the middle of that year when the HSI was at a record high, before a down trend in stock prices was established. Unlike the second half of 1998, there was no steady build-up of positions ahead of the selling pressure in the foreign exchange market. Putting these points together, the picture in October 1997 does not support the view that speculators purposefully established short positions in the stock market and then aggressively sold the HK dollar to push up interest rates and move their short equity positions into profit. The experience of 1997 simply showed that a correlation existed.

As in other markets, hedge funds and other HLIs were not the only institutions to have short positions in Hong Kong's equity, interest-rate and exchange-rate markets. Short positions were also established by businesses – so called 'real money' – which wanted to hedge long positions in China and Hong Kong. Given the liquidity of Hong Kong's financial markets and lack of liquidity in China's, shorting Hong Kong's markets was a way to hedge against possible devaluation of the renminbi. The extent of corporate hedging is not known, although market participants in Hong Kong say that hedging by Hong Kong corporates was relatively low. Most Hong Kong companies seem to have believed that the peg would hold and took advantage of high local interest rates to boost their income. Whatever the case, the hard evidence on hedge fund positions in HSI derivatives indicates that they had substantially larger short positions, both individually and collectively, than corporate hedgers in the stock market.

Exiting positions

The key to making a profit in a flexible-price market is to exit a position with minimal effect on price. The intensity of the pressures in 1998 changed in response to events. The worsening situation in Indonesia had a big impact in January 1998 but these pressures soon subsided and asset prices in the region generally recovered in the first several months of 1998. Pressures re-emerged in May and June as the yen depreciated and concerns took hold about renminbi devaluation at a trigger point of 150 yen to the dollar. These pressures were eased temporarily by the yen/dollar intervention of the Federal Reserve and Bank of Japan in mid-June, but re-emerged in August and September. They only eased after two other events occurred.

The first was the general reduction in leverage and speculative positions by hedge funds and other HLIs after the near-collapse of LTCM in September 1998. The other was the intervention by the HKMA in the Hong Kong equity market from 14–28 August, during which time it bought about $US15 billion in equities. This intervention was triggered by concerns that the intense pressures building up in Hong Kong's financial markets were damaging the functioning of the market and that financial prices had seriously overshot their 'fundamental' value. The authorities strongly believed that the unstable dynamics that had developed in the market were the result of concentrated and aggressive position-taking by HLIs, particularly the macro hedge funds. The intervention was related to the view that the concentration of these positions and aggressive market tactics were set to increase. Indeed, market information suggested that the macro hedge funds might have been colluding to generate a further fall in prices.[2]

The intervention by the HKMA and the generalised unwinding of leveraged positions by hedge funds after the near-collapse of LTCM had a substantial impact on short positions. As is evident from the data on exchange-traded instruments, the short interest-rate positions were sharply wound back (see Figure 4.6) and hedge funds' positions in Hang Seng Index derivatives were closed out mostly during October (see Figure 4.5). Spot and OTC positions were also closed out over the same time.

It is difficult to evaluate the profitability of the short positions. On the one hand, currency positions were mostly continually churned and held by many participants, making it difficult to identify buying and selling prices. On the other hand, short positions in the stock market probably were profitable. Market participants estimate, for example, that the 50,000-odd futures contracts held by the hedge funds had an acquisition value of about $HK23 billion ($US3 billion). At the end of August 1998, this would have implied a profit of around $HK4 billion ($US500 million). Based on the average of the index during the time the short positions were closed out – late September to late October – the implied profit from the HSI futures would have been $HK1.8 billion ($US230 million). This is small relative to the size of the positions and capital of the hedge funds. Certainly, the returns data for some of the major macro hedge funds were negative at this time, so these returns were swamped by losses elsewhere in the portfolio (see Figure 4.10).

An assessment

The Hong Kong experience in 1998 contains a lot of important information about market dynamics and hedge funds. It is clear that there was a series of speculative attacks in its financial markets in 1998 – there were many overseas-based participants in the market for the first time, swap funding for short positions increased, and there were many instances of concentrated and intense selling in unusual circumstances. The double

[2] No further detail is available on this, but it is not necessarily an isolated case. Some market participants in Thailand also say that the macro hedge funds had been thinking of closing out their short baht positions in May and June 1997 before the actual collapse in July, and had talked among themselves about ways to do this at minimum exit cost.

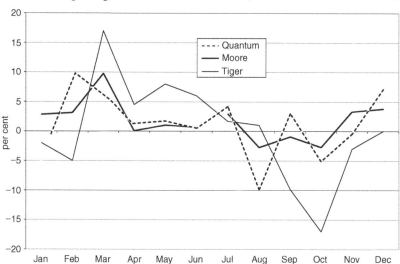

Figure 4.10 Individual macro hedge fund returns

play on stock and exchange-rate/interest-rate markets was a part of this, although no market participant has said publicly that it was involved in such a strategy.

It is also clear that highly leveraged institutions – particularly some of the macro hedge funds – were at the centre of this speculative activity. They had extensive short positions in the full range of Hong Kong's financial markets. As can be seen by the actual positions data presented in the report of the FSF Working Group on HLIs (2000), a handful of hedge funds had the largest short positions in the stock market, at times accounting for half the market. They were also acutely aware of the effect of perceptions of their presence on the other market participants. In particular, given the powerful reputation of macro hedge funds at the time, they were aware that other market participants try to copy their positions in order to benefit from the price dynamics set in train by these positions.

The macro hedge funds had substantial short positions in both stock and currency/interest-rate markets. Given the extent of their short equity positions, they are also the most likely beneficiaries of concentrated selling in the HK dollar and interest-rate markets. That is, since the double play would advantage them more than most other types of institutions, they are most likely to have been the institutions which instigated the double play. This does not mean that all hedge funds – or even all the macro hedge funds – were engaged in this activity, but market participants uniformly assess that they were the institutions at the heart of the strategy.

The data and discussion on hedge funds' positions provided by the FSF Working Group on HLIs (2000) reveal three other dimensions to the behaviour of hedge funds in financial markets. In this case, the hedge funds involved were predominantly the macro hedge funds.

First, the positions were established *after* the Hang Seng Index had already fallen over 35 per cent from its 8 August 1997 peak of 16,647 to the 10,500 range, which was its level in the first half of 1996. In the case of the equity strategy, the positions were only established after a clear 'story' about price dynamics had emerged.

Second, according to the FSF Working Group on HLIs (2000), the position-taking by the two main macro hedge funds involved were positively but imperfectly correlated. These hedge funds moved their positions in a similar way throughout all of 1998, both in the way they established and then reversed their positions.

This does not necessarily mean that the hedge funds were colluding, although that is a possible explanation. What it does show at the very minimum is that the macro hedge funds at times think alike and establish similar positions. These positions can be very large – at one stage, one fund's position in Hang Seng Index futures was equivalent to a third of the market. The effect of this is to amplify the effect of individual large positions in a financial market. As discussed elsewhere in this book, not only do perceptions of these positions affect the position-taking of other market participants, but the unwinding of these positions, forced or otherwise, can have substantial impact on financial prices and possibly the economy.

Third, the positions *increased* sharply after the HKMA started its intervention on 14 August. Market participants reckon that the hedge funds' short positions in Hang Seng Index futures increased by about $HK5 billion during the intervention episode. This shows that the macro hedge funds and other HLIs are aggressive market players. The general increase in hedge funds' short positions was also associated with widely reported criticisms of the HKMA's intervention by some of the hedge funds. On 27 August, for example, Bloomberg quoted Stanley Druckenmiller, then manager of Soros Fund Management's flagship Quantum Fund, criticising the HKMA's defence of the stock market, and saying that the dollar peg was 'silly' and that the stock market would not recover.

As discussed elsewhere in this book, there is nothing at all inherently wrong in selling financial assets. That is how price adjustment occurs.

The concern is really whether the dynamics in financial markets can become unstable – in Hong Kong's case, market integrity was threatened because of highly aggressive behaviour and because positions were so large and concentrated that they left financial prices exposed to large disorderly and discontinuous movements. If the dynamics are unstable, this may lead to overshooting of asset prices from fundamentals.

The view of the authorities was that markets had become seriously destabilised. In an address in Frankfurt on 29 September 1998, the Financial Secretary, Donald Tsang, said:

The HKSAR Government did not buy shares to support the market at any particular level. We bought shares to stop a contrived and extreme market condition which was creating severe instability in the stock, futures and currency markets. The stock and property markets in particular could not find their true levels in such an unsettled environment.

While there was substantial uncertainty about regional economies and there were good economic reasons to short Hong Kong financial markets, there is evidence that financial prices in Hong Kong did overshoot. This is most apparent in the extreme movements generated in stock prices. The Hang Seng Index peaked at 16,673 on 7 August 1997 and troughed at 6,660 almost exactly a year later, on 13 August 1998, a phenomenal 60 per cent fall. The episode was associated with extreme volatility (see Figure 4.11) and unprecedented weakness in the price–

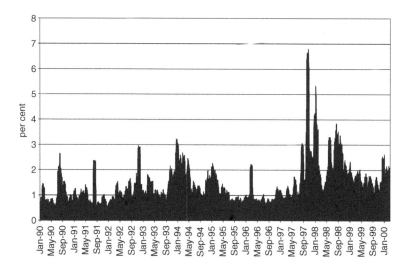

Figure 4.11 Stock price volatility

earnings ratios of Hong Kong stocks (see Figure 4.12), although this is not the only episode of volatility or extreme movement in Hong Kong's asset prices. The notion that fair value for the Hang Seng Index was 4,000 – as some participants with short positions were saying – was hardly credible, even at the time. Price–earnings ratios were already too low by historical standards when the Hang Seng Index was at 7,000.

Overshooting is also apparent in the movement of financial prices after the hedge funds closed their short positions. The Hang Seng Index recovered as short equity positions were closed out, and ended the year over the 10,000 mark, which was a recovery of 50 per cent from the mid-August trough. Property prices also stabilised.

Conclusion

This chapter has outlined how the dynamics unfolded in Hong Kong's financial markets in 1997 and 1998. Given domestic and regional economic fundamentals, shorting of Hong Kong's financial markets was justified, but a number of aggressive concentrated speculative attacks made the dynamics in these markets become unstable at times and led market prices to overshoot their 'fundamental' value.

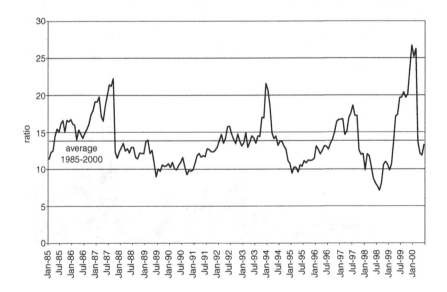

Figure 4.12 Price-earnings ratio, Hang Seng Index

Highly leveraged institutions, and the macro hedge funds in particular, were at the heart of this. The macro hedge funds had large concentrated positions in a range of asset markets, most obviously in the stock market. This substantially affected price formation in asset markets by affecting the willingness of other market participants to establish counter positions. The size of the equity positions meant that their forced unwinding had a substantial impact on price.

There was also a relatively high degree of aggressive behaviour by a range of HLIs in markets at this time – like rumour spreading, spoofing electronic broking, and dealing in quiet markets or trading times – designed to affect the position-taking of other participants in financial markets. It is also apparent that some market participants took advantage of the significant negative correlation that emerged between stock and interest-rate markets at the time, to generate price movements in the stock market which were to their advantage. The macro hedge funds and proprietary trading desks of banks and securities firms were prime beneficiaries of this, although not all HLIs with short positions were necessarily involved in the double play.

5 Indonesia, Malaysia and Singapore

Geographic proximity, ethnic and cultural links, and deep trade integration closely bind the economies and financial markets of Indonesia, Malaysia and Singapore together. In many respects, they are seen as a bloc despite the many substantial differences in their economic development, financial sophistication and regulatory framework. From the perspective of international investors, the circumstances of one affects perceptions of the other two, and this had an important bearing on financial market dynamics and positions in 1997 and 1998, intimately intertwining outcomes in the three countries' financial markets.

The experiences of Indonesia, Malaysia and Singapore in 1997 and 1998 also feature many of the extremes of the east Asian financial crisis. Indonesia, on the one hand, had the most tempestuous experience, with its currency at one stage losing 85 per cent of its value against the dollar and its financial and economic system routed. Singapore, on the other hand, had one of the most stable economies and financial systems of the region, and its asset markets experienced the least disruption and volatility. Indonesia, on the one hand, experienced substantial buying of its currency by macro hedge funds in late 1997 after the falls in regional currencies left many with the view that the initial depreciations had been overdone. Malaysia, on the other hand, experienced some of the most aggressive currency selling by highly leveraged institutions seen in the region, especially in 1998. And, finally, in terms of policy response, Indonesia, on the one hand, shifted to a genuinely floating exchange-rate regime while Malaysia, on the other hand, fixed its exchange rate to the dollar and imposed capital controls.

Their experiences in 1997 and 1998 also provide a range of insights into the behaviour of hedge funds and proprietary trading desks, and the impact that they can have on the dynamics of financial markets. They show how stabilising such institutions can be – like the heavy buying by macro hedge funds in support of the rupiah in late 1997 – and how destabilising they can be – like aggressive trading tactics and correlation plays in Malaysian financial markets in late 1997 and early 1998. They also show how the behaviour of the authorities can discourage speculative activity, as in Singapore, or exacerbate it, as in Malaysia.

The chapter sets out the economic context and describes and analyses the price dynamics that took place in each country. The case studies are set out in alphabetical order.

Indonesia

The economic context

Ahead of the Asian crisis, the standard macroeconomic fundamentals for Indonesia appeared relatively strong. Real growth had been over 7 per cent in the years before the crisis, saving and investment had been around 35 per cent of GDP, inflation below 10 per cent, current-account deficits about 1 per cent or so of GDP, and the fiscal surplus over 1 per cent of GDP (de Brouwer 1999a).

The vulnerability of the economy was revealed in the second half of 1997, as changes in investors' risk preferences towards emerging markets led to falls in financial asset prices and sharply increased the foreign currency exposure of highly leveraged, short-term unhedged borrowers. This vulnerability was also associated with a range of other problems in the economy, including excessive credit growth, overvalued stock and property prices, state-directed lending, decision making centralised on the President, and a weak financial system (Radelet 1999). Non-performing loans were thought to be about 12 per cent before the crisis (Bonin and Huang 2000), and as events unfolded in 1998, the market revised this up substantially, suspecting that between a half to two-thirds of banks' assets were seriously non-performing.

Indonesia underwent a political crisis in 1998, with a laboured transition from President Suharto to President Habibie. For most of the second half of 1997, the dictatorship had been viewed by markets as a reason why Indonesia would be able to avoid contagion from the collapse in the baht in July. This view changed in late 1997 on news reports that Suharto was ill, and as he became uncomfortable with high interest rates and negotiations with the IMF reached a stalemate. Domestic confidence was severely damaged by the IMF-led closure of sixteen banks on 1 November 1997 and by economic and political uncertainty about the election due in March 1998. In January 1998, international confidence was seriously undermined by public conflict with the IMF over budget plans and public criticism of Indonesia by the IMF and the

US Treasury.[1] Domestic and international economic and political tensions continued to adversely affect Indonesia's financial markets in succeeding months (Radelet 1999).

Price dynamics in financial markets

Of all the countries in the region, Indonesia's financial markets underwent the most extreme movements in 1997 and 1998. From peak to trough, the exchange rate depreciated over 85 per cent (from January 1997 to June 1998), three-month interest rates rose from 10.7 per cent to 58 per cent (March 1997 to September 1998), and stock prices fell 65 per cent (July 1997 to September 1998).

These extreme movements in Indonesia's financial markets were dominated by the effects of selling by domestic participants and capital flight, rather than the effects of offshore participants like hedge funds or other HLIs in the market.

In terms of their role, HLIs generally had long positions in the rupiah in 1996, like they did in the baht and ringgit. The positions in the baht started changing in late 1996 and early in 1997, and short positions were established in the rupiah, ringgit and other currencies at around the same time. Some HLIs were thought to be applying strong selling pressure at this time. Short positions were established at around Rp2,400, and the subsequent depreciation, to around the Rp3,000 level in September and Rp3,500 level in October – at this stage a 30 per cent depreciation – made the positions profitable and the currency look oversold. Short positions were then closed out and long positions established.

By October 1997, the macro hedge funds were uniformly long in the rupiah. Not only was Indonesia viewed favourably at this time, but long positions in the rupiah provided speculators with a large short-term interest differential over US rates of at least 20 per cent. People involved in these trades also say that it was easy to avoid local withholding tax on interest earnings, which made these investments even more attractive. Even if the currency did not appreciate, as some thought likely, the interest earnings were sufficient to attract investors' attention. Market participants reckon that HLIs, predominantly hedge funds, had long positions of about $5 billion (about $2\frac{1}{2}$ per cent of GDP). Several large hedge funds had individual long positions of around $1–1\frac{1}{2}$ billion.

---

[1] The Asian crisis website of Nouriel Roubini – at *http://www.stern.edu/nroubini/NOTES* – provides an excellent detailed news summary of events in east Asia in 1997 and 1998.

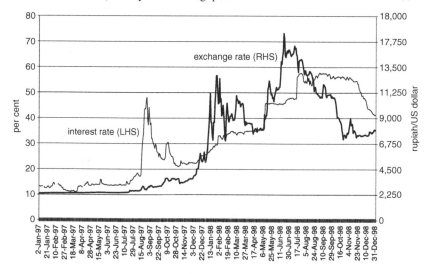

Figure 5.1 Rupiah and Indonesian overnight interest rate

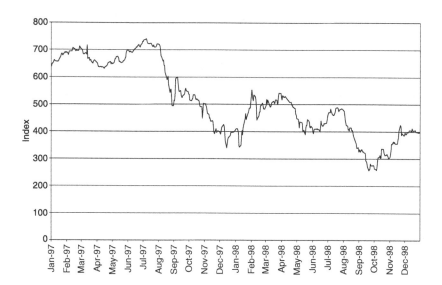

Figure 5.2 Indonesian stock price

As it turned out, the rupiah weakened rather than strengthened, although the interest earnings were some compensation against foreign-exchange losses. The rupiah oscillated around Rp3,500 during November, but depreciated rapidly by a further 30 per cent in December. Markets were rattled by the collapse in public confidence in the banking system after the IMF-directed closure of sixteen banks on 1 November, and by Suharto's decision to revoke the closure of his son's bank later that month. The lift in interest rates to attract deposits undermined the stock market, leading local and foreign investors to sell out. Foreign concerns and uncertainty were exacerbated in December by reports that Suharto was ill.

During November and December 1997, there was substantial domestic capital flight, possibly as much as $30 billion, largely in response to the domestic banking crisis and persecution of ethnic Chinese. Hedge funds mostly closed out their long positions in December. Some positions were held longer, into January and February, and recorded larger foreign-currency losses. George Soros (1999) noted that Soros Fund Management lost a billion dollars on its long rupiah position, which market participants believe to have been in the order of $1½ billion.

In December, as official concerns developed about hedge funds and others establishing short positions in the rupiah, the authorities imposed limits on offshore swap funding in the rupiah. As it turned out, the chaotic state of Indonesian financial markets, especially in the June quarter of 1998, was a sufficient disincentive for large speculative activity. With the domestic banking system paralysed, Jakarta politically and socially unstable and pricing spreads extremely wide, foreign banking operations in Indonesia were substantially wound down and credit lines closed. The bid–ask spread on the rupiah widened dramatically, from a typical 100 points to 1,250 points on occasion (see Figure 5.3).[2] Simply put, neither the opportunity nor the will for foreigners to speculate in Indonesian financial markets was present any longer.

Malaysia

The economic context

The Malaysian economy was relatively robust before the east Asian financial crisis. Economic growth was 8.6 per cent in 1996, its average for the previous five years. Inflation was only 3.6 per cent. Saving and

---

[2] In May 1998, the rupiah retail bid–ask spread at Jakarta airport reached 10,000 rupiah.

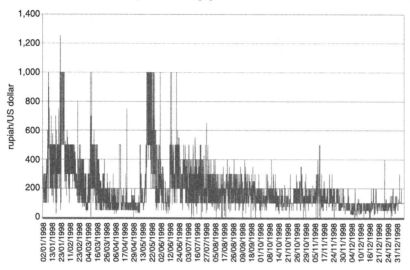

Figure 5.3 Intra-day rupiah bid–ask spread, 1998

investment were over 40 per cent of GDP and government finances were strong: the fiscal surplus was 0.7 per cent in 1996, and had averaged a deficit of only 1 per cent in the previous five years. The current-account deficit in 1996 was 1.8 per cent, narrowing from a deficit of 3.9 per cent in 1995, and external debt was low. The banking system was relatively sound: banks had a risk-weighted capital adequacy ratio of 10.6 per cent and total non-performing loans (NPLs) were 3.7 per cent of assets and were almost fully provisioned. Malaysia's pre-crisis NPLs were much lower than those for Thailand (15 per cent), Indonesia (12 per cent) and Korea (16 per cent) (Bonin and Huang 2000).

There were concerns about rapid credit growth – which reached over 30 per cent in late 1995, well above the average 17 per cent of the first half of the 1990s – the profitability of big-scale development projects, and rising asset prices. The authorities understood that excessive growth in credit and asset prices posed risks for inflation and the health of the banking system, and had started putting measures in place in 1996 and 1997 to limit real-estate lending by banks. As a result, private credit growth had fallen back to the mid 20 per cent range in 1996.

Malaysia's greatest economic vulnerability was the fact that it was a key competitor with Thailand: after Singapore and the Philippines, Thailand is the country whose exports are most similar to those of

Malaysia. The ringgit first came under heavy selling pressures around May 1997 during the pressures on the Thai baht, and these pressures continued after the baht was floated on 2 July.

Domestic political factors had a substantial impact on the assessment of Malaysia. The international perception of Malaysia was affected by reports of conflict between Prime Minister Mahathir Mohamad and Deputy Prime Minister and Finance Minister, Anwar Ibrahim. Anwar, on the one hand, was perceived as an orthodox economist who would basically follow IMF-type policies – even though Malaysia was not on an IMF program – including raising interest rates to stabilise exchange rate expectations. Mahathir, on the other hand, was perceived as an economic nationalist and interventionist, not given to IMF-type policy prescriptions. As conflict between the top two political figures became public, economic and political uncertainty increased, and financial prices became increasingly vulnerable.

As concerns about Thailand's economy intensified, and the problems associated with short-term unhedged foreign-currency borrowing and the stability of the banking system emerged, they spread to other countries in the region. Even though Malaysia had what is generally regarded as a stronger banking system and substantially fewer short-term unhedged foreign exchange exposures,[3] concerns strengthened about economic and financial stability in Malaysia. The ringgit was also viewed by non-residents as the most liquid of the ASEAN currencies after the collapse of the baht, and was seen as a good proxy to hedge regional risks or speculate on regional developments, particularly in Indonesia.

Price dynamics in financial markets

The action in Malaysia's financial markets was concentrated in the foreign-exchange market, but also occurred, to a lesser degree, in the stock market. This action occurred in a series of waves. As mentioned above, the ringgit foreign-exchange market was affected by the pressures on the baht (Figure 5.4), with the ringgit depreciating over 20 per cent in the three months after the baht was floated.

There are four features of Malaysia's foreign-exchange market at this time that continued, more or less, until August 1998. The first is that turnover in the ringgit increased markedly (see Figure 5.5). This was apparent in the spot market only to a limited extent, but was most

---

[3] According to BIS statistics, banks' consolidated cross-border claims with a maturity of less than one year were 49.7 per cent of the total at June 1996 and 56.4 per cent of the total at June 1997, which was less than for all other crisis economies at the time.

Figure 5.4 Ringgit and baht

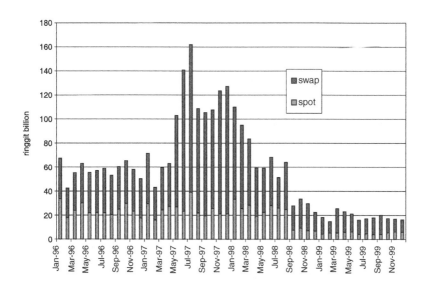

Figure 5.5 Ringgit turnover in Malaysia

evident in the explosion of activity in the ringgit swap market. As explained in Chapter 2, the standard method to establish a short position in a currency is to sell it in the spot market and borrow funds in the swap market to settle the spot sale, which is due in two trading days. This provides the speculator with a currency exposure, the date of which depends on the length of the swap or the willingness of other participants in financial markets to roll the swap over. As elsewhere in the region, there was an increase in the length of swap funding. An increase in swap activity and lengthening of swap contracts are standard signals of increased speculative activity.

At the same time, there was increased activity by non-residents in the ringgit market. Financial institutions which had not before been present in the market became active, including hedge funds. The FSF Working Group on HLIs (2000: 119) reports that hedge funds had 'substantial short positions at this time', with some individual funds believed to have had positions of several billion dollars each. Market participants believe that some of these positions were closed out by the end of the September quarter of 1997.

Third, the authorities did not respond passively to these events. While they let the exchange rate depreciate substantially in response to the selling pressures, they also intervened heavily in the foreign-exchange market at the time, buying at least $5 billion of ringgit in July 1997 (see Figure 5.6). The authorities discouraged local speculation against the ringgit and continued to maintain limits on the net open-position limits of local banks, which are based on banks' capital and dealing capacity. On 4 August 1997, they imposed swap limits of $2 million on banks for non-trade related activities with non-residents. This was intended to prevent offshore parties from establishing a speculative position and funding it through the swap market. This did not stop offshore parties from using outright forwards, or using the offshore ringgit market in Singapore, to establish short positions. Interest rates also rose as the ringgit weakened (see Figure 5.7).

The fourth feature of the ringgit market at this time was the development of 'correlation plays' by some market participants. It is well known by people who work in financial markets that traders use all sorts of tools to instruct them in how to trade financial assets. One popular strategy, especially in times of uncertainty, is to sell and buy an asset based on the correlation of its price with other financial asset prices. From mid-1997, there were essentially two kinds of correlation plays involving the ringgit that became possible – a correlation of the ringgit with the Kuala Lumpur stock-price index, and a correlation of the ringgit with the rupiah.

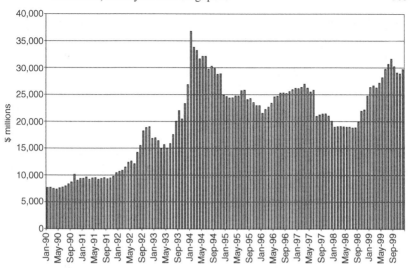

Figure 5.6 Malaysia's foreign exchange reserves

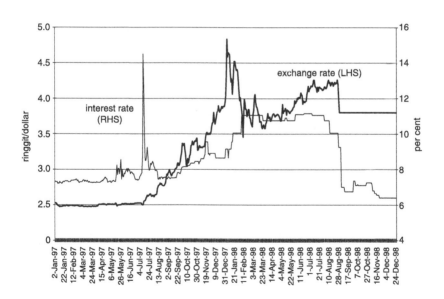

Figure 5.7 Interest rate and the ringgit

Figure 5.8 shows the ringgit and the KL composite stock-price index. As shown in Figure 5.9, the correlation between daily movements in the Malaysian currency and stock price became markedly and significantly negative – that is, a depreciation in the ringgit was associated with a fall in stock prices – whereas previously there had been no systematic relationship between the two.

Some market participants also speak about the possibility of using the trading rule to in fact make profit – establishing short positions in the ringgit and then selling in the stock market to have an effect on the currency, through the operation of the trading rule. This is a 'double play', as occurred in Hong Kong, and, indeed, it may have been where highly leveraged players first learned how to implement a double play in practice. The added dimension in this case was that the correlation play took advantage of the differences in liquidity in the two markets. To the extent that the stock market was less liquid than the foreign-exchange market, a sale of a given value in the stock market would have a relatively larger price impact in the ringgit market. From the 1997 peak to the 1998 trough, Malaysian stock prices fell 80 per cent.

The other correlation play that seems to have been used was between the rupiah and the ringgit. Before the 1997 financial crisis, the baht was the most liquid of the southeast Asian currencies. But after the collapse of

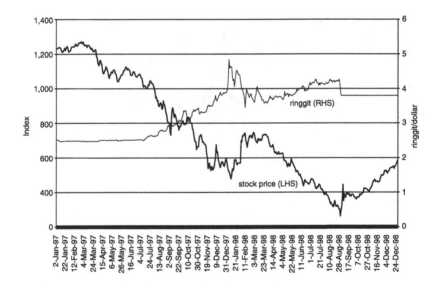

Figure 5.8 Ringgit and Kuala Lumpur composite stock-price index

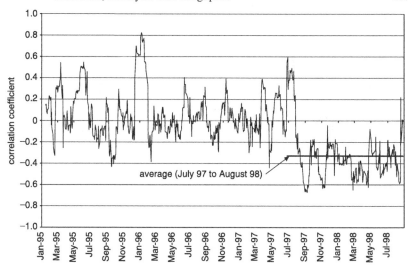

Figure 5.9 Correlation of stock prices and ringgit

the baht in June 1997, the mantle of most liquid currency passed to the ringgit. Given domestic political and economic uncertainty, the market in rupiah was substantially less liquid, more fragile, and more vulnerable to sudden and large shifts in market sentiment. Given the proximity and close links between Indonesia and Malaysia, the ringgit was sensitive to movements in the rupiah.

Figure 5.10 shows the rolling correlation of changes in intra-day offer (that is, selling) rates for the rupiah and the ringgit in the first eight months of 1998 – there are about 20 observations for each trading day. Intra-day changes in both currencies are strongly positively correlated, especially in the first few months of 1998. This provided a trading opportunity. From a trader's point of view, trading small amounts in the rupiah foreign-exchange market could have a substantial impact on the price. By first establishing a short position in the ringgit, and then selling a relatively small amount of rupiah – noisily for maximum price effect – a trader would hope to depreciate the ringgit and close out the short ringgit position. The trade would be profitable if the cross-price effect was large enough, and if the buy order to close out the short position did not push up the price of the currency too much.

Are cross-price effects evident in these currency markets? One way to assess this is to examine whether movements in one currency are systematically predicted by movements in another. If an exchange rate is a

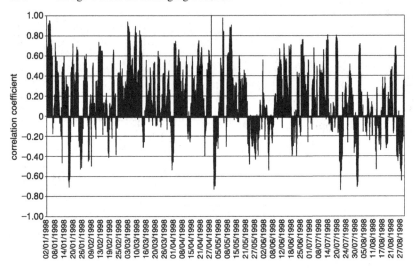

Figure 5.10 Correlation of rupiah and ringgit, January to August 1998

random walk (possibly with drift), then shocks or innovations to the exchange rate should be uncorrelated and should not be explained by movements in any other currency. Table 5.1 presents the results for the ringgit from a vector-autoregression (VAR) model of daily changes in the rupiah and ringgit. The first two columns show that, in general, daily innovations in the ringgit are not systematically explained by past movements in either the ringgit or the rupiah.

But this is not always true over smaller sample periods. As shown in the third and fourth columns of Table 5.1, changes in the rupiah the previous day had a systematic influence on the ringgit during September 1997 and February–March 1998, which is also a period of strong positive intra-day correlation between the rupiah and ringgit (see Figure 5.10).[4] While this obviously does not prove that traders were pushing on the rupiah to make money on the ringgit, it does suggest that such a strategy would have been viable at particular points in time, especially when there was substantial uncertainty in the market.

This has to be kept in context. Traders say that these double plays are risky – the correlation is far from perfect and is sometimes negative. They also say that a wide variety of market participants used these strategies,

---

[4] These periods were selected by examining the plots of coefficients plus/minus 2 standard errors from rolling the VAR over a fixed 20-day window in 1997 and 1998.

Table 5.1. *Innovations to the ringgit*

	2 Jan–31 Dec 1997#	1 Jan–31 Aug 1998#	4 Sep–1 Oct 1997	18 Feb–17 Mar 1998
Intercept	0.04	0.15**	0.50	−0.33
	(0.17)	(0.06)	(0.21)	(0.47)
Δ log ringgit$_{t-1}$	0.11	0.14	−0.55	−0.09
	(0.18)	(0.11)	(0.34)	(0.29)
Δ log rupiah$_{t-1}$	−0.01	−0.01	1.00**	0.28*
	(0.04)	(0.04)	(0.25)	(0.15)
R-bar-squared	0.00	0.01	0.56	0.13
LM Serial Corr.	0.30	0.71	0.93	0.68
Ramsey Reset	0.23	0.03**	0.37	0.87
Normality	0.00**	0.00**	0.70	0.32
Ramsey Hetero.	0.00**	0.00**	0.08*	0.38

Note: standard errors in parentheses; # indicates that standard errors are adjusted for heteroscedasticity using White's method; ** and * indicate significant at the 5 and 10 per cent levels respectively; diagnostic tests report marginal significance. Dependent variable: change in the log of the ringgit.

and that they were more typical of HLIs which churn or regularly turn their positions over, like traders at banks and securities companies and particular macro hedge funds. Other macro hedge funds tend to hold their positions for longer periods rather than churn them. And some macro hedge funds had long positions in the rupiah at the time, making these funds unlikely candidates for this particular play. The scope for the rupiah–ringgit play declined substantially by mid-1998 as the rupiah market collapsed. Not only were severe limits imposed on rupiah business by credit control at the head offices of banks and securities companies, but many institutions simply withdrew from the market after the first few months of 1998.

A further wave of speculative pressure on the ringgit occurred in December 1997 and January 1998, as the economic and political situation in Indonesia deteriorated. In the first few weeks of January, the IMF and US Treasury publicly criticised Indonesia for lack of progress in reform and touted the possibility that the second tranche of the loan to Indonesia would not be disbursed. This shook confidence in Indonesia's financial markets, with sharp flow-on effects to the ringgit.

Pressures on the ringgit were intense: in the first week or so of January, the currency depreciated 15 per cent, from RM3.89 to RM4.65. Currency transactions became unusually large at this time. The typical size for a ringgit transaction is $3–5 million but during

December 1997 and January 1998, transactions of $50–100 million became common. The volume of currency trading (spot and swap) surged to RM50.5 billion in January 1998, compared to an average of RM30 billion in the preceding six months. There was a sharp increase in offshore sales – in Singapore, and, to a lesser degree, in New York, London and Hong Kong – with individual sell orders reaching $200 million and $500 million. Buy–sell spreads on the ringgit also widened from a standard 5 to 15 points to 100 to 500 points and peaked at 1,000 points.

Market participants say that some hedge funds and proprietary trading desks of banks and securities firms had substantial short ringgit positions at this time. One hedge fund, for example, is believed to have had a short ringgit position of around $4 billion at this time. There was an increase in trading at normally quiet times and in rumours in the market, and hedge funds were thought to place sell orders with a range of banks to generate as much price action as possible. Bank Negara Malaysia intervened strongly at this time.

The Prime Minister publicly criticised speculators, and hedge funds in particular, in January 1998. Mahathir is quoted as saying, for example, that '[a]ll these countries have spent 40 years trying to build up their economies and a moron like Soros comes along with a lot of money to speculate and ruin things' (Baily, Farrell and Lund 2000). His comments had two effects on the market, which had a bearing on the intensity of pressures that built up on the ringgit in mid-1998.

First, by drawing the attention of Malaysian corporates to hedge fund activity in the ringgit at a time when macro hedge funds had extremely good reputations, Mahathir made Malaysian corporates fearful of further currency movement. Moreover, by identifying speculation with a lack of patriotism, he forced Malaysian corporates to hide their selling of ringgit, and go offshore to Singapore.

Second, he brought the ringgit to the attention of speculators around the world. Market participants speak of the catalysing effect of Mahathir's comments on the willingness of speculators to take positions against the ringgit. Comments by political leaders in defence of their currencies are usually interpreted by financial markets as a signal of a fundamental or structural economic weakness. To the extent that they signal the intention of the authorities to defend a particular exchange rate, they also attract more speculation because, as discussed in Chapter 2, speculators think that they will be guaranteed liquidity in exiting a position. This focused the market's attention on announcements on reserves and any information about intervention by the central bank. The ferocity, emotionalism and anti-Semitism of Mahathir's comments was an affront to many speculators and widened the motivation of their activity from simply making money to include an element of retribution. In the words of some market participants, Malaysia became an 'ego play'.

While the ringgit was relatively calm for the rest of the first quarter, pressures re-emerged in April 1998 and remained until August. The FSF Working Group on HLIs (2000) notes that as talk of HLI activity in the ringgit increased and the currency depreciated, Malaysian corporates increased their hedging of ringgit exposures. It says that banks in Singapore suggested that Malaysian corporates did not wish to be seen by the authorities to be selling and so went offshore instead of using local markets.

Speculative pressures also increased at the same time, generating a negative feedback between speculation and hedging. Traders say that HLIs knew that talk about the activity of hedge funds in the market would unsettle Malaysian corporates and encourage further selling, and used this reaction to their advantage by selling 'noisily' in the market and in quiet times. They also knew that institutional investors would be required to cut back on Malaysian investments as prices fell, adding further to the downward price momentum. Large short positions in the ringgit were built up and the currency steadily depreciated, reaching RM4.3 to the dollar in mid July.

Most of the speculative and hedging activity took place in Singapore and, to a lesser extent, in London, New York and Hong Kong. As short positions increased, ringgit funds were in short supply because swap funding from Malaysian banks was controlled. Consequently, off-shore ringgit interest rates were bid up, to double and sometimes triple the level of onshore interest rates (Figure 5.11). The cost of overnight funds in the offshore market peaked at 400 per cent at one stage. The ringgit shortage was so great that some participants short sold Malaysian stocks in Singapore to obtain ringgit, and some hotels in Singapore were even requesting Malaysians to use ringgit to pay for their accommodation.

The increase in interest rates on ringgit deposits in Singapore led to a shift from ringgit deposits in Malaysia to Singapore. This was an arbitrage transaction to take advantage of higher deposit rates, and not currency flight since Malaysian households and businesses all the while kept their deposits in ringgit. By the end of August, these deposits amounted to an estimated RM10 billion (2\frac{1}{2}$ billion). According to the FSF Working Group on HLIs (2000), market participants estimate that short ringgit positions held by highly leveraged institutions at this time

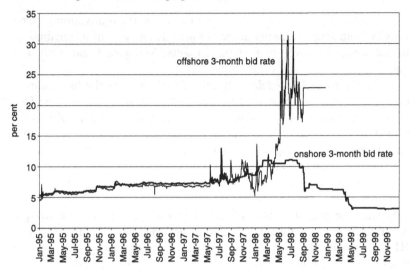

Figure 5.11 Onshore and offshore interbank interest rates

were a multiple of the offshore deposit base, around RM30–40 billion ($7–9 billion) or 15 per cent of GDP.

Offshore interest rates started to decline in mid-August, around the time of Russia's devaluation and debt moratorium. The FSF Report on HLIs (2000) reports that some market participants in Singapore suggested hedge funds had largely covered their short positions by the end of August and that Malaysian households and corporates had started to repatriate deposits. One reason for the closing out of positions was that speculators started to expect some form of controls, although many were surprised at the breadth and depth of controls when they were introduced.

By the end of August 1998, the ringgit had depreciated by 40 per cent and the stock market had declined more than 75 per cent from pre-crisis levels. The Malaysian authorities imposed tightened capital controls on 1 September and fixed the exchange rate a day later. This was seen as a response to these pressures and rising domestic political tension between Mahathir and Anwar, with the sacking and jailing of Anwar occurring just after the imposition of capital controls. The exchange controls effectively cut off the supply of ringgit to the offshore market and – in conjunction with position unwinding after the Russian actions – effectively brought the speculative pressures to an end.

Singapore

The economic context

Singapore's economic fundamentals before the east Asian financial crisis started in mid-1997 were among the strongest in the region. Singapore had grown at an annual average rate of about $8\frac{1}{2}$ per cent from 1990 to 1996, had inflation below 2 per cent, a fiscal surplus of $8\frac{1}{2}$ per cent in 1996, a current account surplus of about 15 per cent of GDP, and low external debt. Corporate gearing was low and the banking system was well supervised and strong.

Singapore's economic and financial strengths were broadly recognised. In its Asian Intelligence Report of 5 August 1998, Asia Political and Economic Risk Consultancy (APERC) rated Singapore as having the economy with the best institutional framework in Asia. In October 1998, *Euromoney* concluded that Singapore was Asia's least risky market.

From the perspective of foreign investors, the country's main vulnerabilities were the global downturn in the electronics industry in 1997 and its proximity to and dependence on other regional economies, and Indonesia in particular. As economies elsewhere in the region contracted and their currencies weakened substantially, the outlook for Singapore's economy and currency also weakened somewhat. The Monetary Authority of Singapore (MAS) targets a weighted basket value of the Singapore dollar, and so the general depreciation of regional currencies was widely expected to result in some depreciation against the dollar. The weights in the target currency basket are not publicly known.

While Singapore is a regional financial centre and has large financial markets, it operates more as a centre for trade in other countries' financial assets than for trade in its own. It is, for example, a key centre for foreign-exchange transactions, mostly the US dollar and convertible regional currencies, like, at the time, the baht, rupiah and ringgit. In April 1998, it accounted for 7 per cent of global foreign exchange activity, with average daily foreign-exchange turnover of $US139 billion in that month. Trade in the Singapore dollar, however, accounted for 13 per cent of this, a relatively small $US17.6 billion. While the currency is freely traded, the authorities expressly limit speculative activity by non-residents.

According to MAS Notice 757, the policy of the MAS 'is not to encourage the internationalisation of the Singapore dollar'. This is effected largely by limiting Singapore dollar credit facilities to non-residents to $S5 million, where credit facilities include bank loans, currency swaps, securities lending and repurchase agreements. Under Notice

757, the MAS also requires banks to consult it before transacting Singapore dollar currency options or option-related products with non-bank financial intermediaries or with non-residents other than for specified commercial or hedging purposes. Banks are not allowed to transact Singapore dollar currency options or related products with each other. This means that the MAS can effectively control the standard mechanism for establishing short positions in its currency, at least in the onshore market. The authorities also forbid short selling of stocks listed on the Singapore stock exchange, effectively closing off opportunities for non-residents to speculate in stocks.

These policies are strictly enforced and financial institutions in Singapore are well aware that they may be subject to full audit by the authorities at any time. As observed by the FSF Working Group on HLIs (2000: 124), '[m]arket participants in Singapore noted that the MAS could exercise moral suasion to limit outright forwards to non-residents, especially when the Singapore dollar is under downward pressure. Market participants noted the "fierce reputation" of the MAS in limiting speculation against the currency.'

Price dynamics in financial markets

Given the economic deterioration and currency weakness in the region, the Singapore dollar started depreciating from July 1997. In the second half of 1997, the currency depreciated 15 per cent, from $S1.43 to $S1.69 (see Figure 5.12). This depreciation was mostly orderly. The authorities actively bought Singapore dollars during these six months, with foreign exchange reserves falling over $US9 billion in the last six months of 1997, with buying concentrated in periods of uncertainty such as August, October and December (see Figure 5.13).

Conditions in Singapore's financial markets became substantially more unsettled in January 1998, as uncertainty about economic and financial stability in Indonesia increased. The Singapore dollar depreciated 5 per cent in the first few weeks of January, three-month interest rates rose from around 7.2 per cent to 12 per cent, and prices on the Singapore stock exchange fell 30 per cent (see Figure 5.14). The MAS intervened strongly in the foreign-exchange market, with foreign-exchange reserves falling $US3 billion in the month.

Despite its formal and informal capital controls, the control of the MAS over the Singapore dollar is not perfect because there is a relatively large offshore market in the currency, based in London and New York, which is about two-thirds the size of the onshore market. As expectations of further currency weakness took hold, speculators would either sell the

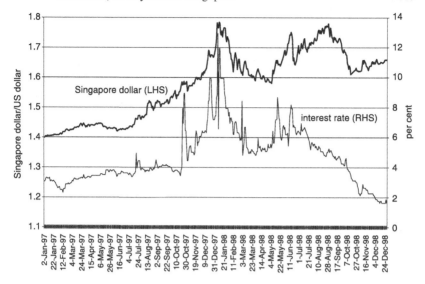

Figure 5.12 Singapore dollar and the three-month interest rate

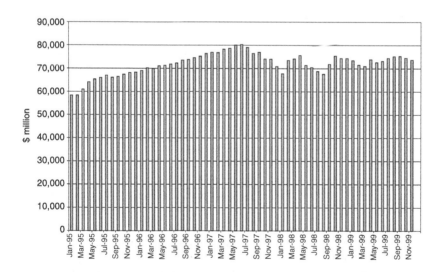

Figure 5.13 Foreign exchange reserves, Singapore

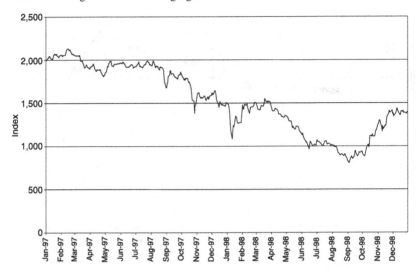

Figure 5.14 Singapore stock prices

Singapore dollar forward or borrow Singapore dollars and sell the currency in the spot market in the expectation of being able to buy it back at a depreciated rate. These periods are associated with the emergence of differentials between onshore and offshore interest rates. From late December 1997 to January 1998, the one-month differential widened substantially, reaching $12\frac{1}{2}$ per cent on 6 and 7 January (see Figure 5.15). There was an unusually high degree of activity by foreign international banks at this time, acting on behalf of hedge funds and on their own account.

These pressures abated, with the currency appreciating $12\frac{1}{2}$ per cent from January to mid May. Pressures then re-emerged, in a renewed bout of regional currency weakness. The FSF Working Group on HLIs (2000) reports that market participants estimated that HLI short Singapore dollar positions in 1998 were around $US1–2 billion (1–2 per cent of GDP), with an average length of three to six months. Most shorting activity was done by the HLIs, with no additional activity by pension or mutual funds.

The FSF Working Group on HLIs (2000: 125) reports that 'the Singapore dollar stabilised in late August and strengthened in subsequent months amid the closing of leveraged positions after the introduction of capital controls in Malaysia, the Russian default and near-collapse of LTCM, and the subsequent improvement in global financial markets.

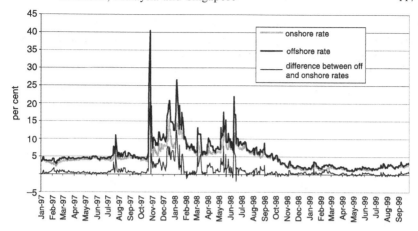

Figure 5.15 Onshore and offshore one-month interest rates, Singapore

According to market participants, the exchange controls in Malaysia helped to give the Singapore-dollar market a firm and credible level against the US dollar for an important bilateral exchange rate. The recovery in the Singapore currency was also helped by a feeling in financial markets by August that regional currencies and assets had been oversold.'

An assessment

The case studies of Indonesia, Malaysia and Singapore provide four valuable insights into the behaviour of hedge funds and other HLIs in emerging-country financial markets.

In the first place, they show clearly that it is an inaccurate caricature of hedge funds to say that they are only ever on the sell side of a market. Macro hedge funds and other HLIs change their positions over time, depending on how their judgment of economic and financial fundamentals evolves. They establish long and short positions depending on their assessment of economic and financial conditions. While hedge funds were short the rupiah in mid-1997, for example, they had shifted to substantial long positions for most of the December quarter of that year.

Second, hedge funds and other HLIs were active in these three countries to varying degrees. Hedge funds appear to have been less active in Indonesia and Singapore than they were in Malaysia. In Indonesia, their activities were largely swamped by domestic participants and capital flight as political and social stability broke down – hedge funds are certainly neither a necessary nor sufficient condition for a financial crisis. In Singapore, effective capital controls were the key feature limiting the fall in the Singapore dollar. The emergence of a non-trivial spread between Singapore onshore and offshore interest rates is *prima facie* evidence of capital controls. Onshore and offshore interest rates for the same asset should be the same if there are no capital controls, which can be tested formally as

$$i_{t,k}^{onshore} = \alpha + \beta i_{t,k}^{offshore} \tag{1}$$

where the null hypothesis is $\alpha = 0$ and $\beta = 1$.

Table 5.2 shows the results for one-month data. Before the crisis, the null hypothesis of closed interest rate parity is not rejected, but it is strongly rejected during the crisis, from October 1997 to October 1998. Singapore's capital controls were effective in driving substantial wedges between local and offshore Singapore-dollar interest rates in 1997 and 1998.

In Malaysia, hedge funds and proprietary trading desks appear to have been very active, and at times were particularly aggressive in selling the currency. Market participants indicate three reasons (not in any particular order) for this. The first is that, as indicated above, Mahathir's anti-western, anti-Semitic and anti-speculator comments acted as a lightning rod in attracting speculative interest in Malaysia, and 'made it personal'. Second, hedge funds needed to make up for the losses they suffered in Indonesia, and felt that they had to approach successive investments more aggressively. Finally, the fact that hedge funds had been on the

Table 5.2. *Closed interest parity, Singapore, One-month on and offshore interest rates*

Period	Average differential (per cent)	Regression of onshore rate on offshore rate	
		α ($\alpha = 0$)	β ($\beta = 1$)
January to June 97	0.48* (0.03)	−0.37 (0.28)	0.98 (0.07)
October 97 to October 98	2.07* (0.17)	2.96* (0.22)	0.46* (0.02)
January to September 99	0.28* (0.03)	0.57* (0.09)	0.61* (0.04)

Note: standard errors are in parentheses; standard errors for α and β are Newey-West adjusted; * indicates significance at the 1 per cent level; data were provided by a bank in Singapore.

buy side in Indonesia and lost, made them wary of the upside in markets and taking long positions. Because of Indonesia, they became inclined to the view that emerging markets were more susceptible to moving down than up, and they became more inclined to sell than buy.

Third, the diverse outcomes for these three countries show just how difficult it is to judge the economic and financial fundamentals of a country. Speculators have to make decisions under uncertainty. In the final analysis, because there is no clear model of the fundamentals, it is difficult to prove whether financial markets overshot or not. Econometric models of these three countries' exchange rates – based on conventional indicators like inflation differentials, productivity differentials, interest differentials, terms of trade, the current account – are not sufficiently stable or 'sensible' in the pre-crisis period to be able to show convincing deviations from fair value in the crisis period.

But it is hard to argue that the falls in asset prices these countries experienced, especially in Indonesia and Malaysia, were justified *ex ante*. The argument that financial prices overshot is more heuristic. Market participants in both the official and private sectors say that exchange rates overshot. The changes in financial prices that occurred, with half to three-quarters of the value of financial assets lost, were unprecedented for such economies. Moreover, basic models, for example based on purchasing power parity, indicate that at June 1997, the rupiah was overvalued by at most 6 per cent, the ringgit by at most 12 per cent, and the Singapore dollar by at most 20 per cent (Chinn 1998; Furman and Stiglitz 1998).

To the extent that real exchange rates had become misaligned, the movement induced by the crisis was out of kilter with the correction that was required. Figure 5.16 shows JP Morgan's estimate of these three countries' real effective exchange rates over the past three decades. There was a modest, at most 10 per cent, appreciation in their real exchange rates in the mid-1990s which was far less than had occurred in some previous episodes of exchange rate correction (like, for example, the appreciation of the ringgit in 1984 and 1985). The correction was unprecedented over the past three decades, with the real effective exchange rates in Indonesia and Malaysia depreciating by 70 per cent and 35 per cent from peak to trough in 1997 and early 1998. While the sign of the adjustment was right, it defies common sense to argue that the size of the adjustment was right *ex ante*.

The fourth insight that comes from comparing Indonesia, Malaysia and Singapore is the importance of a stable well-functioning policy framework. In Indonesia, the collapse of effective policy-making made the crisis a political and social one, and seriously exacerbated the out-

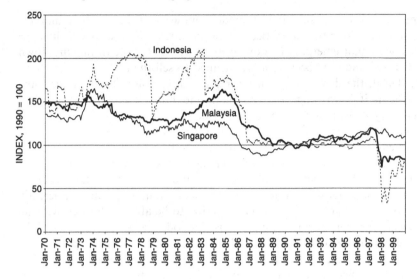

Figure 5.16 Real effective exchange rates

come. In Malaysia, personal and policy conflict between the prime minister and his deputy created uncertainty and hence vulnerability, and the vituperative comments of the prime minister about speculators drew that country to their attention. The public policy process exacerbated the outcome. Policy-making in Singapore, by way of contrast, remained credible and focused, which underpinned that country's successful handling of the crisis.

The success of Singapore during the crisis has two elements, the strength of the economy and capital controls. The economy was structurally very sound, but it was also highly exposed to developments in its two large neighbours, Indonesia and Malaysia. The Singapore dollar did depreciate and appreciate with 'bad' and 'good' news in 1997 and 1998, but the overall movements were modest – a peak to trough nominal depreciation of only 20 per cent – and were consistently orderly. If speculators had been able to freely establish short positions in the currency, they would surely have established larger positions, and the fall in the Singapore dollar could have been substantially greater, given Singapore's proximity to, and integration with, Indonesia and Malaysia. This suggests that the MAS's strict formal and informal control over speculation in onshore markets and its substantial strategic intervention to support the currency (of at least $US20 billion) were the keys to limiting overshooting of the exchange rate.

6   Australia and New Zealand

Given Australia's and New Zealand's deep trade integration with east Asia, the Australian dollar and the NZ dollar depreciated substantially as the east Asian financial crisis progressed and commodity prices fell. Australia and New Zealand have freely floating exchange rates and, in both cases, substantial currency depreciation was welcomed as an effective means to stabilise domestic income in the face of a large adverse foreign-demand shock. But there was a strong view in both the official sector and in financial markets that the currency falls were overdone and that, in Australia, market conditions at times became seriously disorderly.

Highly leveraged institutions were important players in both currency markets and had large concentrated positions. At least in the case of Australia, these large concentrated positions were associated with two undesirable effects. One was explicit aggressive destabilising activity by some HLIs that was designed on specific occasions to move prices to the advantage of those institutions. The other was that the very size and concentration of hedge fund positions affected the willingness of other market participants to take alternative positions, resulting in additional instability in foreign-exchange markets and overshooting of the exchange rate on the downside. These have important implications for market integrity which are explored in the conclusion.

The chapter assesses the economic context for both countries together, but reviews and assesses the market dynamics and activities of HLIs for each country separately.

The economic context

The price movements in asset markets need to be understood in the context of the economic and policy conditions in each country. Figure 6.1 shows GDP growth for Australia and New Zealand in the 1990s. Both countries were growing strongly in the lead up to the Asian financial crisis. Inflationary pressures were very modest: underlying

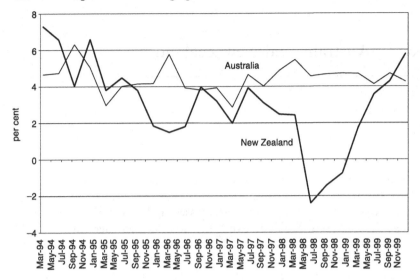

Figure 6.1 GDP growth in Australia and New Zealand

inflation in 1997 was 1.4 per cent in Australia and 1.6 per cent in New Zealand.

Unlike the crisis-affected economies, they also had – and still do have – robust policy regimes. Both countries had fiscal surpluses in 1997 – 0.2 per cent of GDP in Australia and 2 per cent in New Zealand – and well-established inflation targeting regimes to guide monetary policy. Before the crisis, government debt in Australia and New Zealand was 20 per cent and 30 per cent of GDP respectively, well below the OECD average, and is now even lower. The New Zealand banking system is foreign (mostly Australian) owned, and Australian banks were very secure: non-performing assets were only 0.5 per cent of total assets before the east Asian financial crisis – peaking at a minuscule 0.6 per cent during the crisis – and the banks were well capitalised. Firms' foreign currency exposures were also well-hedged (see Appendix 6A).

The vulnerability of both countries to the east Asian financial crisis was seen to lie in their large trade exposures to the region. Half of Australia's merchandise exports, for example, are directed to east Asia, with two-thirds going to non-Japan east Asia. New Zealand sells one third of its exports to east Asia. The contraction in east Asian demand directly affected Australia's and New Zealand's exports, widening both countries' current-account deficits (see Figure 6.2). The deterioration in the current-account deficit was smaller in Australia than in New Zealand because Australian exporters were more able to diversify into alternative markets, including the Middle East. The east Asian financial crisis also put considerable downward pressure on commodity prices and Australia's and New Zealand's terms of trade (see Figure 6.3) which is a traditional determinant of these countries' exchange rates (see Figure 6.4).

In assessing the economic fundamentals of these economies, it is worth keeping in mind that the impact of the region's financial crisis was relatively limited. Throughout the financial crisis, Australia's domestic economy remained strong, with annual growth staying above 4 per cent. Even in the midst of the pressures in 1998, the consensus forecast for Australia's growth in 1998 did not fall below 3.2 per cent, and even the most pessimistic of the mainstream forecasters were predicting a growth slowdown to only around 2 per cent.[1]

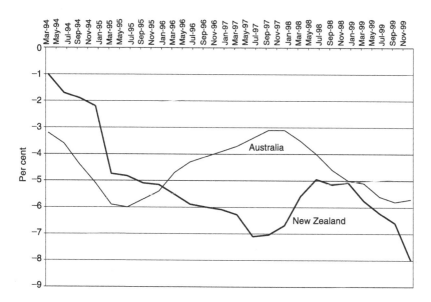

Figure 6.2 Current-account deficits of Australia and New Zealand

---

[1] The resilience of the economy lay in the confluence of several factors: the depreciation of the exchange rate insulated domestic exporters from falls in world prices, some exporters were able to find alternative markets, and domestic confidence and demand remained strong due to interest-rate reductions a year earlier, a reduction in margins in lending rates for both firms and households, and stable monetary policy throughout the crisis. Private demand was also supported by one-off increases in wealth associated with the partial privatisation of Australia's telecom company and the demutualisation of a large insurer/pension fund.

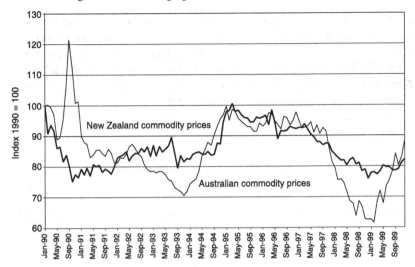

Figure 6.3 Export commodity prices of Australia and New Zealand

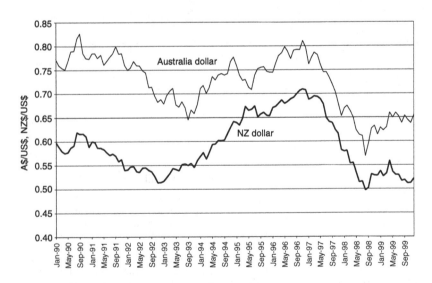

Figure 6.4 US dollar exchange rates of Australia and New Zealand

New Zealand was not able to maintain the momentum of growth, partly because it has a narrower export base and was less successful in finding alternative markets, but also because the central bank ran excessively tight monetary policy (see Figure 6.5). The Reserve Bank of New Zealand encouraged interest rates to rise in late 1997 and early 1998 as the exchange rate depreciated in order to prevent monetary conditions from becoming too easy and inflation rising. This hurt domestic growth at a time when the economy had just been hit by a large external real shock.

Price dynamics in the foreign-exchange market

The Australian dollar and the NZ dollar both experienced substantial movement in 1998 but the two countries' experiences with highly leveraged institutions differed somewhat and it is worthwhile tracing through events in each market separately.

The Australian dollar

The Australian dollar is the seventh most-traded currency in the world, with average daily turnover in April 1998 of $US44.2 billion (BIS 1999).

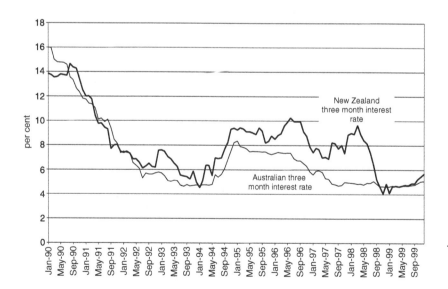

Figure 6.5 Interest rates in Australia and New Zealand

This is much less than for the US dollar ($1,260 billion), mark ($US430 billion) and yen ($US300 billion) but is similar to the Canadian dollar ($US52 billion). Onshore trade in the Australian dollar ($US23.3) is about five times onshore trade in the NZ dollar ($US4.9 billion). About 15 per cent of Australian dollar transactions are with customers who are not financial institutions. The openness, size and liquidity of the market and the fact that Australia is deeply integrated in the east Asian economy combine to make the Australian dollar a useful currency to speculate on, or hedge against, regional developments.

The financial-market pressures experienced by Australia during 1998 took the exchange rate to its weakest level since the currency was floated in December 1983. Figure 6.6 plots the Australian dollar daily in 1997 and 1998 (FSF Working Group on HLIs 2000: Annex E). After peaking at around US81 cents in late 1996, the Australian dollar depreciated gradually through 1997 and the first half of 1998, reflecting the weakening situation in Asia. The depreciation over most of this period was generally fairly smooth, with two key exceptions.

The first was in late May and early June, when market conditions deteriorated rapidly. The currency only recovered after the coordinated Federal Reserve/Bank of Japan intervention to support the yen. The second was in mid-August following the Russian devaluation and domes-

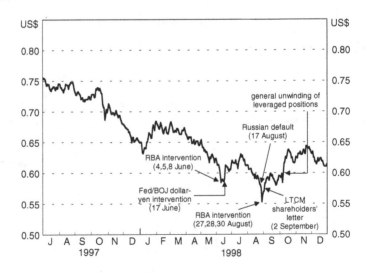

Figure 6.6 Australian dollar

tic debt moratorium. There was an expectation at the time that Russia would sell its commodities stockpile, which would depress world commodity prices and, consequently, 'commodity currencies' like the Australian dollar. The near-collapse of LTCM and seizing-up of US asset markets forced speculators to unwind short positions in the yen and other regional currencies, causing an immediate recovery in regional exchange rates. The Australian dollar rose by almost 7 per cent during one twenty-four-hour period in early October, its largest such rise in the post-float period. By the end of 1998, the currency had returned to its levels in early May, around US63 cents.

According to market participants, hedge funds and other HLIs were important players in the two periods of instability in the Australian dollar market in 1998 (Rankin 1999; RBA 1999b; FSF Working Group on HLIs 2000). Based on wide-ranging discussions with market participants, these reports say that hedge funds and other HLIs were active in three stages.

In the first instance, hedge funds mostly started establishing large short positions from the end of 1997 and the first half of 1998, after the exchange rate had already depreciated by 10 to 15 per cent and a downward trend was clear. The motivation for the positions varied but a recurrent theme is that they were either proxy plays on other less-liquid regional currencies, or were 'bets' on the prospect for a much wider regional crisis that included devaluation of the Chinese renminbi and collapse of the Hong Kong dollar peg.

These positions were generally established steadily and quietly. They were large. Market participants suggest that hedge funds' positions were in the order of $A10–15 billion ($US6–10 billion), equal to about $2\frac{1}{2}$ per cent of Australia's GDP, about half the size of Australia's current account deficit at the time.

These positions were also concentrated, with a couple of the large macro hedge funds each having positions of several billion Australian dollars. Proprietary trading desks of investment banks are thought to have had aggregate short positions in the order of $A3 billion ($US2 billion).

The short positions were established in the conventional way: selling the currency in the spot market and funding the position in the swap market. Turnover in the spot and swap Australian dollar markets increased substantially in 1997 and 1998 (see Figure 6.7).[2] Swap turnover

---

[2] These data are for onshore trade. According to the BIS (1999), in April 1998, about 60 per cent of trade in the Australian dollar was conducted offshore.

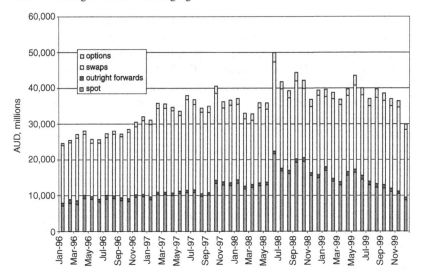

Figure 6.7 Australian dollar onshore turnover

increased by 32 per cent in 1997, and remained at high levels in 1998, especially in June. While data are not available, the duration of pre-funding in the swap market of short positions in the spot Australian dollar market lengthened in the first half of 1998.

The HLI positions are equivalent to about a quarter to a third of average daily turnover in the Australian dollar, which in April 1998 was reported to be $US44.2 billion (BIS 1999). It is wrong to interpret this as indicating that HLI positions were small relative to the market. Most foreign-exchange transactions are in fact the passing of positions between financial intermediaries, who trade and re-bundle positions on and offshore in a search for an ultimate buyer or seller. The share of non-financial customers – so-called 'real money' – in the Australian dollar market is about 15 per cent of total turnover, which means that the HLI positions were equivalent to several days trade.

Shifting the sorts of positions that the macro hedge funds had would have a very substantial impact on the Australian dollar exchange rate, especially if it occurred in a short space of time. While the effect of a currency transaction on the price depends on the particular conditions of the market at the time, Australian dollar traders reckon that the market cannot absorb more than several hundred million dollars of new money at a time without a substantial effect on price. If a fund is to close out a short position of several billion Australian dollars without causing the currency to appreciate substantially, it needs to do so steadily over a period of weeks or else in a surge of selling.

This leads to the second stage. Some macro hedge funds took a more aggressive stance as the exchange rate approached its post-float lows around US60 cents, a time when the market had become particularly sensitive to rumours. Market participants report a range of actions in early June 1998 which substantially unsettled the market. At least one hedge fund signalled to other market players that it was about to 'attack' the Australian dollar, a move which heightened uncertainty and deterred potential buyers from remaining in the market. Investment banks acting for hedge funds also progressively lowered offer prices in the broker market even though they were able to sell all they had on offer at the existing price – that is, they did not sell at 'best price' to other traders. This had the effect of thinning liquidity in the market because traders were left holding loss-making positions.

There was also concentrated selling in periods of thin trading, such as Friday lunchtime and in the cusp between Sydney closing and London opening. The concentrated selling that occurred at lunchtime on Friday 4 June, for example, originated from the Singapore, London and New York offices of one investment bank which was said to be acting on behalf of one macro hedge fund.

As a result of intense market uncertainty in early June, some 'market makers' in the interbank market – the fifteen to twenty or so intermediaries which are always supposed to provide prices for selling and buying Australian dollars – effectively dropped out of the market by delaying making a price or not answering their phones.[3] Another consequence was that exporters, who had been keen buyers of Australian dollars at higher levels, not only stopped buying but began to sell in the expectation that the exchange rate would fall further (RBA 1999b). There was also a noticeable shift to options hedging, even though volatility was high and options were expensive. The Reserve Bank of Australia intervened to buy Australian dollars in early June, buying $A2.6 billion in the periods of concentrated selling. This increased hedge fund positions by about 20 per cent.

The third stage was the hedge funds unwinding and taking profit on their short positions. Short positions established in the first half of 1998 were strongly in profit for a substantial period and so there was ample opportunity for this to be completed. The RBA (1999b) argues that only

---

[3] There are seventy or so market makers in the interbank and broker markets as a whole.

limited profit taking occurred at this time, with hedge funds holding their short positions in the expectation of further falls – one fund said it was targeting a low US50 cent figure.

The Australian dollar did fall further, touching a new record low in late August of US55.3 cents and prompting a further $A0.7 billion of RBA intervention in the spot market and some intervention in the options market in the form of the purchase of a short-dated out-of-the-money call option. This was a particularly attractive form of intervention since banks holding the option have to buy the Australian dollar to hedge the option on their books, particularly as the exchange rate moves to the strike price. This generated a wave of buying that looked, for all intents and purposes, to be sourced from the private sector rather than the central bank. Serious consideration was given at various times to raising interest rates to support the currency.

But events moved very quickly. In late September and early October, the near-collapse of Long-Term Capital Management caused banks to cut back on their funding to all hedge funds. Deprived of credit to fund their short positions and needing to finance other positions, hedge funds were forced to cover those positions by buying in the market. This produced a sharp rise in the exchange rate, back to around US65 cents, roughly where it had been before the hedge funds' selling started six months earlier.

The New Zealand dollar

New Zealand is a small open economy, about one-seventh the size of Australia's. Its financial markets are open, relatively large for an economy of its size, and highly internationalised in the sense that about two-thirds of its bonds and stocks are held by offshore entities. It also has a relatively long history of activity by macro hedge funds in all its financial markets.

The main macro hedge funds have been active in New Zealand since the early 1990s for three reasons. First, a number of key personnel at these funds have strong personal links – and hence familiarity– with the country, either having lived or extensively visited there. When they are in New Zealand, they have access to the country's top policy-makers. Second, the country has an unusually high economic profile because it was at the vanguard of policy reform from the mid-1980s to mid-1990s, which means that people are generally familiar with its economy and focus on what is happening in it. Third, it has offered a number of highly profitable investment opportunities over the years.

The NZ dollar fluctuated substantially over the 1990s, in a prolonged upswing from late 1992 to early 1997, in which it appreciated 30 per cent to US72 cents, followed by a major downswing, in which it depreciated 32 per cent to US48 cents (see Figure 6.4). Macro hedge funds appear to have been active players in both. In the mid-1990s, they established long positions in the NZ dollar, as well as in global NZ government bonds ('kiwis'). Hedge funds – and other speculators – closed out these long positions in 1996 with a profit, well ahead of the turn in the currency.

Market participants say that hedge funds were able to close out their long positions with limited downward effect on the NZ dollar because there was still substantial buying pressure in the market at the time: there was solid demand for the NZ dollar because of large foreign-direct-investment inflows in the second half of 1996 (like the privatisation of New Zealand telecom), large issues of global 'kiwi' bonds, and strong demand for local currency by exporters who hedged at the prevailing high exchange rate because they feared that the NZ dollar would appreciate even further. In the New Zealand case, exporters clearly over-hedged (see Appendix 6A).

While many local companies and exporters anticipated further appreciation – some even talked of parity with the Australian dollar – some macro hedge funds and a few others came to the view in late 1996 that the NZ dollar would fall and started establishing short positions. Their assessment that high interest rates could not be maintained was driven in part by public and private statements by the authorities that the exchange rate was overvalued. The Governor of the RBNZ in fact went to New York around this time and implored the market to sell the NZ dollar. Evidence of a growth slowdown and weakening commodity prices and current-account deficit, combined with the regional turmoil from mid-1997, added to these pressures.

During the second half of 1997, the operation of the RBNZ's monetary conditions index (MCI) – an index of the economic stimulus from interest-rate and exchange-rate settings – also made the shorting strategy more attractive. The RBNZ reacted to the depreciation in the exchange rate by encouraging market interest rates to rise by up to almost 10 per cent in the second half of 1997. This became widely regarded in financial markets as unsustainable for a slowing economy, and intensified shorting activity.

Aggregate short positions in the NZ dollar were large. Market participants reckon that highly leveraged players were the key institutions shorting the NZ dollar. They estimate that total HLI short positions in 1998 reached about $NZ15 billion ($US9 billion) – equivalent to 15 per cent of GDP – and that $NZ10 billion ($US6 billion) of this was held by around half a dozen macro hedge funds (FSF Working Group on HLIs).

These positions were also heavily concentrated: one large macro fund is believed to have had a short position of $NZ5 billion ($US3 billion), and another a position of several billion NZ dollars. Individual proprietary trading desks' positions do not seem to have exceeded $NZ1 billion ($US600 million). The individual hedge funds' long positions in 1995 and 1996 were substantially smaller than their short positions in 1997 and 1998. As in Australia, the bulk of the short positions were established quietly. The behaviour of the macro hedge funds also varied: some funds adopted 'position and hold' strategies, while others actively covered and re-established their positions.

The intense position-taking by macro hedge funds and proprietary trading desks of investment banks is reflected in a rise in offshore activity: during this period, foreign-exchange turnover with offshore counterparties increased and reached three-quarters of total turnover. As for Australia, the short positions were established using swap markets to fund sales in the spot foreign-exchange market.

These positions were very large relative to the size of the market. Market participants reckon that, in general, it is difficult to transact more than $NZ400 billion of new money a day without substantially affecting the price in the market. A $NZ4 billion position, they say, would take about three weeks to be established if it was to have minimum price impact. Of course, this has the counterpoint that unwinding a position needs to be managed very well to prevent price movement adverse to the profit of the position.

The short positions of HLIs generally proved to be profitable. Based on the transactions in which they participated, traders estimate that the bulk of hedge fund positions were established in the low US60 cent range and were reversed in the low US50 cent range – a 17 per cent return. Some positions were particularly profitable, especially for funds which established positions at the peak around US70 cents and reversed them at the trough, below US50 cents – a 29 per cent return.

The sort of aggressive, or what some market participants call 'unprofessional', trading behaviour that occurred in Australia did not arise to any substantial degree in New Zealand, although the trading tactics of some macro hedge funds (especially those which churn their positions) were more aggressive than of others.

The report of the FSF Working Group on HLIs also discusses the role of other players in the market. As mentioned above, exporters feared in 1996 and 1997 that the NZ dollar would continue to appreciate and bought more NZ dollars than they needed to cover their foreign exchange receipts for the coming year (see Appendix 6A). They over-hedged. This had an impact on price dynamics: as the currency depreciated, demand that would usually emerge at such a time was only thin, making the market more one-sided, on the sell side. This appears to have been especially important after the December quarter of 1997, as the exchange rate broke through the low US60 cent range. Importers had also under-hedged – because they also anticipated further appreciation – and they added to the selling momentum. As the currency depreciated, it broke key technical points, triggering options-related selling.

The New Zealand dollar hit a low of US48.6 cents in late August – albeit not as low as the record low of US43.1 cents in March 1985. The currency then strengthened in September and October, following the generalised position unwinding by highly leveraged players after the Russian default and near-collapse of LTCM: on one day in early October it appreciated by over 5 per cent (see Figure 6.8). There was also an abrupt recovery in the stock market, which rose over 15 per cent in the month of October.

Evaluating the episode

Australia and New Zealand provide two interesting examples of large concentrated position-taking by macro hedge funds and others. In both

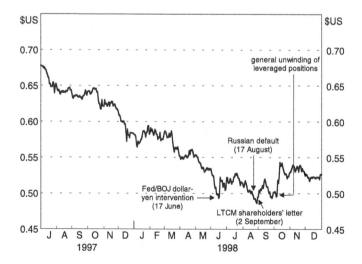

Figure 6.8 New Zealand dollar

countries, the authorities thought that a substantial currency depreciation was necessary to stabilise the domestic economy in the face of a large negative external shock, although this was not fully recognised by the RBNZ until the middle of 1998, at which time it allowed interest rates to fall sharply.

Differences in tactics

The two striking differences between Australia and New Zealand are the occasional highly aggressive tactics of HLIs in the foreign-exchange market – as shown in the June 1998 episode – and the effect of the perceived presence of macro hedge funds on the willingness of other market participants to take contrary positions. There are three feasible explanations for why the Australian dollar experienced more market dislocation than the NZ dollar in 1998.

The first is that positions in the NZ dollar market were too small, compared to positions elsewhere, to warrant special attention. This could be so but market estimates of the size of positions in each currency are not that different – hedge fund short NZ dollar positions are thought to have been $US6 billion, compared to short Australian dollar positions of up to $US9 billion.

The second relates to the liquidity in the NZ dollar market. Hedge funds are acutely aware of the state of liquidity in financial markets in which they have positions – without adequate liquidity, a position cannot be closed without causing price movement adverse to the profitability of that position. Liquidity in the NZ dollar market is very different to that in the Australian dollar market.

In the first place, liquidity in the New Zealand market is highly variable. So-called 'real money' transactions – the demand and supply of NZ dollars by exporters, importers and investors – tend to be large, bulky and relatively infrequent. There are pockets of liquidity, and these can arise in the local time zone or in London or New York trading hours. The relative illiquidity of the NZ dollar market arises because the economy is relatively small and trade transactions are relatively large and seasonal. For example, agricultural and dairy produce is exported through large promotion boards, and international payment for such produce tends to occur in blocks, sometimes with a distinct seasonal pattern. This differs to Australia, where the export, import and investment flows are much larger – because the economy is seven times larger – and more diverse. Real money flows tend to be more even in Australia than in New Zealand.

In addition to this, the number of financial institutions which are prepared to 'make a market' – that is, always willing to provide a buying or selling price for foreign exchange – is substantially smaller in New Zealand than in Australia. There are five NZ dollar market makers, compared to just under seventy Australian dollar market makers. These five NZ dollar market makers play a crucial role in managing liquidity in the NZ dollar market. It is imperative for each market maker in New Zealand to maintain good relations with the other market makers.

The hedge funds which are active in New Zealand understand that liquidity in the NZ dollar market is highly variable and they know the patterns of flows. They also understand that access to liquidity is through a narrow conduit – five institutions – and that all these institutions know that their access to good prices in the market depends on them maintaining good relations with the other four institutions. If an institution or trader develops a reputation for not doing business at 'best price', for example, then other traders quote prices with a wider spread to that institution or trader. What goes around comes around. Variable liquidity and a narrow entry point to liquidity when it is there provide hedge funds and traders alike with a powerful incentive not to dislocate the market. Dumping or ramping large transactions through the NZ dollar market, for example, is more likely to hurt a hedge fund that help it. This is not the case in Australia.

The third reason why the NZ dollar market was subject to less malbehaviour than the Australian dollar market may be because the speculative positions in New Zealand were more profitable than the positions in Australia, and so speculators did not need to generate more selling momentum to be able to close out their positions profitably. As discussed above, hedge fund short positions in the Australian dollar are thought to have been mostly established after a trend was clear, in the mid-US60 cent range. In the case of New Zealand, by late 1996 and early 1997, a short position in the currency was viewed by hedge funds as a 'no brainer'. Positions were established earlier in New Zealand and were more profitable than those in Australia. In Australia, it looks like positions needed a push.

There is another explanation for the different tactics applied in Australia and New Zealand: the two countries' different policies with respect to foreign-exchange intervention. The RBA has intervened on occasion to support the Australian dollar when market conditions have become extremely unsettled, but the RBNZ has not intervened since the currency was floated in 1984.

It is difficult to believe that intervention drove the short positioning in Australia. In the first place, the short positions were mostly established *before* the early June intervention. There were no transactions between hedge funds and the central bank. Furthermore, the intervention in June 1998 was the first major intervention for six years. The RBA does not target a particular level of the exchange rate; its intervention is not predictable and so cannot be relied on to establish or close out positions. In the June episode, it appears that some HLIs were targeting a lower Australian dollar – in the low US50 cent range – but this did not eventuate. The HLIs ended up with a bigger short position and a higher Australian dollar than they anticipated (Rankin 1999). It is also worth noting that market participants consistently say that the central bank's intervention policies were not a factor in driving the shorting of the Australian dollar.

Econometric evidence of overshooting

If there was destabilising speculative activity in the Australian and New Zealand dollar foreign-exchange markets, it should manifest itself in overshooting of these currencies. Rankin (1999) presents the RBA view, arguing that the Australian dollar depreciated more than was justified by fundamentals in mid-1998. The starting point for his analysis is the well-documented correlation of the Australian dollar with commodity prices (Blundell-Wignall, Fahrer and Heath 1994; Tarditi 1996).

To support his claim, Rankin estimates an unrestricted error correction of the month-end Australian dollar/US dollar exchange rate, which is the bilateral rate that accounts for almost all Australian dollar trading, commodity prices for Australia's exports, and the three-month interest differential with the United States. Commodity prices in this case are represented by the Westpac commodity futures index. He estimates the model from 1988 to the end of 1996 and to the end of 1997, and forecasts the exchange rate to mid-1999. In both cases, the forecast value follows the actual rate in depreciating sharply in late 1997, but the actual rate then depreciates substantially more than the forecast rate in mid-1998, the period of speculative attack. Changes in the actual and forecast exchange rates again converge after September 1998.

Another way to see this is by looking at the residuals of a conventional forecasting equation for the Australian dollar. Table 6.1 presents such an equation, using the same definitions of data as Rankin (1999) but estimated from November 1988 to March 2000. Figure 6.9 plots the residuals and a two-standard-error margin for the 1990s.

Table 6.1. *Model of the Australian dollar, November 1988 to March 2000*

Regressor	Coefficient	Standard errror	t-ratio [probability]
Constant	−0.0193	0.1245	−0.15 [.877]
Interest differential (t-1)	0.00191	0.0007	2.59 [.011]
Δ Westpac CFI	0.2489	0.0627	3.97 [.000]
$A/$US (t-1)	−0.072	0.0442	−1.63 [.106]
Westpac CFI (t-1)	−0.0024	0.0255	−0.96 [.924]
R-bar-squared: 0.17		Standard error: 0.022	

Notes: Standard errors are adjusted for heteroscedasticity using White's method.

There are two obvious points to be made. The first is that large deviations from 'fair value' occur relatively frequently – the standard error on monthly movements in the Australian dollar is 2.2 per cent, and in the 1990s a quarter of the monthly movements in the currency were larger than one standard error. There are five occasions in the 1990s when the monthly change in the Australian dollar was significantly larger than what was predicted by the interest differential and change in commodity prices. It is difficult to make the case that 'destabilising speculation' is responsible for most deviations from fair value.

The second is that the deviations of the Australian dollar from fair value in the 1990s are greatest in the period associated with intense

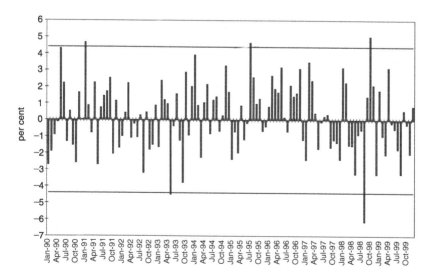

Figure 6.9 Australian dollar residuals

speculative activity by highly leveraged institutions. The two largest residuals are in August 1998, when the Australian dollar depreciated 6.1 per cent *more* than the model predicted – the model predicted a 1 per cent depreciation – and in October 1998, when the Australian dollar appreciated 5 per cent *more* than the model predicted – the model predicted a 0.2 per cent appreciation.

The residuals are also large in May 1998, with the currency depreciating 3.2 per cent more than predicted by fundamentals. The residuals are not out of the ordinary in June 1998, when the actual attack occurred, but this is not surprising since the central bank intervened heavily at the time to support the currency. Overall, the pattern of residuals from fair-value equations corroborates the claim by the authorities that the Australian dollar was seriously overshooting fundamentals on the down side and that this was related to HLI activity.

One standard criticism of these sorts of exchange-rate models is that they are not robust to changes in sample period or specification. This is true in the sense that there is variation in the point estimates and precision of regression coefficient over time. Exchange-rate models are notoriously unstable. But this should not obscure the fact that, unlike many other currencies, movements in the Australian dollar can historically be explained systematically by movements in the commodity prices of Australia's exports (or Australia's terms of trade) and the interest differential with the United States. While the particular values of the residuals from exchange-rate equations may certainly vary, the *pattern* identified above is robust to alternative specifications, and the interpretation is qualitatively correct.

The method used to identify overshooting in the Australian dollar is applied to the NZ dollar, which is also widely regarded in financial markets as a 'commodity currency'. Table 6.2 sets out the model and Figure 6.10 plots the residuals from the estimated equation. The commodity price series is the ANZ Bank's world price index for New Zealand's export commodities. The model is augmented by current and lagged changes in the Australian dollar because the two currencies tend to be traded together in the market.[4] Because of possible simultaneity

---

[4] The Australian-dollar model does not include changes in the NZ dollar because the coefficients are not statistically significant in the instrumental variables estimation. In practice, pricing of the NZ dollar is much more affected by the Australian dollar than the other way round, even though events in the NZ-dollar market do occasionally spill over into the Australian-dollar market. Participants in the Australian/New Zealand-dollar cross-rate market reckon that the $NZ/$US rate affects the $A/$US rate about once for every ten times the $A/$US rate affects the $NZ/$US rate.

Table 6.2. *Model of the NZ dollar, February 1989 to February 2000*

Regressor	Coefficient	Standard error	t-ratio [probability]
Constant	−0.3029	0.1290	−2.348 [0.02]
Interest differential	0.0007	0.0009	0.7585 [0.45]
Δ ANZ WPI	0.1234	0.0542	2.277 [0.02]
Δ $A	0.5474	0.1437	3.811 [0.00]
Δ $A (t-1)	0.1531	0.0591	2.591 [0.01]
$NZ/$US (t-1)	−0.0365	0.0205	−1.782 [0.08]
ANZ WPI (t-1)	0.0593	0.0258	2.298 [0.02]

R-bar-squared: 0.286   Standard error: 0.017

bias arising from including the current Australian dollar rate, the model is estimated using instrumental variables.[5]

The error band for the NZ dollar is also wide and it has only a few more significantly large changes than the Australian dollar. The pattern of big changes in the NZ dollar in 1998 is a little different to that of the Australian dollar, although this is partly by construction since movements in the Australian dollar will have some effect on the NZ dollar in this model. The distinguishing feature of the NZ dollar is that it experienced substantial depreciation in December 1997 and the first half of 1998: from the end of November 1997 to June 1998, the NZ dollar depreciated 12 per cent, while the Australian dollar depreciated only half that amount. The movements in August were much more moderate. It did, however, share a substantial appreciation with the Australian dollar in October 1998.

Conclusion

In Australia and New Zealand, macro hedge funds and other highly leveraged institutions had large concentrated short currency positions in 1997 and, particularly, 1998. In New Zealand in particular, these positions were the mechanism by which the currency depreciated, and currency depreciation was very much a welcome process since it helped insulate these economies from the adverse real external shock they experi-

---

[5] The instruments are the NZ interest differential, the lag log levels of the NZ dollar and ANZ WPI, the change in the log of the ANZ WPI, the first and second lags of the log change in the Australian dollar, and the first log difference of the Westpac Commodity Futures Index.

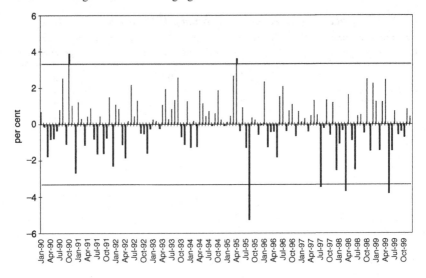

Figure 6.10 NZ dollar residuals

enced as east Asian markets slowed and commodity prices fell. These economies were, however, fundamentally sound and did not suffer from the vulnerabilities that existed in the east Asian crisis economies.

There is extensive anecdotal evidence from accounts by the Reserve Bank of Australia (1999a, b) and the Financial Stability Forum Working Group on HLIs (2000) that highly leveraged institutions – and macro hedge funds in particular – at times destabilised price dynamics in the foreign-exchange market which led to overshooting of the exchange rate.

The destabilising process is most evident in the case of Australia in June and August 1998. It is apparent in a pure speculative attack in early June when a hedge fund announced to traders that it was going to force the currency down further, after it had already depreciated 25 per cent, and rapidly sold unusually large volumes of Australian dollars in quiet periods. This had a chilling effect on the market, forcing many buyers out, and liquidity all but dried up making the market vulnerable to a further sharp fall. In August, there is no evidence of an attack as such, but the presence of large concentrated positions by the hedge funds, which at that time enjoyed a particularly strong reputation, again adversely affected the willingness of other market participants to take contrary positions.

These effects led to substantial overshooting of the Australian and New Zealand dollars. In the first place, the depreciation of the

Australian dollar at this time was significantly larger than predicted by conventional commodity-price/interest-differential currency models. This affected the NZ dollar. Furthermore, the contraction of credit extended to hedge funds after the near-collapse of LTCM in September, and the subsequent turmoil in US asset markets, led to a rapid unwinding of short positions in the Australian and New Zealand dollars. This unwinding led to the most dramatic one-day rises in these currencies in their post-war history. In Australia, the reversal of the short positions took the currency back to the level that prevailed before the bulk of the hedge fund short positions were established.

These cases are important because they show that large players in mid-sized financial markets are able to materially affect price dynamics at times even in countries with flexible exchange rates. As it turned out, the overshooting on the downside did not substantially affect the economy because it was soon reversed as a result of the crisis that was occurring in US financial markets due to the near-collapse of LTCM. But had that event not occurred, it is not clear that things would have turned out so well. The authorities were concerned that continuing currency instability would undermine domestic confidence. Discussion with market participants indicated that some exporters were starting to reverse their market activity, from being buyers at an historically low rate to selling in the expectation of buying Australian dollars at an even substantially lower rate in the near future. There was also serious consideration given to raising interest rates to support the currency, which, if it had happened would have slowed growth, as occurred in Canada and New Zealand, and caused a loss of jobs.

These cases also show, as argued by Rankin (1999), that the policy recommendation that deep financial markets are important in ensuring stability is not necessarily the case. Australia, like Hong Kong and South Africa, was vulnerable to proxy plays and proxy hedges because its market for its currency is so deep and liquid. While these economies certainly benefit from financial integration, it is not necessarily without risk. If these risks are to be reduced, an international policy response to deal with threats to market integrity is necessary, an issue which is addressed in Chapter 9.

Appendix 6A: Hedging strategies in Australia and New Zealand

Firms hedge their exposures in a number of ways. Balance-sheet exposures are hedged by matching the currency denomination of assets and liabilities or by using financial instruments, especially swaps. Cash flows and profit and loss are hedged by matching the currency denomination of inflows and outflows or by using financial instruments, especially forwards and options. Some firms also use 'natural hedges'. In Australia, for example, the well-established correlation of the Australian dollar and commodity prices provides commodity exporters with a natural hedge against unfavourable movements in US dollar denominated commodity prices – the Australian dollar tends to depreciate when commodity prices fall, stabilising Australian-dollar incomes.

Listed firms which are not financial intermediaries only use derivatives to hedge risks associated with interest rate, foreign currency or commodity exposures. They do *not* trade them on their account and are generally very wary of speculative positions. This is a direct legacy of the experience of the 1980s, when a number of firms took open speculative positions in foreign exchange and subsequently recorded substantial losses. There is also a general aversion among firms and households to unhedged foreign-currency positions. Encouraged by their banks, some firms and households in the mid-1980s took low-interest Swiss-franc loans without taking forward cover. Subsequently, the Australian dollar depreciated by about 30 per cent, in response to deteriorating terms of trade, and their Australian-dollar interest costs rose substantially, leaving a permanent impression on the dangers of unhedged borrowing. These experiences had a cathartic effect on the management foreign-exchange-rate risk by corporates in Australia.

Listed companies generally structure their balance sheets to create natural foreign-currency hedges between assets and liabilities. This typically involves tying the currency denomination of borrowing to their assets through foreign currency swaps. Commercial banks in Australia are also risk averse in managing foreign exchange risks and do not hold large open positions. Funds managers follow a variety of strategies, depending on in-house risk-management practices and the customer's risk preferences.

The way firms manage the exchange-rate risk associated with their transactions depends on the nature of, and market for, the good or service for which they are exchanging value. Accordingly, hedging strategies vary considerably between exporters and importers, between export sectors, and between firms in a given sector. While revenues may be sensitive to exchange-rate movements at the individual firm level, they are more stable in aggregate across industrial sectors, across exports and across the economy as a whole, indicating that risk is well diversified.

The hedging profile of exporters varies substantially between sectors, with the structure of a hedge tied to characteristics of the good which they sell, including its product cycle, durability and differentiability from other goods. For example, hedging by gold producers can extend to a dozen years, given long lead times in discovery and extraction, and the durability and homogeneous nature of the commodity. Hedging by agricultural producers, by way of contrast, is generally tied to the seasonal cycle. But even within a sector, firms can take very different strategies, with some firms having a full, partial or zero hedging strategy with widely varying mixes of forward and option cover at a range of prices.

Firms use foreign-exchange hedging much more than they use commodity-price hedging (although, again, there are substantial differences between sectors and firms). The primary reason for this is that the market for foreign-exchange cover is substantially deeper and cheaper than the market for commodities. Often, the local market for hedging instruments is insufficiently developed, although gold is an important exception. In some cases, the exporter is also too large relative to the size of even the international market to be able to cover prices extensively.

Many firms have also sought more flexible hedging devices, expressing more interest in options than before. Growth in options has exceeded that in forwards, although forwards are still used more widely (by about four to one). Options can be very expensive, however, and more so when markets are volatile, which acts to contain the shift to options. Companies also talk about using cheaper out-of-the-money options as a device to control the risk of big movements. They are very sensitive to their position relative to competitors and fear being 'caught out'.

In contrast to exporters, importers (especially at the retail level) tend to hedge only for relatively short periods of time, typically three or four months, since they prefer flexibility in supply and buy their goods on short contracts. While changes in exchange rates are passed through fairly quickly into the prices of imported goods 'at the docks', they are generally passed only very slowly into the prices of imported goods at the retail level. Given that import hedging is typically short term in nature, changes in hedging strategy are unlikely to affect the speed of pass-through of exchange rate changes into consumer price inflation.

Hedging behaviour in New Zealand is similar to that in Australia. In general, firms in New Zealand have a three-year hedging profile. Market participants reckon that firms hedge 80 per cent of their foreign-exchange exposures in the first year, 60 per cent of their exposures two years out, and 40 per cent of their exposures three years out. In 1997, they hedged more than 100 per cent of their foreign-currency exposures.

While there are many large firms active in the foreign-currency derivatives market in Australia, one large firm, the NZ Dairy Board, dominates the NZ dollar derivatives market, particularly the options market.

7   Models of market dynamics

Economists have long been puzzled by substantial overshooting of asset prices from their perceived fundamental value. The sharp rise and subsequent crash of the UK stock market in October 1987, for example, provoked a flurry of research examining the regularity of such events and trying to explain how they could occur.[1] In elementary rational-expectations models, movements in prices occur because market participants receive new information. But many movements in asset prices, even large and sustained ones, appear not to be explained by new information.

The literature on the microstructure of financial markets seeks to address some of these issues, and shows that movements in prices can occur for many reasons, including because of the trading mechanism itself, the types of trades made, and the strategies of different types of traders (O'Hara 1995).[2] The aim of this chapter is not to summarise the already large and expanding literature on market microstructure but to selectively identify and set out some of the main models that are relevant to the issue of this book: how, as shown by the experiences of 1997 and 1998 in east Asian financial markets, large informed players can affect financial-market dynamics.

The exposition in this chapter comprises three parts. The first looks at the literature on herding in financial markets, focusing on semi-rational herding models with noise traders and rational herding models due to information cascades and principal-agent concerns.[3] The emphasis is on the preconditions for herding to occur and its effect on market prices. The second part examines the literature on manipulation in financial markets. The third briefly looks at so-called third-generation models of multiple equilibria in economies, with particular focus on models with

---

[1] For example, see Gennotte and Leland (1990) and De Long, *et al.* (1990a, b).

[2] There are, of course, many factors that can be relevant in explaining market dynamics, including hedging activity (Gennotte and Leland 1990).

[3] There are also irrational models of herding; Devenow and Welch (1996) provide a good set of references.

financial markets. The conclusion provides a summary of the issues raised by the theoretical literature.

Herding

The phenomenon of herding in financial markets has been observed and thought about for a long time, as attested to by the following comments by Keynes (1936: 157):

> Investment based on genuine long-term expectation is so difficult . . . as to be scarcely practicable. He who attempts it must surely . . . run greater risks than he who tries to guess better than the crowd how the crowd will behave.

and Devenow and Welch (1996: 603):

> Imitation and mimicry are perhaps among our most basic instincts. Herding can be found in fashion and fads, just as in such simple decisions as to how to best commute and what research to work on. There is an especially prominent belief, not only among practitioners but also among financial economists (when asked in conversation), that investors are influenced by the decisions of other investors and that this influence is a first-order effect. In the financial realm, herding could potentially be universal.

Herding is an important feature not only of financial markets but also many features of human behaviour (Becker 1991; Hirshleifer 1995). The exposition on herding in this chapter concentrates on three coordination mechanisms. The first focuses on the interaction of rational informed speculators with 'noise traders', which is a model of semi-rational herding since one set of participants does not seek to maximise its welfare. The second focuses on fully rational market participants and information cascades, and the third focuses on fully rational market participants and principal-agent concerns. This covers only a part of the literature on herding and is clearly selective.[4]

---

[4] Devenow and Welch (1996) and Brunnermeier (1998a) provide excellent surveys on herding. Rational herding can also arise when the payoff to an agent increases as the number of agents adopting the strategy increases. The literature on payoff externalities covers a range of activities, including bank runs, market liquidity and acquiring information (Devenow and Welch 1996). As applied to financial markets, the key idea is that under certain circumstances, traders and managers may find it worthwhile to acquire further information only if others do; they herd in the sense that collectively they do not acquire further information: see Brennan (1990), Froot, Scharfstein and Stein (1992), Hirshleifer, Subrahmanyam and Titman (1994) and Vives (1995). Froot, Scharfstein and Stein (1992) argue, for example, that herding occurs if speculators have short horizons – they herd on the same information, trying to learn what other informed traders know. There can be multiple herding equilibria, and herding speculators may even choose to study information that is completely unrelated to fundamentals.

Noise trading

Kyle (1985) coined the term 'noise traders' to represent those market participants who base their trading decisions on rules, sentiment, or 'pseudo signals' like rumours or the advice of market gurus. They do not base their trading decisions on economic or financial fundamentals, which implies that changes in investor sentiment are not fully offset by arbitrage activity and so can have price effects (De Long, *et al.* 1990a, b). Shleifer and Summers (1990) argue that noise traders are not rational investors.[5] The models that incorporate noise trading, therefore, are not based solely on rationally acting agents.

De Long, *et al.* (1990a) set out the main model which analyses the effects on price dynamics of noise trading – represented in this case by traders who buy or sell depending on whether prices rose or fell in the previous period – in combination with informed rational speculators and passive value-seeking investors who simply buy or sell when the price is above or below fundamentals, regardless of price dynamics. Their model, which is set out in Appendix 7A, has important implications for thinking about the fundamental valuation of financial assets and the stability of speculation.

In the model, the market price of the risky financial asset deviates from its fundamental value in the short and the medium term. For a given noisy signal about future positive returns, informed rational speculators buy the risky asset from passive value-seeking investors, forcing the price of the risky asset up above its fair value in the expectation of feedback buying. Subsequent feedback buying by noise traders forces the price up even further, in response to which speculators close out their long positions and go short. Passive value-seeking investors also sell, adding to the selling pressure. Asset prices fall and converge to their fundamental value in the long run.

The interaction of feedback traders, passive investors and strategic rational speculators causes market prices to deviate from their fundamental value in the short and medium term – in periods 1 and 2 – but return to their true value in the long term, period 3.[6] This is shown in

[5] This is a somewhat controversial statement. If information is asymmetric, then prices perform two functions – market clearing and information aggregation, which implies that the sequence of prices may also be informative. In this case, uninformed traders may learn information from watching how prices unfold, thus providing 'one explanation for the pervasive use of technical analysis in markets that are supposed to be efficient' (O'Hara 1995: 160). Traynor and Ferguson (1985), for example, set out a model where past price processes help a trader determine whether his private information is already incorporated in prices.

[6] This is by construction: the model does not allow for multiple equilibria.

Figure 7.1.[7] The fundamental price of the risky asset increases in period 1 from 0 to $\phi/2$ (where ϕ is an element of the stochastic return on the risky asset) when this noisy signal about the first element of the stochastic return is received by speculators. It further rises to ϕ in period 2, which is also its value in period 3.

The market price also rises in period 1 and period 2 but in both cases it rises more than is justified by fundamentals. The market price falls in period 3 to its fundamental value. There is positive correlation in market prices in the short to medium term, but negative correlation in the longer term as fundamental value asserts itself. Asset price overshooting occurs in this model because of the interaction between feedback traders, passive value-seeking investors and rational informed speculators who take advantage of the reactions of all players.

With a noisy signal of a positive shock to returns, the model predicts that feedback traders are either neutral or long the risky asset because prices are either constant or rising in all the periods relevant to their profile, and it predicts that passive value-seeking investors are either short or neutral because prices are always above or equal to fundamental value. Informed rational speculators, by way of contrast, are initially long the risky asset, as prices rise, and then go short as prices peak. The crucial difference is that they earn profits from short-term trading

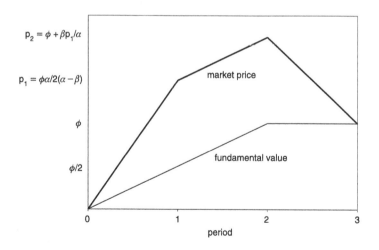

Figure 7.1 Price dynamics in the De Long, *et al.* (1990a) model

---

[7] See Appendix 7A for an explanation of the parameter values.

based on the reaction of other players and the effect of each set of players' position changes on price dynamics.

The model also makes a major contribution to thinking about dynamics in financial markets by showing that speculation is not always stabilising. Friedman (1953) argued that speculation is *necessarily* stabilising since speculators buy when the price is low and sell when it is high; if they do otherwise, they go out of business. The model set out by De Long, *et al.* (1990a) shows that Friedman's assessment is not a general proposition. Speculators may in fact buy rather than sell at a high price because they reckon that the price can go even higher because of feedback pressures. The same holds analogously for buying at a low price: speculators may sell at low prices because such action can induce feedback and force prices even lower for a period of time. 'Trading by rational speculators destabilizes prices because it triggers positive feedback trading by other investors' (De Long, *et al.* 1990a: 380).

The same rational investor can expect price trends to continue in the short run – and indeed exploit this to make profit – and revert to their true or fundamental value in the long run.[8] This proposition has strong empirical content. Cutler, Poterba and Summers (1990a) document that the predictions of the model occur in practice – for example, that excess returns on many financial assets are positively correlated in the short run and negatively correlated in the long run. Frankel and Froot (1988) find that market participants expect price changes to trigger others in the same direction, even if market participants think that prices will revert to fundamentals in the long run.

The model is relevant to thinking about the effects that large well-regarded speculative players can have on market behaviour and price dynamics. While there is an obvious danger in over-characterising and generalising market participants, the three types of players in the model broadly correspond to participants in financial markets in east Asia in 1997 and 1998 as discussed in previous chapters. Loosely speaking, institutions like some of the prop desks and small speculators have the attributes of feedback traders, looking to mimic the trades of hedge funds and responding to the price dynamics at times set in train by them. Institutions like mutual and pension funds have the attributes of passive value-seekers.[9] The macro hedge funds, and to a lesser extent some of the prop

---

[8] See also Cutler, Poterba and Summers (1990b). De Long, *et al.* (1990b) and De Long, *et al.* (1991) show that feedback trading can be profitable.

[9] This is consistent with the empirical observation by Nofsinger and Sias (1999), in their comprehensive study of herding and feedback by institutional investors, that institutional investors like mutual funds and pension funds, at the margin, buy undervalued stocks and sell overvalued stocks.

desks, have the attributes of informed rational speculators. Not only are they finely tuned to the trading strategies and positions of other players in the market, but their size and universally acclaimed analytical and trading skills make them the prime player on which to herd.

Indeed, it is important to keep in mind that De Long, *et al.* (1990a) motivated their model at the time on observations that hedge funds are key lead players in financial markets. They were particularly taken by George Soros' (1987) description of his strategy of buying or selling in anticipation of the purchases or sales by other market participants; feedback trading and fads are a well-established part of the market, and the key to success is not to counter the irrational wave of enthusiasm but to ride it and sell out at (around) its peak. The quintessential strategy of macro hedge funds is to identify the reaction function of other market participants and estimate how their demands – and hence market liquidity and price – will evolve under changing economic and financial conditions. Feedback traders are one such predictable group, as are those participants whose demand is largely exogenous like, for example in foreign-exchange markets, exporters, importers and investors.[10]

Information cascades

Information cascades, which is a term coined by Welch (1992), refer to situations where players optimally ignore their own private information about the likelihood of outcomes, and instead base their decisions on the information conveyed by the actions of other earlier players. Decisions are made sequentially rather than simultaneously by players, with later players learning from the actions of earlier players rather than from their information signals. In some cases, the actions of earlier players are so persuasive, that later players unconditionally imitate them, even if they have other divergent information.

Hirshleifer (1995: 188–89) sums up the key idea in the following way: 'learning by observing others can explain the conformity, idiosyncrasy, and fragility of social behaviour. When people can observe one another's behaviour, they very often end up making the same choices; thus localized conformity. If the early movers erred, followers are likely to imitate the mistake; hence idiosyncrasy. If later on a few people start behaving differently for whatever reason, then a sudden phase change can occur in which the old convention is swept away by the new, hence fragility'. The model has been applied to a wide range of behaviours.

---

[10] In the literature, these types of players are also called liquidity traders.

The information-cascade model of herding has two important implications for understanding the events in east Asia's financial markets in 1997 and 1998. The first is general: even rational market participants may at times ignore their own private information and follow the actions of earlier participants because the information in other people's collective actions overwhelms the individual's private information. This is more likely to occur when some participants have – or are perceived to have – superior information. The macro hedge funds were perceived as having superior information in two important respects.

First, in 1997 and 1998, macro hedge funds were universally acknowledged by market participants as having the best reputation of all financial-market participants in understanding east Asian economies and financial markets. In this respect, macro hedge funds were important because of their skill, not necessarily because of their size. It is worth remembering that the reputation of macro hedge funds was not sullied until 1999 and 2000, when they changed their strategies in relation to the US stock market. Their reputation in east Asian markets was in place all through 1998. This was despite the losses in Indonesia in 1997 because in that case everyone agreed that the bet was a good one *ex ante*. And it was despite the near-collapse of LTCM in September/October 1998 because that case was a relative-value fund event, not a macro hedge fund event.

Second, macro hedge funds were also universally acknowledged as the only institutions with accurate knowledge about what everyone else thought crucial to understanding the future direction of financial prices: hedge funds' positions in financial markets. In this respect, the informational advantage of the hedge funds was intrinsically related to their size – other participants were only interested in knowing hedge funds' positions in these markets because the positions were big relative to the size of the market and hence would have an impact on price dynamics. The upshot is that hedge funds' information was superior and some market participants were prepared to copy what they perceived to be the actions of hedge funds, rather than use their private information.

The second implication of the information cascade model is more specific: these models show the fundamental importance of the first player. The first player is important because his action carries more influence than anyone else on later players' actions. This is because the first player chooses to act in the way he does because he has information, whereas later players may act because they either have information or are just following someone else. As discussed below, in models where people can choose their place in the sequence of action, the first player has more or better information than other players, and this has an additional impact on subsequent players. Market participants say that hedge funds were the first players in a number of east Asian financial markets, either at the start of the play, as in Thailand in 1997, New Zealand in 1997 and Malaysia in 1998, or at the start of a new wave of selling, as in Australia and Hong Kong. In these cases, the macro hedge funds played an important signalling role to the rest of the market.

The first models of information cascades were set out by Bannerjee (1992), Bikhchandani, Hirshleifer and Welch (1992), and Welch (1992). These models are variants on a common theme: it can unequivocally be in the interests of later players to copy the actions of earlier players rather than base their actions on their own information.

Consider Bannerjee's (1992) model.[11] There are many assets, and they are indexed in a continuous line from 0 to 1, starting at $i = 0$. The ith asset is called $a(i)$. People have to choose one asset in which to invest. The excess return on all the assets is zero, except for one, i^+ which has a positive excess return. Naturally, everyone would like to know which asset this is, but no one does. Some people have an idea of which asset it may be, since each person faces a probability, α, that he receives a signal that I^+ is i'. The probability that the signal is true is β. If the signal is false, then it is drawn randomly from a continuous line from 0 to 1: the implication is that $\beta > \beta - 1$, and hence that a person who follows his signal is more likely to be right than wrong.

People make their decisions in random sequential order. Each person knows the decisions of previous people, but not whether these people received a signal. It stands to reason that the first person makes his decision without knowing anything about other people's decisions. No one knows whether the decisions that have been made were successful until after the last person has made his decision. In short, a person knows the actions of those who acted before but not those people's signals or the success of the actions.

Bannerjee (1992) sets out three decision rules:

1. A decision maker always chooses $i = 0$ when he has no signal of his own and when everyone else has chosen $i = 0$.
2. A decision maker always follows his own signal when he is indifferent between following previous actions or his own signal.
3. A decision maker always chooses to follow the previous decision maker with the highest i when he is indifferent between following more than one of the previous decision makers.

These rules imply a set of outcomes where information cascading and herding can arise. It is worth bearing in mind that the second rule makes

[11] Brunnermeier (1998) summarises the differences between the models.

cascading and feedback *less* likely. Figure 7.2 sets out the decision tree for the first three players in the sequence, and shows how cascades can arise.

If the first player does not receive a signal, he chooses $i_{1,ns}$. If he receives a signal, i', he follows it and choses $i_{1,s} = i'_1$, where the number in the subscript refers to the player and the subscripts s and ns refer to the choice of i when the player receives a signal or does not receive a signal. The action of the first player reveals more than that of any other player since he only chooses $i \neq 0$ if he has a signal. Other later players might chose $i \neq 0$ because they are following their own signal or because they are following another earlier player. Since there is no earlier player than player 1, the selection of $i \neq 0$ can only be because he has a signal; player 1's action necessarily reveals his signal.

If the second player does not receive a signal, he follows the first player, choosing $i_{1,s}$ if player 1 chose $i_{1,s}$ and $i = 0$ if player 1 chose $i = 0$. If player 2 receives a signal, he follows it, regardless of what the first player did.

If the third player does not receive a signal, he follows the other players. If both of the previous players chose $i = 0$, player 3 does too. If one of the previous players chose $i \neq 0$, then player 3 follows, and if both the two previous players chose $i \neq 0$, then player 3 follows the player who chose the highest i if the choices differ from each other. If the third player receives a signal, he follows it unless both people before him have chosen the same option (so long as this option is not $i = 0$).

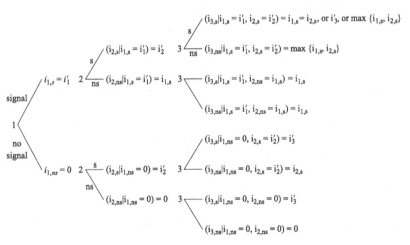

Figure 7.2 The decision tree

If the two players before player 3 have made the same choice and this choice conflicts with his own signal, player 3 will ignore his private information and follow the action of the other two players. Bannerjee (1992: 805) explains that

the third person knows that the first person must have a signal, since otherwise she would have chosen $i = 0$. The first person's choice is therefore at least as good as the third person's signal. Further, the first person has someone who followed her. This is some extra support for the first person's choice, since it is more likely to happen when the first person is right than when she is wrong. It is therefore always better to follow the first person.

An information cascade is now in process since successive players will follow suit for the same reason, even if they have a signal that differs from the choices made by previous players. The stability of cascades may be precarious, however, and subject to change with only relatively minor shocks (Bannerjee 1992; Bikhchandani, Hirshleifer and Welch 1992). A number of important variations have been developed. If the accuracy or power of the signal differs between individuals, then players whose information is less accurate will be more inclined to follow players whose information is more accurate, so long as players can distinguish between themselves on the basis of these characteristics (Bikhchandani, Hirshleifer and Welch 1992; Zhang 1997).

In terms of players in east Asian financial markets in 1997 and 1998, macro hedge funds were widely regarded as the players with the key information, in the ways set out above. In terms of the predictions of the Bikhchandani, Hirshleifer and Welch (1992) and Zhang (1997) models, market players were more likely to follow hedge funds since they were perceived as having a clear informational advantage at the time.

The player sequence in these models is exogenous. Bikhchandani, Hirshleifer and Welch (1992) consider a more general setting in which players can put off their decision to wait for more information, although there is a cost to delay. In this framework, 'the cost of deciding early is lowest for the individual with the highest precision' (1992: 1002), and so individuals with better information tend to act before others. Since this is understood, the actions of the first players are more likely to be imitated by other players. In Zhang's (1997) model, players initially wait but the player with the best quality information acts first and the second player, knowing this, follows him rather than his own signal. In this respect, endogenising the play sequence and introducing differences in the quality of information make cascades and herding more likely.

By choosing early, players at the start of a sequence show that they have an investment opportunity and hence affect later players (Chamley and Gale 1994). But it is not all one-sided (Brunnermeier 1998a; Gul and Lundholm 1995). The first player is able to partially infer the signals of other later players by the fact that they have delayed their action. This biases the action of the first player to later players and generates clustering in outcomes – in terms of Gul and Lundholm's (1995) model, people's forecasts are closer together when sequencing is endogenous rather than exogenous.

Bikhchandani, Hirshleifer and Welch (1992) also discuss the empirical and experimental literature that says that the more uncertain an individual is, the more susceptible that individual is to following others who are perceived as having information. This is also relevant to the events of 1997 and 1998 when financial markets were highly uncertain and susceptible to following 'trading rules' or people with good judgment or influence.

Avery and Zemsky (1998) have challenged the relevance of the information-cascade model to financial markets. The basic models discussed above assume that prices are fixed. This can 'undo' information-cascade models: if price changes, not only is the situation faced by later players in the sequence different to that of earlier players, but there is a continuous stream of new information coming to the market which undermines the cascade.[12] Devenow and Welch (1996) argue that information-cascade models are still relevant so long as prices do not move instantaneously and smoothly, such as when the market maker does not know that the price has moved because of some other player's private information.

While Avery and Zemsky (1998) challenge the relevance of information cascades in financial markets where all participants are rational and price reflects all publicly available information, they show that herding and price overshooting are robust to the operation of the price mechanism so long as there is compound uncertainty. As the dimensions of uncertainty in a market increase, the capacity of a single price to reveal information diminishes, and herding can become more prevalent and its effects on price more extreme. In short, the price mechanism works less well when uncertainty is multidimensional.

To show this, Avery and Zemsky (1998) identify three types of uncertainty, which add increasing layers of complexity and consequently reduced clarity to the price mechanism.

The first is *value uncertainty*, where the market is uncertain about the value of the asset. If the signal about the value of the asset is above the

---

[12] In an information cascade, no new information is made available when later players imitate earlier players. If prices change, this is no longer the case since market participants now have new information. Avery and Zemsky (1998: 728) define herding as a player acting contrary to his own signal and following other earlier players.

market price, traders buy it; they sell it if the signal is below the market price. There is only one dimension of uncertainty among market participants, and the new current price contains all the information they need to make their trading decisions. Since the history of the price does not reveal any additional information, herding does not arise.

The second is *event uncertainty*, where the market is uncertain whether the value of the asset has changed from its initial expected value (Easley and O'Hara 1992). In models where prices contain all publicly available information, rational traders only act when there is an information asymmetry between them and the market maker who sets the price. In Avery and Zemsky (1998), the information asymmetry is that informed traders know that an event has occurred but the market maker does not, and this gives the informed traders an advantage in interpreting the asset's trading history.

Herding occurs when three conditions hold: when the information in the history of trade overwhelms an individual's information about value uncertainty, when the likelihood of an information event is high, and when the bid–ask spread does not deter would-be herders from trading. As the market maker observes the herding and learns that an event has occurred, he widens the bid–ask spread and the herding ends. Asset price overshooting associated with event uncertainty is bounded and relatively small.

The third dimension is *composition uncertainty*, where the market is uncertain *ex ante* about the proportion of traders who are well-informed about the information event and those who are not. Composition uncertainty arises when the probability of traders being different types is not common knowledge. It can lead to a preponderance of activity on one side, with the effect that prices deviate substantially from fair value.

Herding occurs in this case when market participants have difficulty in distinguishing between the case in which the market is composed of well-informed traders and the case in which the market is composed of poorly informed traders who are herding. The conditions for a well-informed market to look the same as a poorly informed market with herding are difficult to satisfy. First, the information event that occurs must be very unlikely. Second, the market must generally be well informed, so that the market maker initially dismisses the possibility that it is not a well-informed market. Third, informed traders' signals all point to the same state. If these conditions are satisfied, 'then a poorly informed market with herding behaves exactly like a well-informed market and nothing is learned about composition uncertainty if there is herding. These effects combine to create highly volatile prices when the market is poorly informed about an information event' (Avery and Zemsky 1998: 737).

This model is helpful in understanding the possible influence of market dynamics on asset prices in east Asia in 1997 and 1998. It shows that rational herding occurs and can become more serious as the dimensions of uncertainty in a market increase. In this model, herding is not a general phenomenon because the degree and type of uncertainty required for it to occur are not general phenomena. But the degree, type and dimensions of uncertainty that occurred in regional financial markets in 1997 and 1998 were certainly well above the norm.

Principal-agent concerns

Rational herding can also occur when traders or managers optimally decide to 'run with the pack' in order to protect their reputation. If the performance of a trader or manager is evaluated relative to that of other traders or managers, then the trader or manager may prefer to mimic the actions of others rather than use their private information. Under certain circumstances, traders and managers 'will be more favourably evaluated if they follow the decisions of others than if they behave in a contrarian fashion' (Scharfstein and Stein 1990: 466).

The idea that traders and managers optimally act to protect their own interests and reputation, rather than those of their principals, is not a new one. Keynes (1936: 158) observed that 'worldly wisdom teaches that it is better for reputation to fail conventionally than to succeed unconventionally'. The issue has been explored with respect to financial markets in a number of papers, including Scharfstein and Stein (1990), Graham (1994) and Zwiebel (1995).

Scharfstein and Stein (1990), the key paper in this literature, set out a model where managers can be either smart – that is, they receive informative signals about the value of the investment – or dumb – that is, they receive a purely noisy signal. Neither can initially identify their type, but managers are evaluated on the profitability of their investments and on the similarity of their action with that of other managers.

There are unpredictable factors which affect the value of the investment made by managers, but these factors are systematic in the sense that smart managers receive identical signals. If the prediction errors of managers were completely uncorrelated, the market could update its assessment of their evaluation just by looking at their performance. If forecast errors are correlated, however, the market obtains information by comparing managers.

A manager who makes a mistake is evaluated less harshly if his colleagues made a similar bad investment: blame is shared. Smart managers receive the same signal but dumb ones just receive noise, so if a manager mimics the actions of others, his action suggests that he has received a signal which is correlated with that of others, and hence is more likely to be smart. If the decision turns out bad, then he is not blamed for being dumb but is just judged to have been unlucky. If he takes a contrarian position, however, then, all else equal, he is more likely to be perceived as dumb and takes the blame if the investment turns out bad. If managers are assessed on absolute and relative performance, they are, therefore, more inclined to follow other managers than use their own private information. If the manager who acts first has a better reputation than the manager who follows, then he will have excessive influence on the actions of managers who act later.

The model is relevant to understanding the effect of hedge funds on other players in markets. As explained above, the macro hedge funds had a very powerful reputation in east Asia in 1997 and 1998, and were universally perceived as the leaders in analysis and market know-how. Traders and managers of other institutions active in regional financial markets – like the prop desks of banks and securities companies – who wanted to protect or enhance their own reputations had a powerful incentive to be seen to be making positions similar to those of the macro hedge funds. Herding by other players would occur regardless of the intention of the hedge funds at a given time.

An interesting feature of Scharfstein and Stein's (1990) model is that it relies on 'good' managers' signals being correlated. Scharfstein and Stein (1990: 468) confess that 'this feature may seem slightly unnatural' but it makes a lot of sense in the context of hedge funds in east Asia in 1997 and 1998. Macro hedge funds placed similar positions in markets in the region. This 'correlation of signals' is most unlikely to have been due to explicit collusion, but is due to the fact that the traders and managers at these funds thought very much alike, looked at the same features of economies and financial markets in making their decisions, and talked a lot to each other. The model makes sense.

Market manipulation

Manipulation – actual and attempted – of asset prices has a long history. Allen and Gale (1992) refer to some colourful instances of stock price manipulation over the past three centuries. In the early 1600s, brokers engaged in rumour-mongering and concentrated selling on the Amsterdam Stock Exchange to frighten other investors, force large price falls, and buy stock at cheap prices. They also refer (504) to Jacob Little who, in the late 1800s, was nicknamed the 'Great Bear of Wall Street' and was said 'to gorge and digest more stock in one day than the weight of the bulk of his body in certificates', first short selling a company's stock, then spreading rumours about its insolvency and covering his short position. This type of manipulation is illegal on exchanges, although not in over-the-counter foreign-exchange markets.

Allen and Gale (1992) identify three types of manipulation. The first is *action-based manipulation*, or manipulation based on actions that change the actual or perceived value of assets. Examples include the Harlem Railway case, where sellers short sold Harlem Railway stock but had to buy the stock back at inflated prices, and the American Steel and Wire Company case, where the owners of some mills short sold stock in their company, closed down the mills which forced the stock price down, and then closed out their short positions and reopened the mills.

The second is *information-based manipulation*, or manipulation based on releasing false information or spreading rumours. Examples include the *New York Daily News* journalist, Raleigh T. Curtis, who conspired with a trading pool run by John J. Levinson to write favourably about stocks that the pool had bought.

The third is *trade-based manipulation*, or manipulation intended to alter the price of an asset simply by buying or selling it. Such manipulation is aimed at allowing the speculator to buy at low prices and sell at high ones. 'Cornering' a market and 'short squeezes' are classic examples of trade-based manipulation (Brunnermeier 1998a).

In the United States, the first two forms of manipulation were made illegal for stocks after the 1929 stock market collapse, under the Securities Exchange Act 1934. The general view is that measures to contain action-based and information-based manipulation in the stock market have been successful (Allen and Gale 1992), and analysis of the first two types of manipulation is no longer prominent in the academic literature.[13]

---

[13] Vila (1989), Benabou and Laroque (1992) and Bagnoli and Lipman (1996) are exceptions. Vila (1989) sets out models where a speculator colludes with another buyer before a takeover bid is announced, and when a speculator shorts a stock, releases false information, and then closes out the position at a profit. Bagnoli and Lipman (1996) set out a model where the speculator takes a position, colludes with another player who announces a bid, and then closes out the position at a profit. Benabou and Laroque (1992) set out a model where a player who has inside information and is regarded as credible, makes misleading statements to profit from pre-established positions. Repeated games can occur: manipulators' reputations need not be destroyed completely because information is noisy and manipulation can not be perfectly detected (Brunnermeier 1998).

But action-based and information-based manipulation still matter for over-the-counter (OTC) markets, especially those for foreign exchange. Even if regulations and codes of conduct are made for OTC markets, they are largely unenforceable because there is no effective governance mechanism in OTC markets.[14] Indeed, many of the instances of rumours, concentrated selling and other aggressive behaviour that market participants say occurred in east Asian financial markets in 1997 and 1998, were in the form of action-based and information-based manipulation.

One reason why there is less focus on action-based and information-based manipulation in foreign-exchange markets is because these markets are, in theory, infinite and are characterised as being so large that they are populated by many small agents acting individually and atomistically. They tend to be regarded as an example of perfectly competitive markets.[15] Unlike commodity markets in which supply of the commodity is fixed, the stock of foreign exchange is not fixed and, at the limit, is infinite: the market cannot be cornered.

This is true as far as it goes, but it ignores the fact that liquidity in markets is not constant and may in fact be highly variable (O'Hara 1995). Liquidity is notoriously difficult to define but it is well established in practice and theory that the willingness of buyers and sellers to trade varies over time, and so the effect of a trade on price depends heavily on the conditions prevailing at the time (Kyle 1985; Gennotte and Leland 1990; O'Hara 1995). If players can affect the decisions of other participants – specifically their willingness to take positions in the market – by action-based and information-based manipulation, they can affect liquidity and hence price formation in a market.

As noted above, the academic literature has concentrated on the issue of trade-based manipulation. The literature indicates that trade-based manipulation is only profitable under certain conditions. The starting point is that profitable trade-based manipulation is impossible in a perfectly efficient market (Jarrow 1992), where all participants are price takers and the price contains all agents' information. Traders who try to profit from buying high and selling low can only do so if other players make losses, but no player trades with the would-be manipulator if he expects to lose. Markets need to be inefficient if trade-based manipulation

---

[14] There are codes of conduct, like the Association Cambiste Internationale (ACI) code for foreign-exchange dealers, but these codes do not cover this sort of behaviour and are purely voluntary.

[15] Market practitioners tend to reject the view that foreign-exchange markets are atomistic. They point out that while there are many traders in foreign exchange, there are 20 or so financial intermediaries around the world that dominate markets.

is to occur or be profitable. The literature has focused on three main types of inefficiencies.

The first is when traders have – or are perceived to have – different quality information. One example is the model set out by Allen and Gale (1992). They assume that the asset is not highly traded and that there are three types of traders: small uninformed and 'passive' investors who are risk averse; informed large investors who are risk neutral and buy or sell the asset if its price is below or above that warranted by fundamentals; and uninformed large investors who are also risk neutral and want to manipulate the market.

Suppose the informed large investor thinks that the asset is undervalued and expects its price to rise. He buys the asset but his buying sends a signal to others that the asset is good value and the price rises. The signal, however, is noisy and passive investors do not force the price up to its true value immediately because they are risk averse and limit their buying. At some point, the informed investor closes his position and makes a profit if the sale price is higher than the purchase price.

The point of Allen and Gale's (1992) model is to show that the uninformed large player can make a profit from trade-based manipulation if he is able to pass himself off as an informed investor to small passive investors. If the informed large investor is not in the market, the would-be manipulator can pretend that his action is that of an informed investor who has received an informative signal about the asset. An information asymmetry lies at the heart of this, and other similar models.

The second inefficiency may be because there are differences between related markets, such as differences in liquidity between spot and futures markets. Brunnermeier (1998b: 3) considers the instance where the spot market is less liquid than the futures market: 'Liquidity allows a trader to go long into futures without affecting the prices of futures significantly. The trader can then buy the underlying stocks after having established his futures position. If the spot market is illiquid, the price rises and he can short squeeze other traders. Other traders who are short futures have to buy the underlying stock in order to deliver.' The price impact – and hence profit – is magnified.[16]

The third inefficiency that enables would-be manipulators to make profit is the presence of noise or feedback traders, since these traders base their decisions to buy or sell on extraneous information rather than fundamental information. This was shown in De Long, *et al.* (1990a, b) but it has also been set out in other models.

[16] See Kumar and Seppi (1992).

Brunnermeier (1998b), for example, sets out a Bayesian Nash equilibrium model – that is, an equilibrium where all players take the strategies of other players as given and are aware that their trade affects price – with three types of players: informed risk-neutral traders, liquidity traders (whose demand for the risky asset is exogenous) and a market maker who determines the price on the basis of the order flow in each period. An informed trader receives an imprecise signal about the value of an asset. This information will become public at some later stage, and the informed trader knows what the price impact will be when this happens. His sole motive for trading is to exploit his superior information about the fundamental value of the asset, and he does this twice – when he receives the signal and when the information in the signal becomes public. Other players know he receives a signal but do not know its content.

After receiving an imprecise negative signal, for example, the informed trader short sells the asset with the expectation that he will reverse his position and buy the asset back when the information becomes public, at which time other traders will be selling. The more the informed player sells, the more the price falls, and the greater is the overshoot below the true value implied by the signal. Up to some limit, this is in the informed trader's interests since it means that the price signal to other players is worse, and hence his buying opportunity when the information becomes public is better.

Other players trade on the basis of a mix of the signals they receive and use technical analysis to try to back out other players' demands. Since they do not receive the same signals, other players cannot identify the price effect of the informed trader's early trade. Brunnermeier (1998b) argues that players with such an informational advantage will trade more aggressively, in the sense of establishing larger positions than otherwise. He identifies speculative and manipulative components to the actions of the informed trader: the informed trader speculates in the sense that he trades in the expectation of unwinding the position in the next period, and he manipulates the market in the sense that he acts intentionally to move the price to enhance his informational advantage and financial gain in the next period.

For the reasons discussed above, Brunnermeier's (1998b) model of trade-based manipulation is helpful in thinking about hedge funds and financial market dynamics in east Asia in 1997 and 1998. Market participants tend to describe macro hedge funds' strategies as establishing the bulk of their positions quietly and then generating noise and uncertainty in order to generate flows to enable them to close out their short positions with minimal price effect adverse to their profit.

Multiple equilibria

The notion that more than one equilibrium is possible as the outcome of a series of economic events has gained wide acceptance over the past few years. There is a growing literature showing, for example, that financial and currency crises are not necessarily the outcome of fundamental policy inconsistencies or weak economic fundamentals. Recent work explicitly models the role of traders in financial markets – including the interaction of large and small traders – in causing a shift in the economy from a relatively strong to a relatively weak equilibrium.

There are many models of multiple equilibria.[17] The first-generation models explain currency crises under a fixed rate regime as the result of speculators rapidly selling the currency because they foresee foreign-exchange reserves being exhausted (Krugman 1979; Flood and Garber 1984). Second-generation models explain currency crises as the result of a policy inconsistency between maintaining the peg and abandoning it – as, for example, if policymakers want to keep the peg to tie down inflation expectations but also face political pressure to devalue to stimulate growth in the economy and employment – which is resolved by a speculative attack if the costs of defending the fixed rate increase when market participants expect the fixity to break (Obstfeld 1994).

In both the first- and second-generation models, speculators are simply bringing forward a correction in the exchange rate that would have occurred anyway. 'In effect, financial markets simply bring home the news, albeit sooner than the country might have wanted to hear it . . . Financial markets simply force the issue, and indeed must do so as long as investors are forward looking' (Krugman 1997: 5).

The third-generation models present a situation where a currency crisis is not a completely preordained event: crises can become self-fulfilling in economies with sufficiently, but not completely, weak fundamentals when market participants think that a crisis can occur if others sell and in fact do themselves sell because they come to think that others will sell (Krugman 1996, 1997). In an economy with some vulnerability, pessimistic expectations can become self-fulfilling. It is important to note that the economy must be in some intermediate state between completely sound and completely weak fundamentals for such a crisis to occur.

Obstfeld's (1996) exposition on self-fulfilling attacks includes a simple example, shown in Figure 7.3. There are two traders who each have money assets of $6. A trader must pay $1 to speculate, and if the peg breaks, the currency depreciates by 50 per cent. In case 3A, the autho-

---

[17] See Krugman (1997) for a general overview.

	Trader 2 hold	Trader 2 sell
Trader 1 hold	0, 0	0, −1
Trader 1 sell	−1, 0	−1, 1

(a) R = $6, each trader has $6

	Trader 2 hold	Trader 2 sell
Trader 1 hold	0, 0	0, 2
Trader 1 sell	2, 0	−½, ½

(b) R = $20, each trader has $6, cost of position is $1

	Trader 2 hold	Trader 2 sell
Trader 1 hold	0, 0	0, −1
Trader 1 sell	−1, 0	1½, 1½

(c) R = $10, each trader has $6, cost of position is $1

Figure 7.3 Nash equilibrium payoffs under different fundamentals

rities have reserves of $20 – the good fundamentals case – which exceeds speculators' individual and combined funds. If a trader speculates, he always loses $1. The sole Nash equilibrium is that neither trader sells the currency, and so the peg survives.

In case 3B, reserves are low – the bad fundamentals case – and each trader can individually sell the currency and force a devaluation, in which case he makes a net gain of $2. If both traders sell, the net return is just $½. Sell–sell is the sole Nash equilibrium.

In case 3C, reserves are at an intermediate level, $10, at which neither player acting individually can break the peg and turn a profit. If both players can coordinate a play, however, they each make a net gain of $1½. There are two Nash equilibria. The first is that both traders hold. This is a Nash equilibrium since neither trader has an incentive to adopt a sell strategy once the other has adopted a hold strategy. The second is that both traders sell. This is also a Nash equilibrium since neither trader has an incentive to hold once the other has sold. There are two possible equilibria. Once one party attacks, so will the other and expectations of the collapse of the peg becomes self-fulfilling.

Of itself, the size of either player is not relevant in this model unless the big player can take out the peg by itself. Yam (1999) argues that size is relevant in case 3C when there are many players because in such a game, a large player is more able to coordinate or guide the activities of other, smaller players. Accordingly, he argues that self-fulfilling attacks are *relatively* more likely to occur when the market is dominated by large traders.

Corsetti, *et al.* (2000) explicitly model the effect of large and small traders in financial markets and the conditions for multiple economic equilibria. Their model of speculative attack against a currency peg has three implications which are relevant to the analysis of large players in financial markets.

First, the presence of a large player raises the probability of an attack on a peg since a large trader makes smaller traders adopt more aggressive trading strategies: 'the large trader injects a degree of strategic fragility to the market' (2000: 3). The presence of a large player makes an economy with a higher level of economic fundamentals vulnerable to successful speculative attack.

Second, the influence of the large trader is even greater when he is better informed than the smaller traders. If the large trader has less information, his presence makes little or no difference to small traders' strategies. This fits clearly with how traders in east Asian financial markets focused on large players in 1997 and 1998. On the one hand, traders intently and intensively focused on the operations of the macro hedge funds, which they perceived as having the greatest insight into regional economies and markets and the greatest influence on price dynamics. On the other hand, they did not react nearly as much to the operation of mutual funds and pension funds because these institutions were not thought to have any additional information.

Third, the influence of the large trader is even greater – and, in this case, substantially so – when the large trader's position is revealed to small traders before they trade. When the large trader moves first and other traders know this, his action acts as a powerful signal to them, providing the fulcrum for a coordinated attack on the peg. 'To the extent that a speculative attack is the resolution of a coordination problem among the traders, the enhanced opportunity [provided by the signal embodied in the first move by the large player] to orchestrate a coordinated attack helps to resolve this collective action problem' (Corsetti, *et al.* 2000: 3). This underpins Yam's (1999) observation that coordinated attacks are more likely in the presence of large traders.

Conclusion

The mainstream response in the United States to the east Asian financial crisis in 1997 and 1998 has underplayed the role of financial market dynamics in generating asset price overshooting. The 1970s and 1980s textbook view of the world is that financial markets are efficient and market dynamics irrelevant. This view ignores a substantial literature that has developed in the past decade to explain inexplicably large and sustained movements in the prices of financial assets.

This literature has focused on the possibility of asset prices substantially deviating from fundamental value for extended periods of time due to herding, manipulation and multiple equilibria in financial markets. There are two key elements to these models. Either there are participants in financial markets who use feedback trading rules, which gives rise to the opportunity for other players to exploit this reaction function for their own short-term advantage, or there are substantial information asymmetries between market participants which the better-informed players are able to exploit to their advantage, not least because they know that the less-well-informed players will try to follow them to try to capture their information edge.

Both of these elements were apparent in east Asian financial markets in 1997 and 1998. Market participants all point to the macro hedge funds and, to a lesser extent, the proprietary trading desks of banks and securities companies as the players which were in the best position to exploit these elements at the time.

In the first place, feedback trading was – and remains – a key feature of financial markets and market participants all note the consummate skills of the macro hedge funds in understanding the reaction functions of other market participants in east Asian financial markets in 1997 and 1998. In particular, macro hedge funds are regarded as having had the best understanding of how market participants respond to price movements. Market participants also note the ability of macro hedge funds and prop desks at the time to trigger feedback trading, by using various techniques – outlined in earlier chapters – to encourage other players to adopt particular strategies or refrain from entering the market.

Market participants also agree that the macro hedge funds had two key informational advantages in east Asia in 1997 and 1998. The first was that they understood the strengths and vulnerabilities of economies and the flux in liquidity in financial markets in the region better than any other type of institutional investor at the time. The macro hedge funds had the analytical edge and had the ability to move quickly in markets. The second informational advantage was that the macro hedge funds knew what everyone else wanted to know: they knew their positions and strategies. This was important because size matters to price and the macro hedge funds were the biggest players in many of these markets. The first informational advantage relates to the perceived superior analytical skill of the macro hedge funds; the second to their sheer size in regional financial markets.

Appendix 7A

De Long, *et al.* (1990a) set out a four-period model (from period 0 to period 3), with three players and two assets. The three players are feedback traders (*f*), who buy and sell depending on whether prices rose or fell in the previous period, passive investors (*e*) who seek value by buying when prices are above fundamentals and selling when prices are below, and rational speculators (*r*) who maximise inter-temporal utility and take account of the reaction function of all other players, exploiting short-run price dynamics for their own gain. The proportion of investors which are rational speculators is μ and the proportion which are passive is $1 - \mu$.

The two assets are cash and a risky asset. Cash is supplied perfectly elastically and provides no net return. The risky asset is in zero net supply and pays a dividend, δ, in the final period. The dividend payable in period 3 has two stochastic components. The first, Φ, has a zero mean and three possible values: $-\phi$, 0 and ϕ. It becomes known publicly in period 2 but a signal about it, ε, is released in period 1. Only rational speculators use the signal. The second stochastic component in the dividend is θ, and it is normally distributed with a zero mean and variance, σ_θ^2.

De Long, *et al.* (1990a) assume that investors receive a positive signal, ϕ, about Φ in period 1 (the results are symmetric for a negative signal). Signals are noisy and can be true or false with the following probability:

$$\Pr(\varepsilon = \phi, \Phi = \phi) = 0.25$$
$$\Pr(\varepsilon = \phi, \Phi = 0) = 0.25$$
$$\Pr(\varepsilon = -\phi, \Phi = -\phi) = 0.25$$
$$\Pr(\varepsilon = -\phi, \Phi = 0) = 0.25$$

A positive (negative) signal can indicate that Φ is either positive (negative) or zero. Accordingly, if a positive signal is received, $\phi/2$ is the fundamental value of the risky asset in period 1 for period 2.

The key result in this model is that prices overshoot fundamentals. To show this, it is necessary to solve for the prices in the system. Prices in the first period, period 0, are normalised at zero, $p_0 = 0$. Prices in period 3 are equal to the dividend paid at that time, $p_3 = \Phi + \theta$. Given that there are two states of the world possible in period 2 – that is, $\Phi = \phi$ and $\Phi = 0$ – denoted by states *a* (the good state) and *b* (the bad state), there are three unknowns to find, p_1, p_{2a} and p_{2b}. Three excess demand equations for each period/state of the world are needed to find the three unknown prices.

The general excess demand equation for period 1 is

$$0 = D_1^f + \mu D_1^r + (1 - \mu)D_1^e \tag{7A.1}$$

where D signifies the demand for the risky asset, the subscript refers to the period, and the superscript the investor type: feedback trader (f), rational speculator (r), and passive investor (e). Equation (7A.1) reduces to

$$0 = \mu D_1^r - \alpha^e(1 - \mu)p_1. \tag{7A.2}$$

There is no feedback demand in period 1 because feedback traders respond to past, not current, changes in price, and there has not yet been any price movement. To be time-consistent, the asset demand by rational investors is solved by backward induction from the final time point, and is derived below after expressions for period 2 asset demands have been obtained. Passive value-seeking investors buy low and sell high, and their demand is assumed to be negatively related to the current price of the risky asset, $-\alpha^e p_1$, where the superscript e indicates passive investor.

The general excess demand equation for period 2 is

$$0 = D_2^f + \mu D_2^r + (1 - \mu)D_2^e \tag{7A.3}$$

which is equal to

$$0 = \beta(p_1 - p_0) + \mu \alpha^r(\Phi - p_2) + \alpha^e(1 - \mu)(\Phi - p_2) \tag{7A.4}$$

where β is the positive feedback coefficient of feedback traders to past price changes. Rational and passive investors demand the risky asset in period 2 if the information about returns revealed at that time indicates that prices are below fundamentals. In the opposite case, they short sell the asset.

The asset demands of rational investors are derived from the maximisation of expected utility. Demand for the risky asset in period 2 is determined in the following way. The return on the risky asset known at period 2 is Φ. The wealth (W) constraint at period 2 is

$$W_2 = p_2(W_1 - D_2^r) + \Phi D_2^r \tag{7A.5a}$$

which can be rewritten as

$$W_2 = p_2 W_1 + (\Phi - p_2)D_2^r \tag{7A.5b}$$

where D_2^r is speculators' demand for the risky asset in period 2. Speculators' expected utility is assumed to exhibit constant absolute risk aversion (CARA) in the form

$$V(W) = \exp(-\gamma W). \tag{7A.6}$$

Assuming that returns are normally distributed, the expected utility of wealth in period 2 is

$$E[V(W_2)] = -\exp\left(-\gamma\left\{E[W_2] - \frac{\gamma}{2}VAR[W_2]\right\}\right), \tag{7A.7}$$

which is equal to

$$E[V(W_2)] = -\exp\left(-\gamma\left\{p_2 W_1 + (\Phi - p_2) - \frac{\gamma}{2}D_2^{r\,2}\sigma_\theta^2\right\}\right). \tag{7A.8}$$

Differentiating Equation (7A.8) with respect to D_2^r, the rational investor's asset demand in period 2 is

$$D_2^r = \frac{(\Phi - p_2)}{\gamma\sigma_\theta^2} = \alpha^r(\Phi - p_2) \tag{7A.9}$$

where $\alpha^r = 1/\gamma\sigma_\theta^2$, γ is the coefficient of risk aversion, and σ_θ^2 is the variance of the second stochastic element in the dividend. In the case of rational investors, α^r has a specific meaning and derivation. By way of contrast, the responsiveness coefficient that is used to describe passive investors' demands, α^e, is not derived formally. For analytical convenience, these responsiveness coefficients are assumed to be equal, $\alpha^e = \alpha^r$. Given this and noting that $p_0 = 0$, the period 2 excess demand equation becomes

$$0 = \beta p_1 + \alpha(\Phi - p_2). \tag{7A.10}$$

Given the positive signal, ε, about ϕ, there are two possible states in period 2, which implies two possible outcomes for Equation (7A.10),

$$0 = \beta p_1 + \alpha(\phi - p_{2a}) \text{ for state } a, \text{ and} \tag{7A.11a}$$

$$0 = \beta p_1 - \alpha p_{2b} \text{ for state } b. \tag{7A.11b}$$

Demand for the risky asset in period 1 is obtained by maximising utility from the certain-equivalent wealth in both states of the world in period 2. The certain-equivalent wealth in state $2a$, $CE(W_{2a})$, comprises three terms: wealth at the end of period 1, the gains on the portfolio between period 1 and period 2, and the certainty equivalent of expected gains from period 2 to period 3:

$$CE(W_{2a}) = p_1 W_1 + D_1^r(p_{2a} - p_1) + CE(D_2^r(p_3 - p_{2a})) \tag{7A.12}$$

where D is demand for the risky asset.

For normally distributed returns and a CARA utility function, the certainty equivalent of the expected gains between period 2 and period 3 is

$$CE(D_2^r(p_3 - p_{2a})) = E[D_2^r(p_3 - p_{2a})] - \frac{\gamma}{2} VAR[D_2^r(p_3 - p_{2a})].$$

(7A.13)

Noting that $p_3 = \phi + \theta$ in the good state of the world, substituting in Equation (7A.9), and noting that $\alpha = 1/\gamma\sigma_\theta^2$, Equation (7A.13) simplifies to

$$CE(D_2^r(p_3 - p_{2a})) = \frac{\alpha}{2}(\phi - p_{2a})^2.$$

(7A.14)

Certain-equivalent wealth in state $2a$ is

$$CE(W_{2a}) = p_1 W_1 + D_1^r(p_{2a} - p_1) + \frac{\alpha}{2}(p_{2a} - \phi)^2.$$

(7A.15)

Analogously, certain-equivalent wealth in state $2b$ is

$$CE(W_{2b}) = p_1 W_1 + D_1^r(p_{2b} - p_1) + \frac{\alpha p_{2a}^2}{2}.$$

(7A.16)

Assuming the same CARA utility function as before, the maximand of expected utility over the distribution of period 2 certain equivalent wealth is

$$\max EU[W] = \max EU[0.5 W_{2a} + 0.5 W_{2b}]$$
$$= -\exp\left\{-\gamma\left\{E[W|\phi] - \frac{\gamma}{2} VAR[W|\phi]\right\}\right\}.$$

(7A.17)

Substituting Equations (7A.15) and (7A.16) into Equation (7A.17) yields

$$\max EU[W_2] = -\exp\left\{-\frac{\gamma}{2}\left\{D_1^r(p_{2a} + p_{2b} - 2p_1)\right.\right.$$
$$\left.\left. + \frac{\alpha}{2}\left((p_{2a} - \phi)^2 + p_{2b}^2\right) - \frac{\gamma}{2} D_1^{r2}(p_{2a} - p_{2b})^2\right\}\right\}.$$

(7A.18)

Maximising Equation (7A.18) with respect to D_1^r yields rational speculators' demand for the risky asset in period 1,

$$D_1^r = \frac{p_{2a} + p_{2b} - 2p_1}{\gamma(p_{2a} - p_{2b})^2}.$$

(7A.19)

The three unknown prices, p_1, p_{2a} and p_{2b}, can now be solved using Equations (7A.2), (7A.11a) and (7A.11b), yielding

$$p_1 = \frac{\phi}{2}\frac{\alpha}{\alpha - \beta}\frac{1}{1 + \frac{\phi^2}{4\sigma_\theta^2}\frac{\alpha}{\alpha - \beta}\frac{1 - \mu}{\mu}}$$

(7A.20a)

which simplifies to

$$p_1 = \frac{\phi\alpha}{2(\alpha - \beta)} \text{ when } \mu = 1, \tag{7A.20b}$$

$$p_{2a} = \frac{\beta}{\alpha}p_1 + \phi \text{ and} \tag{7A.21}$$

$$p_{2b} = \frac{\beta}{\alpha}p_1. \tag{7A.22}$$

8   Inferring hedge fund positions from returns data

Knowing the positions of hedge funds in financial markets is critical in evaluating the effect that they may have on the dynamics of financial markets. In the first place, knowing positions is necessary to evaluate how changes in positions affect financial prices. And knowing positions of hedge funds, as well as those of other market participants, is necessary to evaluate how hedge funds' positions affect the positions of other market players.

The problem is that data on market positions are proprietary information and are not publicly available: this creates a serious evidentiary problem. Analysts have tried to work around this by using various methods to infer hedge funds' positions in various markets. One method is to talk with a wide range of market participants and obtain market estimates of positions at particular points in time. But these data are anecdotal and are not available in times series format, and so they do not lend themselves to econometric analysis.

Brown, Goetzman and Park (1998) have suggested another way to get around the lack of data. They argued that positions can be inferred from the aggregate returns and net asset values of individual hedge funds. Returns and net asset values are more or less publicly available information. Noting that the aggregate return to a fund is the weighted sum of the individual returns on the constituent assets, they infer positions by multiplying a fund's net asset value by the coefficients from a regression of the aggregate return on the returns of individual assets that they think may be in the portfolio. These coefficients represent the asset weights.

On the basis of these estimates, Brown, Goetzman and Park (1998), Fung and Hsieh (1999), and Fung, Hsieh and Tsatsaronis (1999), among others, have argued that hedge funds' positions in emerging markets in 1997 were small and had no impact on key financial prices in these economies. These papers have been influential in US thinking about the role of hedge funds in emerging markets: Brown, Goetzman and Park (1998), for example, was quoted by the IMF study on hedge

171

funds and market dynamics (Chadha and Jansen 1998: 27) and the President's Working on Financial Markets (1999: A7–8) as prime evidence that hedge funds did not destabilise financial markets in east Asia. The paper by Fung and Hsieh (1999) has also had a strong influence on the thinking of US officials.

This chapter outlines some of the pitfalls of the analysis using this method. After presenting the results of these papers, it argues first that many of the estimates either do not pass the 'common sense' test or are at odds with the estimates provided by market participants. It then presents six reasons why the method is unreliable. An artificial portfolio is constructed to test the accuracy of the method. For both monthly and weekly returns, the inferred positions are seriously misleading with respect to the magnitude, sign and timing of the true positions, and they give false signals about changes in the true positions. The upshot is that, unfortunately, positions inferred from returns data using the method pioneered by Brown, Goetzman and Park (1998) are not a viable substitute for actual positions data.

The Brown, Goetzman and Park method

One method of estimating positions that has become popular in the empirical literature is to infer positions from returns data. Brown, Goetzman and Park (1998), Fung and Hsieh (1999), and Fung, Hsieh and Tsatsaronis (1999), for example, are influential papers in which the authors use the aggregate returns data of individual macro hedge funds to attempt to 'back out' positions of hedge funds in various markets.

Brown, Goetzman and Park (1998) examine the impact of hedge funds on the ringgit and a basket of Asian currencies in 1997. Fung and Hsieh (1999) examine the impact of hedge funds in a range of financial crises in the past couple of decades – the 1987 US stock price collapse, the 1992 ERM crisis, the 1993 global bond rally, the 1994 bond market turbulence, the 1994–95 Mexican crisis, and the 1997 Asian financial crisis – and Fung, Hsieh and Tsatsaronis (1999) concentrate on the impact of hedge funds in the east Asian financial crisis.

The method is motivated by the insight of Sharpe (1992) that factor analysis can be used to reconstruct aggregate returns from the returns of constituent asset classes. The method uses simple time-series techniques rather than latent variables analysis to deduce positions, and is referred to in this book as the Brown, Goetzman and Park method. It is straightforward. The return on fund i at time t can be represented as the linear combination of returns to a set of assets,

$$r_{it} = \sum_{k=1}^{K} \beta_{kt} r_{kt} + e_{it} \tag{8.1}$$

where $\sum_{k=1}^{K} \beta_{kt} = 1$ and $\beta_{kt} > 0$. The coefficients in Equation (8.1) represent the portfolio weights of the various asset classes. Accordingly, the total exposure to each asset class, k, at time t can be calculated as $x_{itk} = \beta_{kt} NAV_{it}$ where x is the exposure and NAV_{it} represents the net asset value of fund i at time t.

As Brown, Goetzman and Park (1998) explain, the coefficients in Equation (8.1) are estimated in a series of rolling OLS regressions with a very small fixed sample of at least k observations. In practice, they relax the positivity constraint on the coefficients to allow for both positive and negative positions in assets, and they relax the constraint that the coefficients sum to one because they limit the number of asset classes included in the regression. They also include a constant to capture possible excess returns from, for example, managerial performance. The estimating equation is

$$r_{it} = \beta_0 + \sum_{k=1}^{K} \beta_{kt} r_{kt} + e_{it} \tag{8.2}$$

without any of the restrictions of Equation (8.1) imposed.

The analyst faces a difficult trade-off between choosing a sufficiently representative group of asset prices in the regression and a sufficiently small sample period so that specific-period effects are not swamped and diluted by period-average effects. On the one hand, including more asset classes in the regression is likely to improve the 'fit' of the estimating equation, since hedge funds typically invest in a wide range of assets. The coefficients from including the returns of only one or two assets are likely to be biased.

On the other hand, including more variables means that more observations are needed to calculate the position at each point in time. To the extent that more variables are included, the sample period has to be greater to generate sufficient degrees of freedom, with the consequence that the coefficients and position estimates are an average for a number of points in time rather than the coefficient and position estimate for a particular point in time. This makes it difficult to draw firm conclusions about a fund's portfolio at each point in time and how it evolves over time.

Analysts have taken a number of approaches to deal with the trade-off. Brown, Goetzman and Park (1998), for example, are interested in assessing the Malaysian Prime Minister's claim that macro hedge funds were responsible for the sharp depreciation in the ringgit in 1997.[1] They initially restrict their estimation of Equation (8.2) to regressing monthly hedge fund returns on a constant and monthly changes in the ringgit. They fix the sample length at four months, giving them two degrees of freedom, and roll the estimating equation from January 1994 to October 1997.

They aggregate the results for the twelve hedge funds in their sample, and conclude that hedge funds' aggregate positions in the ringgit fluctuated substantially, reaching long positions of $100 billion around March 1995 and March 1997, and short positions of $200 billion in November 1995 and March 1996 and $100 billion in July 1997. These positions are uncorrelated with movements in the ringgit. Based on their estimates, they say that hedge fund short ringgit positions were in fact closed out in June to August 1997, leading them to conclude that 'hedge fund managers – the speculators – were supplying liquidity to a rapidly falling market . . . [and it] is tempting to suggest that they cushioned the rapid fall of the ringgit, rather than hastened it' (Brown, Goetzman and Park 1998: 9).

In this exercise, they deal with the trade-off between including sufficient representative assets in the estimating equation and minimising averaging effects by opting for the latter. They recognise the trade-off and caution that, given that they only include the ringgit as an explanatory variable, the estimated ringgit position may include positions in other assets which have returns that are correlated with the ringgit. As an alternative, they use weekly returns for two hedge funds and estimate weekly positions using the same methodology, but with the exceptions that they include exposure to major currencies and estimate the equation over a fixed sample of twelve weeks. They conclude that these two hedge funds' positions were uncorrelated, highly variable and particularly modest in 1997. Their assessment is: 'Again, no evidence that these representative managers were the culprits in the crash' (*ibid.*: 13).

Fung and Hsieh (1999), and Fung, Hsieh and Tsatsaronis (1999) also use the rolling regression method set out by Brown, Goetzman and Park (1998). Fung, Hsieh and Tsatsaronis (1999) first repeat Brown, Goetzman and Park's regression of monthly aggregate returns on changes in the ringgit but include the S&P as another independent variable and estimate the equation with a fixed window of six months. Fung and Hsieh (1999)

---

[1] They also assess whether the hedge funds caused the Asian crisis by repeating the exercise with a basket of Asian currencies. They conclude that the hedge funds had relatively small short positions in Asian currencies.

also include the S&P in their monthly regressions, and test for monthly positions for both the baht and ringgit.

Fung and Hsieh (1999) and Fung, Hsieh and Tsatsaronis (1999) then use weekly and daily data on returns for twelve hedge funds to increase the degrees of freedom, and include a wide menu of asset returns in the estimating equation, including changes in stock prices, bond prices and exchange rates for a range of developed and developing economies. Both papers use a step-wise procedure to obtain the best fitting equation: they initially include changes in a wide variety of asset prices as independent variables and sequentially eliminate insignificant regressors.

Based on the analysis of daily and weekly data, they conclude that the macro hedge funds had a range of complex positions in financial markets but that their positions in Asian currencies were relatively modest. They estimate that the short positions of the twelve macro hedge funds in their sample reached a maximum of $4\frac{1}{2}$ billion in the baht in June 1997, $1\frac{1}{4}$ billion in the ringgit in August 1997, and $3 billion in the won in August 1997. The estimated short positions were held for a very short period and hedge funds were substantial buyers at the peak time of the crisis, which they interpret as proof that macro hedge funds are not feedback traders (that is, they do not sell when the market is weak, thereby putting more downward pressure on the market). They estimate that hedge funds were only ever long in the rupiah – about $\frac{3}{4}$ billion in December 1997.

An evaluation of the method

Are the estimates of hedge funds' positions in these papers accurate? Without knowing the actual positions, it is obvious that one cannot answer this definitively. But there are two broad ways to evaluate the estimates of hedge fund positions, and both of these suggest caution in relying on the estimates of hedge fund positions in these papers.

The first is whether they pass a 'common sense' test. This essentially involves comparing the size and timing of estimated positions to other information about, say, the size of the markets involved and estimates of positions provided by key participants in financial markets.

Consider, for example, the estimates of ringgit positions in Brown, Goetzman and Park (1998). These do not pass a basic common-sense test. The estimates fluctuate several times between short positions of $100 billion and long positions over $200 billion over a few years. With 1997 GDP of US$80 billion (at end-1997 exchange rates), a ringgit position of US$200 billion amounts to $2\frac{1}{2}$ times GDP. It is inconceivable that such positions could be built up and liquidated in a month with no effect on the exchange rate.

The estimates are also unbelievable when compared to the volume of onshore interbank transactions. Brown, Goetzman and Park's (1998) estimate of hedge funds' ringgit positions accounts for multiples of annual turnover in the onshore spot market: ringgit/US dollar transactions totalled $270 billion in 1996 (60 per cent of which were swaps) and $430 billion in 1997 (75 per cent of which were swaps). While considerable hedge fund activity in the ringgit occurred offshore, in Singapore, the foreign-exchange transactions that would have to accompany positions of hundreds of billions of dollars would be well beyond the scale of local and regional foreign-exchange markets. Market participants say that they are also in excess of position changes in the dollar, yen and euro markets. It is also highly unlikely that banks and securities firms would have allowed hedge funds to have had ringgit positions of the size implied by Brown, Goetzman and Park (1998).

The position estimates in Fung and Hsieh (1999) and Fung, Hsieh and Tsatsaronis (1999) are substantially more modest than those in Brown, Goetzman and Park (1998). While they are more sensible, they are also substantially smaller than the estimates of expert market participants. As discussed in Chapter 3, market participants reckon that the hedge funds' short baht positions in mid-1997 were in the order of $10–15 billion, with a couple of the larger funds having individual positions of between US$3–4 billion. This is two to three times the size of positions estimated in Fung and Hsieh (1999) and Fung, Hsieh and Tsatsaronis (1999). The size and timing of the long position in the rupiah is also at odds with what market participants generally think – they tend to say that the long rupiah positions were larger and that they were established earlier, around October, and only closed out in the first few months of 1998. The difference between the two sets of estimates can only be resolved if individual hedge fund data were available.

One striking feature of the results in Fung and Hsieh (1999) and Fung, Hsieh and Tsatsaronis (1999) is that they estimate that hedge funds had a short won position of $3 billion in August 1997. This is a curious result for two reasons. The first is that market participants reckon that hedge funds were not involved in the won foreign-exchange market for the simple reason that they – as non-residents – could not obtain access to the swap facilities necessary to fund short positions. The second reason is that the overwhelming consensus in July and August 1997 was that currency turmoil was limited to the baht, and certainly only to southeast Asia. At the time, most analysts, including at many hedge funds, viewed Korea as relatively safe from the turmoil and so it is odd to see substantial short positions being established and quickly removed in the currency at the time.

The second way to assess the estimates of hedge funds is to ascertain whether the estimation procedure itself is credible. There are at least six reasons to doubt its reliability.

The first reason is that the precision of the estimates depends on estimating the regression with the full set of individual asset returns. Brown, Goetzman and Park (1998) estimate positions in the ringgit by regressing aggregate returns only on the change in the ringgit. Hedge funds invest in many and varied asset classes, and it is generally acknowledged that ringgit positions in 1997 and 1998 were small relative to the total positions of hedge funds. The estimates from a bivariate regression may be misleading since total returns are in reality affected by a myriad of asset returns and such a regression focuses explanation on just one variable. The papers by Fung and Hsieh (1999) and Fung, Hsieh and Tsatsaronis (1999) are a substantial improvement in technique – and hence more credible – because they include a substantially wider set of assets.

The second reason to doubt the accuracy of the estimates is that they are averages of positions over the sample period, rather than estimates of positions at a particular point in time. In the case of Brown, Goetzman and Park (1998), the sample period is four months. In the monthly estimates of Fung and Hsieh (1999) and Fung, Hsieh and Tsatsaronis (1999), it is six months. If a position is established and then reversed in one month, the coefficient estimated in a regression using returns over a number of months will tend to underestimate the position in that month since it is affected by the other months in which there was no effect. This may explain why the positions estimated by Fung and Hsieh (1999) and Fung, Hsieh and Tsatsaronis (1999) are substantially below market estimates. This criticism will also apply to positions estimated from daily and weekly data over long sample periods.

The third reason to doubt the accuracy of the estimates is that they are calculated with very few degrees of freedom. Brown, Goetzman and Park (1998) have only two degrees of freedom – two regressors and four observations. The standard errors on the estimates must be quite large, although these figures are not generally reported by the authors. Most applied econometricians would be sceptical of the accuracy of point estimates that are obtained with almost no degrees of freedom.

The fourth reason to doubt the accuracy of the method is that the selection of the weights is highly judgmental and the authors do not provide the reader with tests of the robustness of the outcomes. For instance, Fung and Hsieh (1999) say that they experiment with different fixed-sample window periods, but they do not say which window 'works best', how the estimates vary and whether they use one or cherry pick from a combination of different windows to obtain their estimates.

The fifth reason to doubt the accuracy of the position estimates is that they infer weights on individual assets from changes in asset prices which may not be relevant to individual asset returns, thereby introducing measurement error. For example, the authors attempt to back out hedge funds' US equity positions from the S&P index. Investing in a stock market index is antithetical to the strategy of hedge funds; it is what mutual funds do. Equity investments of hedge funds are much more complex, and, as discussed in Chapter 2, are typically a combination of equity long and short positions. The returns on these positions have been positively correlated with stock-market indices in recent years, but far from perfectly. The criticism also holds for evaluating currency positions. Hedge funds' currency returns are determined by the difference between spot prices and the prices in options and forwards. These returns are likely to be less than perfectly correlated with changes in exchange rates over a particular period.

The sixth reason to doubt the accuracy of the method used by Brown, Goetzman and Park (1998), Fung and Hsieh (1999) and Fung, Hsieh and Tsatsaronis (1999) is that it performs very poorly in identifying positions when the technique is applied to an artificial portfolio with known positions in markets.

To test the accuracy of the method, an artificial portfolio was constructed for an individual hedge fund with $10 billion in funds under management and a mix of positions in US equities and Asian currencies. The hedge fund is arbitrarily assumed to invest 60 per cent of its funds in US equities (the Dow), 12 per cent in the yen, 8 per cent in the ringgit, 8 per cent in the Australian dollar, 7 per cent in the Singapore dollar, and 5 per cent in the rupiah. The fund is long in the US equity market over the full sample period, but it has a time-varying mix of short and long positions in the Asian currencies.

The aggregate monthly return to the hedge fund is the weighted sum of the monthly returns in the individual asset classes. While the positions are chosen arbitrarily, the returns are evaluated using actual financial prices.[2] Currency positions are held for several months but it is assumed that they are established using one-month forward exchange rates, and they are revalued each month at, coincidentally, the same market prices that are

[2] The currencies are defined in units of US dollars, so a rise represents a depreciation. The one-month forward rates are calculated as the spot rate plus the one-month interest differential with the United States.

used to estimate Equation (8.2). This should help the Brown, Goetzman and Park method identify the asset weights.

The return on the US stock market is the percentage change in the Dow Jones Index over the month. If the hedge fund is long a currency, it has bought the currency forward and will receive it at a specified date in the future under the forward contract. It then sells these proceeds in the spot market at that time, and if the currency has appreciated relative to the forward rate, it will have made a positive return in that month. If the hedge fund is short a currency, it has sold the currency forward and has to buy it back in the spot market on a specified date in the future to meet its obligation under the forward contract. If the spot rate has depreciated relative to the forward rate, it will have made a positive return. Figure 8.1 shows the fund's aggregate return and the returns on two of the component assets, the Dow and the ringgit, using historical price data and assuming that the hedge fund was consistently long the Dow and was long the ringgit in 1997 but short the ringgit in 1998. Given that the Dow has a 60 per cent weight in the portfolio, it dominates the aggregate returns series.

The aggregate monthly return is regressed on changes in each of the six assets over a particular window. Figure 8.2 shows the actual ringgit position and the ringgit position that is inferred using the technique pioneered

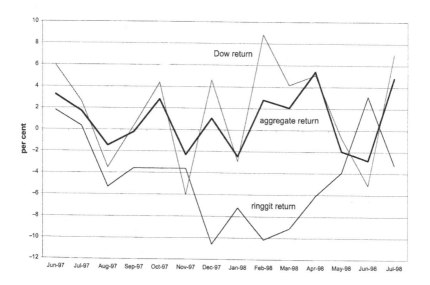

Figure 8.1 Portfolio returns

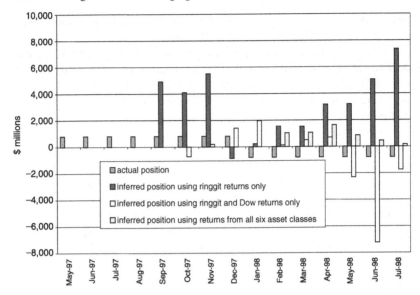

Figure 8.2 Actual and inferred ringgit positions

by Brown, Goetzman and Park (1998) when different data sets are included and sample periods varied. Figure 8.3 shows the same for the US equity position.

Consider, first, the estimated ringgit positions. The fund has a long ringgit position from May to December 1997 and switches to a short position in January 1998 which it holds until July of that year. Three different sets of inferred positions are shown in Figure 8.2. The first set is the ringgit position inferred from a set of rolling regressions of the fund's aggregate monthly return on a constant and monthly changes in the ringgit for a fixed sample window of four months (giving two degrees of freedom). This is what Brown, Goetzman and Park (1998) do, and is referred to below as the Brown, Goetzman and Park model.

The second set is the ringgit position inferred from a set of rolling regressions of the fund's aggregate monthly return on a constant and monthly changes in the ringgit and the Dow for a fixed sample of five months (giving two degrees of freedom). This is what Fung and Hsieh (1999) and Fung, Hsieh and Tsatsaronis (1999) do, and is referred to below as the truncated Fung and Hsieh model.

The third set is the ringgit position inferred from a set of rolling regressions of the fund's aggregate monthly return on a constant and monthly

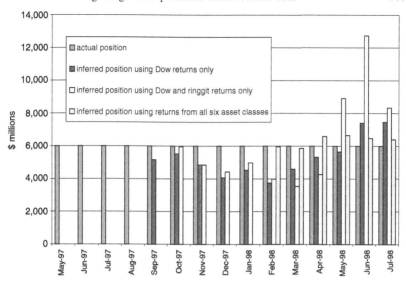

Figure 8.3 Actual and inferred Dow positions

changes in all of the six relevant asset classes for a fixed sample of nine months (giving two degrees of freedom). This is what Fung and Hsieh (1999) and Fung, Hsieh and Tsatsaronis (1999) intend to do in their piecewise regression, and is referred to below as the extended Fung and Hsieh model.

The inferred ringgit positions differ substantially from the actual ringgit position and from each other. In general, the inferred positions are misleading with respect to the magnitude, sign and the timing of the true positions, and they give false signals about changes in the true position. Consider these in turn.

The magnitudes for the Brown, Goetzman and Park model are typically several multiples greater than the true ringgit position. The magnitudes are more sensible for the truncated and extended Fung and Hsieh models, but at one stage the truncated Fung and Hsieh model also becomes deeply unrepresentative of the true position. The extended Fung and Hsieh model is the most accurate in terms of magnitude. This is not surprising since the estimates in this model are conditioned on the full information set.

The signs of the ringgit position are also incorrectly inferred at times in all three cases. The extended Fung and Hsieh model gives the wrong sign. The timing of the change in the ringgit position is also not reflected in the inferred positions. The position change in the Brown, Goetzman and Park model and the truncated Fung and Hsieh model occurs one or two months before the actual change in the position. The extended Fung and Hsieh model is unable to identify a change in position. It provides relatively few coefficient estimates because it takes so many observations to estimate the model.

The Brown, Goetzman and Park model and the truncated Fung and Hsieh model provide false signals about changes in the sign of the ringgit position. That is, they say that positions are changed more than they actually are. While the actual position only shifts once, from long to short in the middle of the sample, they estimate two shifts in position.

The estimates for the Dow positions appear more accurate (see Figure 8.3), but it is worth observing that the Dow returns dominate aggregate returns and the underlying true positions are constant. The truncated and extended Fung and Hsieh models both yield position estimates that have the right sign and do not give false signals about the sign of positions, but this is not surprising given that the sign of the true position does not change.

The magnitudes are not accurately identified. The truncated model, in particular, produces position estimates that vary substantially over a nine-month period from \$6 billion to \$$3\frac{3}{4}$ billion to almost \$13 billion – even though the true position is constant. The extended Fung and Hsieh model is more accurate, but this may not be robust to portfolios which feature significant position changes in key financial variables.

Figure 8.4 shows the inferred positions in the Dow when a period of short equity positions is included in the dataset, in this case from December 1997 to February 1998. The inferred positions from the Brown, Goetzman and Park model and from the truncated Fung and Hsieh model eventually pick up the change in position, albeit with a three-month lag. The extended Fung and Hsieh model misses the change in positions completely. The magnitudes of the inferred positions are also wrong.

The Dow results represent a 'best case' test for the method since the equity position is established in the Dow and the Dow is included as a regressor. In reality, hedge funds do not establish positions in an index – it is indeed the antithesis of their strategy. As discussed in Chapter 2, hedge fund returns from equity market investments are positively but only partially correlated with stock-market indices.

The upshot from this exercise is that it is difficult to put much credence on estimates of hedge fund positions using the method proposed by Brown, Goetzman and Park (1998) and used by Fung and Hsieh (1999) and Fung, Hsieh and Tsatsaronis (1999). The signals about

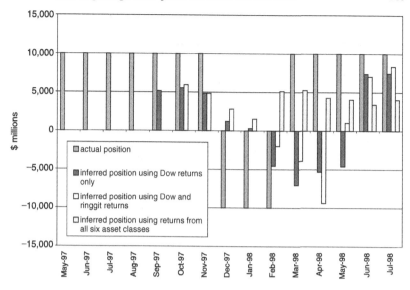

Figure 8.4 Actual and inferred Dow positions with changing positions

hedge fund positions can be seriously misleading, particularly in the case of smaller asset classes. The reconstruction method is not powerful enough to accurately identify positions over time.

The solution is not simply to use higher-frequency data. The problems that arose with monthly data also arise when daily or weekly data are used. The exercise conducted above was repeated for weekly data, with the Fund holding a long position in the Dow for the full period. The fund was assumed to be shifting between long and short positions in the ringgit, as shown in Figure 8.5.

Two changes were made to the estimation process to make the test more realistic. First, noting that the positions are inferred from a regression of aggregate returns on individual asset price changes, a wedge was introduced by using Wednesday data to estimate the fund's aggregate return and using Friday data to estimate the weekly asset price movements. This recognises that the prices used to mark the portfolio to market may not correspond exactly to the data used by the econometrician to back out positions. The second change was to assume that while the hedge fund's stock-market position is in the Dow, the econometrician does not know this and uses the NASDAQ to represent the US stock market, which is only imperfectly correlated with the Dow. This makes

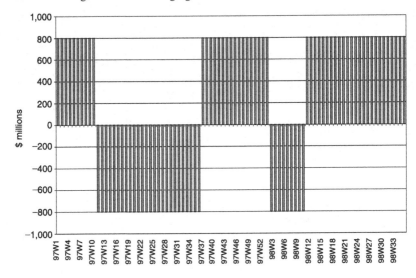

Figure 8.5 Long and short positions in the ringgit

sense since hedge funds positions in equity markets are typically complex and rarely a straightforward position on an index.

The fund's aggregate returns are regressed on the end-week change in asset prices. Figure 8.6 shows the inferred weekly ringgit positions derived from the regression of aggregate returns on a constant and end-week changes in the prices of the six assets in the fund's portfolio. The fixed sample window for each rolling regression is eight weeks, which provides one degree of freedom. While the sign of the inferred positions is sometimes correct – notably at the end of the sample – it is obvious that the magnitudes are completely unrepresentative of the size of the actual positions and that there are many false signals about changes in positions. Although the results are not shown here, lengthening the sample window does not materially improve the accuracy of the estimates.

Conclusion

There is wide interest in knowing the positions of hedge funds and other financial institutions in order to understand the effect these positions may have at times on other participants in financial markets and on the dynamics of asset price determination. Such information, however, is private and belongs to the firms involved.

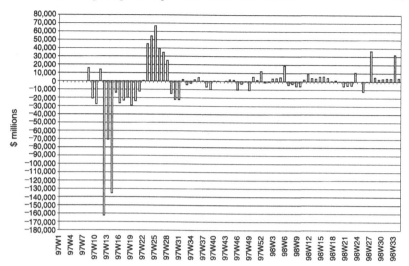

Figure 8.6 Weekly ringgit positions inferred from a regression of aggregate

Some analysts have sought ways to overcome this problem. Brown, Goetzman and Park (1998) have proposed a method to infer hedge funds' positions from data on hedge funds' returns. They regress aggregate returns of individual hedge funds on the returns of a few assets that they think may have been in hedge fund portfolios.[3] They then multiply the coefficients from these regressions by each fund's net asset value at each point in time to obtain estimates of positions in various assets. This method has been used by others, most notably Fung and Hsieh (1999) and Fung, Hsieh and Tsatsaronis (1999). It has also been influential in the debate in the United States about the role of hedge funds in financial markets (Chadha and Jansen 1998; President's Working Group on Financial Markets 1999).

This chapter has argued that the estimates from this method are not reliable. In the first place, the derived estimates are either unreasonable when compared to the size of the markets involved or at odds with estimates of positions made by expert participants in financial markets. To an extent, this objection is subjective and can only be resolved if hedge funds' positions in financial markets were publicly available.

[3] They include the dollar exchange rate against the pound sterling, mark, yen and Mexican peso. This is an odd selection since the macro hedge funds typically have equity and fixed-interest positions.

But, more fundamentally, the method is itself not reliable. The size and pattern of the estimated positions depend on the conditioning variables included in the regression and on the number of observations in the sample. These two effects work in opposite ways: increasing the number of relevant variables in the regression should make the estimates more accurate, but including more variables means using a longer sample for each regression and makes it more difficult to identify accurately the position at each point in time. The estimates are also obtained with almost no degrees of freedom and are highly imprecise.

The accuracy of the method was also tested by constructing an artificial portfolio and examining whether the method accurately identified the positions in that portfolio. It did not. The inferred positions differed substantially from the actual positions. In general, the inferred positions were misleading with respect to the magnitude, sign and the timing of the true positions, and they gave false signals about changes in the true position. The problems are not corrected by using higher-frequency data. This suggests caution in using the Brown, Goetzman and Park method to infer position data from returns data, and in over-interpreting movements in the inferred positions. More generally, the technique does not resolve the need to know actual positions of hedge funds if the issue of how these institutions, and others like them, affect market dynamics is to be resolved.

9 Looking forward

Despite the turmoil of recent years, hedge funds, including the macro funds, are here to stay and are likely to increase their influence in financial markets in the years to come. This chapter examines the reasons why hedge funds will remain important to financial markets and institutions, and then explores what this means for policy.

The policy analysis is structured in four parts. Given the experiences with highly leveraged institutions in recent years and the continuing important role of HLIs in markets around the world, the policy discussion starts with an analysis of the case for policy action, and then sets out three core principles which should underpin such action. Four proposals are then analysed: greater transparency of HLI operations, including public disclosure of aggregate positions by institutional class; imposing margining on all swap and repurchase facilities; the introduction of a code of conduct for financial market participants; and possibly regulating electronic broking in foreign-exchange markets. The policy analysis concludes with an assessment of the merits of direct and indirect regulation of HLI activity, including a discussion on the direct measures taken by some countries in east Asia to limit offshore speculative activity.

The endpiece concludes the chapter and the book.

The future of hedge funds

Following the LTCM debacle in the September quarter of 1998, a number of commentators predicted that the hedge funds' days were over. *The Economist* (17–23 October 1998: 25) opined that 'the brouhaha about hedge funds is . . . misplaced' because banks now properly control lending to them. 'Many [hedge funds] are already shadows of their former selves'.

The reality has turned out somewhat differently. While some celebrated hedge funds have either closed up or reduced the size of their operations, the industry as a whole has continued to expand strongly and continues to be regarded as an essential part of the financial landscape.[1] In an article entitled 'Hedge funds set to bloom', one commentator has even pronounced that the 'future may belong to hedge funds' (*The Financial Times* 28 June 1999). The OECD (1999: 7) has argued that 'hedge funds have become an integral component of the new financial landscape and are considered by most observers to be a permanent feature'. The view that the calamities of 1997 and 1998 were but a temporary setback for hedge funds reflects an understanding of the importance of institutions like these in the world-wide regime of liberalised flexible-price financial markets that currently exists.

Hedge funds are here to stay . . .

There are two key reasons why hedge funds are here to stay and set to expand. The first is that they can offer a range of superior risk-adjusted returns to investors. As discussed in Chapter 2, hedge funds can provide higher average return, lower variability and better chances of gains relative to losses in their portfolios. They are specialised expert funds seeking absolute returns rather than simply trying to match benchmark returns. The returns of different types of hedge fund also tend to be relatively uncorrelated with each other and with market benchmarks, and so they offer an opportunity for portfolio diversification. Indeed, Goldman Sachs and Financial Risk Management (2000) argues that including a relatively small set of hedge funds in a portfolio reduces variability of returns but not the level of returns.

For these reasons, funds of funds – that is, funds which invest in a range of hedge funds – have also become an increasingly popular way to obtain relatively high returns provided by hedge funds but at the same time reduce the riskiness of investing in one type of hedge fund. Even Japanese trading companies are starting to get into the business! For example, an American subsidiary of Nissho Iwai, Nissho Iwai American Corporation, is reported to be opening an internal fund of funds to outside investors like Japanese institutional investors and high net-worth individuals in 2001 (MAR/Week 24 August 2000).[2] Figure 9.1 shows Van Hedge's estimates of median returns for all hedge funds and for funds of funds in their database. The returns for funds of funds track average hedge funds' returns well.

---

[1] See, for example, *The Financial Times* 28 June 1999 and 6 September 2000, and *Risk* November 1998: 17.
[2] Japanese insurance companies are already investors in US hedge funds.

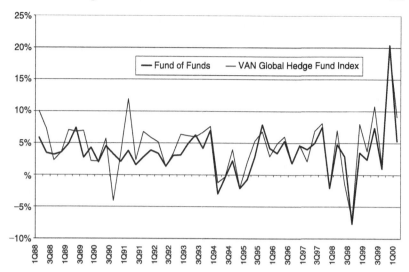

Figure 9.1 Returns on returns of all assets in the portfolio

The second reason to expect continued growth in the hedge-fund sector is that they are becoming increasingly important to other financial institutions. The diversification opportunities provided by hedge funds is making them increasingly attractive to other institutional investors, such as pension or superannuation funds and insurance companies. Market participants are reported to have estimated that US pension funds are set to invest a trillion dollars in hedge funds between 2000 and 2002.[3] Based on the estimates of hedge funds' assets provided by the President's Working Party on Financial Markets (1999), this is five times the existing capital of hedge funds. Managers at pension funds are regularly approached to direct a portion of their assets into hedge funds to diversify their risk portfolio.[4]

Not only are hedge funds attractive to institutional investors, but they are also attractive to banks and securities companies. The growth in hedge funds means that they will continue to be extremely important clients of investment banks and securities companies. Hedge funds are important to banks and securities companies for two reasons.

[3] 'Hedge funds set to bloom', *The Financial Times* 28 June 1999. Similarly, there are regular stories in hedge fund publications, like those of MAR/Hedge for example, about institutional investors investing in hedge funds.
[4] For example, see 'Hedge Funds on Comeback Trail', *Australian Financial Review* 15 March 1999. Managers of pension funds also say that they are regularly approached by hedge funds for business.

The first is because they are big clients. The OECD (1999) notes that banks provide two basic services to hedge funds. The first is prime brokerage services, including office space and technology. Prime brokerage is important to banks not just because of the revenue it provides, but because it allows banks and securities companies to 'track' global asset movements, which they can use for their own trading purposes or can on-sell to other clients.

Banks and securities companies also provide niche services, including specific financial products such as equity derivatives and foreign-exchange services. These can be very important to banks: 'because some hedge funds often transact in enormous size, there are specialist derivatives desks dedicated solely to hedge fund clients' and hedge funds are very big users of swaps and credit derivatives provided by banks (OECD 1999: 8–9). This means trading revenue as well as the opportunity to make money from front-running on the trading flows.

The second reason why hedge funds are important to other financial institutions is because the hedge funds provide useful services or advice to these institutions; there is a symbiotic relationship between banks and hedge funds. In a very real sense, banks and other financial intermediaries can profitably outsource particular operations to hedge funds since, by investing in, or lending to, hedge funds, banks and others can earn returns in areas in which they neither have the necessary resources nor skills. Some of the arbitrage-type activities run by hedge funds – ranging for example from special situations and mergers arbitrage to commodity trading – require considerable expertise, and it is often more profitable for banks and other financial intermediaries to invest in these rather than to run such operations themselves. The hedge funds have also tended to be market leaders in innovation in financial markets, and close relations with such funds provide banks and other financial institutions with crucial access to new product lines and thinking.

This remains true not only for the United States but also increasingly for Europe. In the past, hedge funds have been mainly active in the US equity and bond markets, foreign-exchange markets and emerging markets. But they are set to become increasingly more involved in Europe because European capital markets are opening up, restructuring and becoming larger, partly as a result of the introduction of the euro in January 1999. There is also a greater shift to market instruments through securitisation, and credit derivatives, which all point to increased opportunities for hedge funds (Moonen 1999).

The relationship between banks and hedge funds has changed somewhat after the LTCM debacle. Before the crisis, there was a tendency for banks to market a range of hedge-fund-type products, and to run in-house funds – their proprietary trading desks – or funds of funds. There was also a tendency for the managers or traders in these operations to leave the banks and set up their own hedge fund, so banks were continually struggling to maintain the quality of their own operations.

After the crisis, the tendency has been for banks to either close down or more tightly restrict their proprietary trading desks because of concerns about risk and the amount of capital needed to support these operations. What they now tend to do is invest directly in funds by providing seed capital to nascent hedge funds and putting capital into existing ones, which they manage through their asset management operations. Whatever the case, formal and informal staff connections remain important, and staff still move between banks and hedge funds.

. . . including the macro hedge funds

While the number of hedge funds and assets under their management continue to grow, macro hedge funds have fared substantially less well. According to MAR/Hedge, the number of macro hedge funds fell from fifty-eight to forty-six in the first seven months of 2000, with assets under management falling 29 per cent from $24.9 billion to $17.7 billion. This dramatic fall has been led by the gradual closure of Julian Robertson's Tiger Fund and the generalised winding back of Soros Fund Management.

There were two factors behind the decline of the macro hedge funds in 2000. The first was that they had become so big during the 1990s that it was difficult to hide their market positions and limit front-running by banks, securities houses and other speculators, and hence limit adverse price movement in advance of them closing out positions. George Soros was quoted as saying, for example, that his 'Quantum Fund is far too big and its activities too closely watched by the market to be able to operate successfully' in an environment of highly volatile markets.[5]

The second factor was that the opportunities in currency and fixed-interest markets, which are the traditional strengths of the macro hedge funds, were no longer as great. After the turmoil in emerging markets in 1997, 1998 and 1999, emerging market asset prices did not offer the same opportunity for large movement, at least on the downside, which limited the possibilities to make large gains from asset price movements. The risk appetites of all investors had also fallen, which limited the desire for large position-taking.

[5] 'Quantum leap becomes a plunge', *Australian Financial Review* 1 May 2000.

The opportunities that did remain – like the apparent bubble in the US equity market – did not work out for some of the macro hedge funds. Julian Robertson's exit from the macro hedge fund business, for example, was driven by his assessment that conventional models of evaluating stock-market fundamental value were no longer working. After resisting going long in technology stocks, Soros Fund Management's Quantum Fund shifted to substantial long positions in such stocks in October 1999, but suffered greatly when the NASDAQ fell 35 per cent in March 2000. The Fund ultimately succumbed to pressure to follow the market and it suffered as a result.

The wind-back in macro hedge funds in 2000 has led some to the view that they are now a spent force and irrelevant to decision makers, either in the market or in policy institutions (Frankel and Roubini 2000). Such a view is short-sighted and premature. While there has been a decline in the number of macro hedge funds and assets under management, their asset base still remains large by hedge fund standards.

The macro hedge funds have been in a process of structural adjustment, and are likely to become more focused once this is complete. From a practical perspective, it is difficult to focus on business when the organisation is being substantially restructured. Soros Fund Management (SFM), for example, underwent a series of major changes to its structure and senior management during 1999 and 2000. In mid-2000, SFM's flagship fund, the Quantum Fund, was replaced by the Quantum Endowment Fund, and the *Asian Wall Street Journal* (16 June 2000) reported that it started with assets of $6.5 billion, with half the assets directed at macro and arbitrage plays and half at stock picking. MAR/Hedge Weekly (3 August 2000) reports that $2 billion of the Quantum Endowment Fund is now directed at currency plays. This augurs a return to business.

One aspect of the structural adjustment at macro hedge funds has been the turnover and exit of many senior and experienced staff. Many of these people have set up, or are in the process of setting up, their own, smaller operations to engage in a range of market strategies. In this sense, the relative decline of the very large macro hedge funds has propagated many smaller macro hedge funds which have the potential to grow over time in both number and size. This spawning process may see a stronger, larger and more diverse macro-hedge-fund sector in the future.

Policy issues

The financial crises that affected emerging and industrialised economies alike throughout 1997, 1998 and 1999 have not led to the demise of hedge funds and other highly leveraged institutions. While macro hedge funds have been in major consolidation mode in 2000, neither they nor the hedge-fund sector as a whole is set to disappear from the financial landscape. Rather, they are set to become more important and decision makers cannot simply ignore them.

The case for policy action

It is widely recognised that there are three rationales for regulating financial institutions: to protect investors in key financial institutions, especially those who lack the skills to evaluate the soundness of these institutions; to limit systemic risks and so ensure the safety of the financial system as a whole; and, finally, to protect the integrity of a market and ensure an efficient price-discovery process, which includes preventing institutions from cornering or manipulating a market (Eichengreen, et al. 1998; Sharma 1998). The 1998 IMF study led by Eichengreen and Mathieson concluded that hedge funds did not warrant additional regulation on any of these three grounds.

Given that investment in hedge funds has been limited to very rich individuals and endowments, they argued that there was no investor-protection rationale for regulating hedge funds. There is general agreement that this is right, although the growing interest of institutional investors, like pension/superannuation funds and insurance companies, in hedge funds may be making this less clear cut.

Investment by pension funds and others in hedge funds raises two interesting issues. On the one hand, access to hedge fund returns might be an effective way for these institutional investors to increase returns on a risk-adjusted basis, and this would presumably support long-term saving. On the other hand, some pension funds and insurance companies may lack the expertise to properly assess the many proposals made to them by hedge funds, and this may put long-term saving at risk, implying the need for some prudential limit on such investment. This in itself does not mean that hedge funds should be regulated. If it proves desirable to limit investment by institutional investors in hedge funds, it is probably more effective and efficient to do this through the regulation of pension funds and insurance companies.[6]

---

[6] This is not a universally shared view. There are proposals, mainly made by Europeans, for the direct prudential regulation of hedge funds. These would include licensing, minimum capital standards, large exposure limits, reporting and disclosure, and risk management standards for hedge funds. At this stage, these proposals do not have wider international support.

Following the views of the US and UK governments, Eichengreen, *et al.* (1998) also dismissed the need to regulate hedge funds on the basis of systemic risk. To quote them:

Regulators in the United States and the United Kingdom, the countries in which banks and brokers are most active as counterparties and creditors to hedge funds, seem generally satisfied that these institutions are adequately managing their exposure to hedge funds, which therefore pose no special problems of systemic risk, although they have been known to express concern that the difficulty of obtaining information on hedge funds complicates the efforts of the counterparties to assess the creditworthiness of potential hedge fund customers and that not all banks have the expertise necessary to evaluate the credit risk associated with some hedge funds' complicated derivatives holdings.   (14)

The second half of that sentence was prescient, and events have overtaken the assessment that hedge funds pose no systemic risk. In light of the near-collapse of LTCM in September 1998, the Federal Reserve organised that fund's credit providers to bail it out. The President's Working Group on Financial Markets (1999: 18), which was set up to examine the issues raised by the episode, argued that

the LTCM Fund held a great variety of relatively large positions with numerous trading partners. Those positions, combined with the market volatility and lack of liquidity might have led to a series of dramatic and punishing events for LTCM's trading counterparties and the markets themselves in the event of a default by the LTCM Fund.

It judged that the threat to system stability arose through excessive leverage,[7] which was itself due to poor counterparty risk management by the fund's credit providers and poor risk management within hedge funds. The FSF Working Group on HLIs (2000) endorsed this assessment. As discussed in Chapter 3, several official and private-sector reports have argued for better market and liquidity risk management by hedge funds, better credit risk management by credit providers, and for more disclosure by hedge funds to credit providers. The FSF Working Group on HLIs (2000) focused on market-based solutions to rectify the market failure revealed by the over-leveraging of LTCM. While it explicitly rejected the option of direct regulation, it did leave this open as an option if its preferred measures were not successful.[8]

---

[7] To quote (page 29): 'The central public policy issue raised by the LTCM episode is how to constrain excessive leverage more effectively.'

[8] It also rejected an alternative proposal, mainly made by some European countries, to improve counterparty risk management by the introduction of an international HLI credit register. The idea is that firms with material exposures to HLIs would contribute information to an international centralised system of on- and off-balance-sheet lending to HLIs.

The third ground for regulation is the maintenance of market integrity, which is broadly defined as ensuring that markets are 'fair and efficient' (FSF Working Group on HLIs 2000: 125). Here, one might have thought that the events of 1998 would have led to a reassessment of the capacity of highly leveraged institutions to adversely affect the integrity of financial markets. The argument of this book, and the clear implication of the report of the FSF Working Group on HLIs (2000), is that some of the macro hedge funds and proprietary trading desks of certain US and European banks and securities firms did at times materially contribute to instability in east Asian financial markets and economies in 1997 and 1998. This occurred in two respects.

First, the actual or perceived presence of large players with powerful reputations often tended to exaggerate position-taking and the one-sidedness of markets, leading to overshooting of asset prices. Second, some highly leveraged players used particularly aggressive tactics in some markets at particular periods of vulnerability, which deterred contrary position-taking and increased further the one-sidedness of markets. Some large players also seem to have used their size and reputation to unsettle the market. The assessment the IMF made in 1998 about the role of large players like hedge funds has been overtaken by more careful analysis of the issues and by subsequent events.

Senior central bankers in the region have argued that market integrity was adversely affected during the crisis. Joseph Yam (1999: 168), Chief Executive of the HKMA, for example has argued:

It should be stressed that in principle there is nothing objectionable to any market participants, including HLIs, taking a view on the market and positioning itself accordingly. Speculators in essence buy low/sell high, or sell high/buy low, thereby providing the much-needed liquidity to markets and helping to bring the value of the underlying assets to their equilibrium levels. The issue here is

---

Footnote 8 (continued)
  Aggregated data on credit to HLI counterparties would be available to those counterparties, supervisors and other authorities on a confidential basis. While recognising the potential benefit of being able to precisely identify credit exposures, especially in a crisis, the FSF Working Group on HLIs (2000: 34–35) judged that an international credit register 'is likely to be a more costly and less robust approach to monitoring the leverage of large HLIs than a regime of mandated disclosure which targeted HLIs directly or a voluntary scheme that succeeded in capturing all relevant institutions.' It expressed particular concern that it is much more difficult to assess credit risk for derivative products than simple loans, and that the process would be expensive and require substantial international coordination since data would have to be compiled quickly and frequently, given that positions and prices can substantially change on a day-to-day basis. The Working Group said it may also be appropriate to re-examine the case for a credit register if its recommendations fail to achieve their objectives.

the way in which some HLIs, particularly certain hedge funds, conduct their trading activities, and the impact that these activities may have on the price discovery mechanism in financial markets.

Similarly, Bob Rankin (1999: 155), Head of International Department at the Reserve Bank of Australia, has argued that

in the June 1998 episode [in the Australian dollar market], the hedge funds acted with the apparent intention to then force a change in the price. They were not merely transacting to take advantage of expected events, but they were doing so in a way which seemed intended to try to influence the course of events, posing a risk to market integrity.

While a reassessment of the possible effect of HLIs on market integrity has been widespread, it has not been universal. The views have largely split, on the one hand, between Asia and Europe where policy-makers do perceive a potential threat to market integrity, and, on the other hand, the United States where policy-makers have so far adopted the contrary view.

The Market Dynamics Study Group of the FSF Working Group on HLIs was set up to examine the role of HLIs in 1998 in the dynamics of mid-sized markets, including Australia, Hong Kong, Malaysia, New Zealand, Singapore and South Africa. While keeping in mind that HLIs are diverse institutions and just one of many players in financial markets, the Study Group reported that the actual or perceived positioning of a few large players – specifically a few macro hedge funds – itself had an adverse effect on position-taking by other market participants, and that some HLIs used a range of particularly aggressive trading tactics, designed to materially influence price formation in financial markets.

The Study Group, however, could not agree on whether the market integrity had been undermined:

The judgement as to whether … HLI positions are destabilizing has to be made on a case-by-case basis. Several members of the study group believe that large HLI positions exacerbated the situations in several of the case-study economies in 1998, contributing to potentially unstable market dynamics and significant spillovers. These group members are of the view that HLI positions and tactics can at times represent a significant independent source of pressure. Some other group members do not think that there is sufficient evidence to advance such judgments on the basis of the 1998 experience, given the uncertainty prevailing in markets at that time. They believe that the impact of HLIs on markets is likely to be very short-lived and that, provided the fundamentals are strong, HLI positions and strategies are unlikely to present a major independent driving force in market dynamics.   (FSF Working Group on HLIs 2000: 126)

And on the issue of aggressive trading practices, the report stated:

The group is concerned about the possible impact on market dynamics of some of the aggressive practices cited in the case-study economies during 1998; it is not, however, able to reach a conclusion on the scale of these practices, whether manipulation was involved and their impact on market integrity. Some members believe that the threshold for assessing manipulation can be set too high and that some of the aggressive practices raise important issues for market integrity. They are of the view that there is sufficient evidence to suggest attempted manipulation can and does occur in foreign exchange markets and should be a serious source of concern for policymakers.   (*ibid.*)

As is generally well known, the split in the report reflected the difference in views between the representatives of the US government and those of other governments and international institutions. The lack of consensus – and, more particularly, the fact that the United States does not see market-integrity issues as relevant at this stage – means that a global policy approach to this particular issue is currently unlikely. This puts the emphasis on national and regional policy solutions, and, indeed, the US position on market integrity is one of many factors behind the push for greater regional financial cooperation in east Asia excluding the United States.[9]

Principles in designing policy

In designing a policy response, it is helpful to keep (at least) three core principles in mind in order to maximise the success of policy.

The first principle is to avoid directing the policy response solely at the previous crisis, to try to win in retrospect the battle that was lost.

---

[9] While there is deep and broad support for US economic engagement and strategic involvement in east Asia, there is also now a pervasive sense that the United States is not a reliable ally in financial policy, and that east Asia needs to establish some financial arrangements and institutions of its own to serve its interests. While it is a complex phenomenon, the 'new Asian regionalism' has been sparked, in part, by a series of deeply felt grievances towards the United States. Thai and Malaysian authorities feel that the United States did not adequately support them in the crisis, and only helped Korea because of that country's strategic importance and because of the involvement of US banks. There is a sense in the region that the United States acted to destabilise Indonesia in early 1998 to overthrow Suharto. Hong Kong and China were upset by the absence of US support for the Hong Kong authorities' intervention in the stock market in September 1998. There is also a widespread sense that the US authorities have been inconsistent in their treatment of the issue of hedge funds: the Fed was prepared early on to get involved in the bail-out of LTCM because it feared that, left to themselves, US financial markets would become seriously destabilised by the unwinding of hedge funds' positions, but when it came to official representations from many east Asian governments that HLIs were destabilising regional financial markets in 1997 and 1998, the Fed and US Treasury demanded formal evidence of the level required in a court of law. Whatever the merits of these views, east Asia has become inclined to the view that the financial interests of the United States do not necessarily coincide with those of the region.

Financial crises have occurred many times in history, and will undoubtedly occur again. There are elements of difference in each, be they in the triggers, the nature or the depth of the crisis, which make it important to design a generalised policy response. It is also important that the forward-looking policy response be reasoned rather than emotional or dominated by a desire for retribution.

The second principle is that it is fundamental to look beyond the actual players and institutions that were important in the last crisis, and instead focus on the underlying market and political forces at work. Just because one crisis is dominated by a particular institution or set of institutions, it does not follow that they will be the key players next time around. Nor does it mean that a different set of players would not have been important had a different set of policies been in place. Focusing on one set of institutions may simply create pressure for a new set of institutions to emerge, and may make policy-makers complacent. It is also vital to keep things in perspective, not only being aware of the costs of a particular system but also recognising its benefits.

The third principle is that, given that the problem is global, it may be better to look for coordinated global policy solutions, all the while paying attention to possible national and regional solutions that can complement a global response. If a global response is not feasible, then a national or regional response may be necessary. Policy-makers need to look at the whole menu of possible policy responses.

These three principles are directly relevant to policy issues in relation to hedge funds in east Asia. Given the important role of a few large macro hedge funds in the east Asian financial crisis, there has been a tendency to talk about the 'problem of hedge funds', especially the macro hedge funds. But to simply see the solution in terms of limiting hedge funds' activity would be short-sighted and ultimately self-defeating: the policy response needs to be general rather than specific to a set of institutions if it is to be effective in generating stability.

The experience of financial regulators in the post-war period has been that directing laws and regulations to control one set of institutions just gives rise to evasion and creates a new set of as-yet-unregulated institutions – this is Goodhart's Law. Just as tightly regulating banks, for example, has consistently generated disintermediation of the financial services to non-bank financial institutions, so too would tight regulation of hedge funds lead to them emerging in some other as-yet-unregulated form, perhaps by forcing them offshore into unregulated jurisdictions or by shifting activity to proprietary trading desks. Even if a few hedge funds played a key role in regional financial-market turmoil, directing policy solutions solely at the hedge funds could prove self-defeating.

There is another, more subtle, dimension to this. Attempting to suppress the speculative pressures by focusing on hedge funds can lay the seeds for further, different speculative attacks or crises in the future. Excessive focus on non-resident speculators can be counter-productive if it deflects attention from the need to maintain consistent and sustainable macro and financial policies, and if it distracts policy-makers from the possibility of speculation by residents. It may also force residents to hide their activities from the authorities, undermining the integrity of the system as a whole. It can lead to complacency if policy-makers think they have all bases covered and residents think that the risk of another set of asset price falls is negligible because the authorities will not let a crisis happen again.

This is particularly important in east Asia since there is a substantial body of opinion in the region in favour of regional common currency arrangements, suggesting that countries in the region tie their exchange rates to either a common basket peg or an Asian currency unit.[10] Given the diversity of the economies in the region, such a system would probably require relatively frequent realignment.[11] Policy-makers tend to be reactive rather than proactive in recognising fundamental pressures on an exchange rate, which would make the system vulnerable to domestic and external speculation. Fixed exchange rates in countries with divergent economic fundamentals are to macro hedge funds what a red rag is to a bull.

There is also a tendency in the region to think that speculation in general is undesirable, and that hedge funds, which are the contemporary embodiment of speculation, should be kept out of regional financial markets as much as possible. While the argument of this book has been that a few macro hedge funds and, to a lesser extent, the prop desks were at the heart of the asset price overshooting in east Asia in 1997 and 1998, it does not follow that their involvement in regional markets should be avoided. Indeed, it may be the opposite, so long as appropriate safeguards are put in place.

In the first place, there are many thousands of hedge funds, with the many types of hedge funds involved in financial markets having widely varying risk appetites and being engaged in many and diverse activities. They are a key source of innovation, depth and liquidity in financial

---

[10] On a common basket peg, see Ito, Sasaki and Ogawa (1998), Dornbusch and Park (1999), Williamson (1999), Kawai and Akiyama (2000), Kawai and Takagi (2000), Murase (2000) and Yoshino, Kaji and Suzuki (2000). On a regional currency unit, see Moon, Rhee and Yoon (2000) and Moon and Rhee (2001).

[11] See de Brouwer (2001).

markets, and will become increasingly so. The future *is* on the side of hedge funds.

Hedge funds are the most important class of pure speculator in financial markets, and speculation is vital in financial markets because it provides depth and liquidity. Because speculators have appetites for risk, they are the means by which other, risk-averse participants in markets can shift or hedge risk. The events of recent years should not be allowed to obscure the fact that speculators are an essential element in managing financial risk. In other words, having tried so hard to show that speculation can at times be destabilising, policy-makers and analysts should not fall into the trap of thinking that speculation is *always* destabilising. Nor should they fall into the trap of thinking that speculative selling is necessarily destabilising.

The focus on the dangers of hedge funds and speculation does not necessarily serve the region's interests. In the first place, there is a strong desire in the region to develop intra-regional financial markets – like regional bond markets, domestic-currency commodity markets, and bilateral currency markets like, for example, a yen–won market (Sakakibara 2001) – but these will never develop sufficient instruments and depth if speculators are excluded or their trading tightly controlled. Hedge funds are necessary to the full development of regional financial markets. It is ironic that the development of regional financial markets is proposed as a way to reduce the region's dependence on global capital, but that such development can only happen if globally active institutions like hedge funds are involved.

More generally, allowing hedge fund activity is necessary in developing financial innovation in the region. East Asia, including Japan, can never become a leader in international finance so long as hedge funds are suppressed in the region. Hedge funds are active in all major financial centres, most notably New York. This is not an accident: New York and some other financial centres, like London for example, are centres of financial dynamism and creativity with a mainstream business and social culture of entrepreneurship and competition. The suppression of hedge funds implicitly entails the suppression of financial engineering and dynamism which are so necessary to being a leader in international finance. Given its scale and dynamic culture, it will always be a major challenge for any financial centre to rival New York.

The real issue for policy-makers is whether the elements that lead to destabilising speculation can be controlled and kept in order. There are four policy proposals for dealing with the problems raised by the macro hedge funds and proprietary trading desks in east Asia in 1997 and 1998, which will be discussed later. These proposals are directed at one or more of four objectives:

1. to reduce the potential of HLIs to create systemic risk in financial institutions and systems;
2. to ensure that material players in financial markets are subject to adequate supervision and market discipline;
3. to reduce the potential of HLIs to destabilise financial markets;
4. to ensure that decision makers – that is, authorities and market participants – have adequate information about the activities of material players in financial markets.

The crucial test is whether a proposal helps or hinders these objectives. If a particular proposal supports one or more of these objectives, it should be considered so long as it can be implemented without excessive high cost or creating a substantial negative externality.

The policy changes that the international community has made in the past year or so have focused on improving counterparty risk management between credit providers and hedge funds and improving risk management within HLIs, although little substantive progress has been made (see Chapter 2). These are important and welcome initiatives but the concerns raised by the experience of HLIs in east Asia are broader than those raised by the LTCM debacle.

The region's experience has raised concerns that, by the very size and concentration of their positions, hedge funds and proprietary trading desks can have an undue impact on the dynamics of financial markets, particularly when they can dominate other players. The size of these positions is of concern because the reversal of large positions may cause excessive price movement, especially if positions are unwound rapidly, and because actual or perceived large positions may cause other players to adopt similar positions or refrain from taking contrary positions, making movements in asset prices larger than they would otherwise be. There is also a concern that these market participants at times can also make use of unduly aggressive trading tactics to influence price formation in asset markets.

To the extent that improved counterparty risk management reduces the occurrence of large shifts in portfolios and positions, the initiatives already taken support financial stability: reducing the probability of large shifts in large positions goes part of the way in addressing the region's concerns. But, clearly, it does not address the main concerns – the effect of large positions themselves and aggressive behaviour – raised by recent experience.

Improved counterparty risk management is intended to act as a market-based constraint on excessive leverage, but, while desirable in itself, it does not necessarily limit large position-taking in financial markets. Aggregate on- and off-balance-sheet leverage at the macro funds in 1997 and 1998 was relatively modest, but the size of funds' positions in east Asia was *not* constrained by their credit providers. As discussed in Chapters 2 and 3, the positions of the large macro funds in east Asia were infinitely leveraged: these funds faced no effective credit constraint in establishing positions.

Similarly, large positions may not be a problem from a credit perspective if they are part of a proxy hedge. In this case, a market participant hedges an exposure in one market by establishing, for example, the opposite position in another market which is positively correlated with the first market. This is a standard risk management tool, and is effective so long as the correlations between markets persist. But from the perspective of the market used as the proxy hedge, it can be destabilising if the positions are large relative to that market, as occurred in South Africa in mid-1998 and Australia in August 1998. Again, the size and speed of change in positions is what matters to the country which is used as a proxy hedge; the fact that the strategy is an appropriate risk-management tool is irrelevant.

There are four main proposals to limit position-taking and manipulative activities by highly leveraged institutions. These are to require public disclosure of positions, to require banks to impose margins on all hedge funds and other borrowers when providing swap or repurchase facilities, to implement a code of conduct for participants in financial markets, and possibly to introduce regulations on foreign-exchange trading undertaken using electronic broking systems. The challenge in implementing these reforms is to limit the destabilising effects that can arise with speculation and maximise the benefits, like increased efficiency and liquidity.

It is worth observing that none of these four proposals is currently under active consideration by international bodies. Disclosure of positions has been considered but has, for the time being, been rejected. In December 1998, the augmented G-10 Committee on the Global Financial System set up a Working Group on Aggregate Positions, informally called the Patat Group, to examine the scope for collecting and disseminating aggregate data on markets. Despite support from many of the countries and financial institutions involved in discussions, the G-10 Central Bank Governors, led by the Federal Reserve, decided in November 1999 not to pursue such a policy at this stage.

Disclosure of positions

One way to influence position-taking by highly leveraged institutions is to increase the transparency of their operations by, for example, requiring the reporting of their positions in financial markets.[12] Brown, Goetzman and Park (1998), Fung and Hsieh (1999) and Fung, Hsieh and Tsatsaronis (1999) argue that funds' positions can be inferred from their returns, but the previous chapter showed that inferred positions could be seriously misleading: there is no substitute for the facts. The value of having information about positions is twofold.

First, greater transparency about the risk exposure and market positions of HLIs would provide important information to the authorities about the sustainability of current policy settings and lead to policy changes occurring earlier rather than later. Following the east Asian financial crisis, the international policy discussion on transparency focused on raising the standards of disclosure by governments (G-22 Working Group on Transparency and Accountability 1998). But transparency is a two-way street: just as the private sector needs to understand what is going on in the official sector to make properly informed decisions, so too does the official sector need to understand what is going on in the private sector. HLIs, and hedge funds in particular, are key institutions in financial markets but very little is known about them. This information asymmetry is not sustainable.

Second, greater transparency about the risk exposure and market positions of HLIs may affect the decision making of other market participants in a manner which would support stability in financial markets without loss of efficiency. For example, institutions may refrain from taking large positions if they know that either the authorities or the market knows something about their positions, and other market participants may be willing to take contrary positions if they reckon that position-taking in a market has become unsustainably one-sided.

The core issues are what is disclosed, to whom, and when. Consider the last point first. Positions can be reported in real time or with a lag. Given the current state of technology, real-time reporting may be possible but it would also be highly complex and costly. It is probably more realistic to release information on a periodic basis with a lag – say monthly data with a one month lag.[13] Past recent data is still probably relevant and informative, at least on an aggregate basis, since large aggregate positions are

---

[12] The FSF Working Group on HLIs (2000) contains a partial discussion of these issues.

[13] This corresponds to the requirements imposed on the official sector. The Patat Group, which reported to the augmented G-10 Committee on the Global Financial System, argued for a quarterly release of aggregate positions.

probably still in place if there has been little price movement in the meantime.

There are various combinations of reporting that are possible. For example, positions could be reported only to supervisors and regulators or they could be reported publicly to other market participants. Furthermore, positions could be reported by individual institution or they could be reported in aggregate by class of institution, say bank, securities firm, insurance company, pension fund, mutual fund, hedge fund or other. Table 9.1 sets out a matrix summarising the potential benefits and costs associated with these different combinations of position reporting.

Consider, first, the case of reporting individual HLI positions to supervisors and regulators or publicly to the rest of the market. The advantage of having the authorities know individual positions is that they can then identify the precise sources of risk in a market. But the disadvantages of this course are twofold.

First, having detailed institutional information may lead to pressures on the authorities to act to protect individual institutions even if there is no formal responsibility for supervising that institution. This could be a serious possibility. Australia's asset price bubble and associated (mild) banking crisis in the late 1980s provides an example of how this can happen. While the central bank was not responsible for building societies – the Australian equivalent of America's savings and loan associations – it did collect a wide range of information about them. It formed a private assessment that some building societies were developing problems but it did not act on its assessment since it had no legal responsibility or jurisdiction. The central bank was later sued, unsuccessfully, for damages by the State Government of Victoria and was subject to some public criticism.

A modification that would substantially mitigate the moral-hazard effects that may be created by regular detailed reporting is to restrict reporting to the disclosure of large material positions in financial markets. In this case, only information on positions is reported, and only positions that are material to the market are reported. A similar system in fact already exists in the United States: banks, corporations, broker-dealers, mutual funds and hedge funds in the United States are required to report spot, forward and derivative transactions for the top five traded currencies to the US Treasury on a weekly, monthly or quarterly basis, depending on how large a player they are. Transactions are not an indication of positions, but the principle that *selected* data can be collected by large players in markets without creating moral hazard has been clearly established.

Table 9.1. *Matrix of transparency of positions in financial markets*

Reporting	By individual institution	In aggregate (i.e., by institution class)
To supervisors	**pros** • know exactly where vulnerabilities lie. **cons** • implicit guarantee to reporting institutions. • information may be used by the authorities against individual parties.	**pros** • know broad trends and vulnerabilities in financial market. • no implicit guarantee to individual reporting institutions. **cons** • need credible collection agency. • need to have secure data collection so that confidentiality of individual positions is repeated.
Publicly, to other market participants	**pros** • all players have full information. **cons** • no one takes positions – liquidity falls.	**pros** • all players know broad trends and vulnerabilities in a market. • removes the timing advantage of large players in releasing information. • other players take contrary positions – liquidity rises, volatility falls. • banks that monitor flows can benchmark and check the accuracy of their information. **cons** • other players mimic large positions – volatility rises. • banks that monitor flows lose their informational advantage.

The second concern about reporting of individual positions to the authorities is that the authorities themselves may use this information in a heavy-handed manner against particular institutions, which may be detrimental to individual institutions and to the development and operation of the country's financial markets. This argument is probably overstated. Speculative positions in east Asia during 1997 and 1998 were almost exclusively established in offshore markets – short positions in Australia, Hong Kong and Malaysia, for example, were established in Singapore, London and New York rather than in domestic markets. Even if the domestic authorities knew who was actually taking the positions, there is virtually nothing they could have done unilaterally. Action would really have depended on the policy response of offshore authorities, particularly those in the United States.

Offshore authorities are unlikely to be willing to use information about individual institutions to the detriment either of their own markets or of institutions domiciled or based in their jurisdiction. Most authorities engage in close dialogue and liaison with banks and other institutions in their jurisdiction, and so tend to have some idea of the positions of HLIs in financial markets. Certainly, in the various forums that have considered the events of 1997 and 1998, offshore authorities do not appear to have been forthcoming with such information. Indeed, the lack of formal reporting of positions gives these authorities 'plausible deniability' in saying that institutions based in their jurisdiction are not destabilising financial markets elsewhere.

In addition to supervisory authorities, individual positions could also be disclosed publicly to all other market participants. The main advantage of this is that it provides full information to the market. The main disadvantage is that it would most likely seriously reduce trading by HLIs and adversely affect liquidity in financial markets. It would not eliminate speculative trading – from the world-wide success of casinos, it is clear that people still gamble even if others know their bet – but the loss of anonymity in markets would substantially reduce it. For this reason, no one seriously proposes full market disclosure of individual positions.

The alternative to disclosure of market positions of individual institutions is disclosure of aggregate positions by institutional class. The advantages of such disclosure to the authorities in individual countries is twofold. First, it provides a broad picture on position-taking in financial markets without pointing the finger at any one particular institution. From the authorities' perspective, the first thing they would do with data on individual positions is aggregate them to get a sense of the pressures in financial markets. If this is the case, they may just as well receive aggregate data, although this would have to include a measure of the concentration of positions. The second advantage is that the pressure to implicitly guarantee reporting institutions is substantially weakened if the authorities only receive aggregate data: if they do not know what each institution is doing, the pressure to support an individual institution dissipates.

There are two disadvantages of providing aggregate positions, but neither would seem to be a serious flaw. The first is finding an institution that can collect and process the information efficiently, quickly and without compromising confidentiality requirements. The institution with the best experience and record in this regard is the Swiss-based Bank for International Settlements (BIS), which has a solid reputation and already collects detailed information on cross-border asset flows by banks and other financial institutions.

The other disadvantage in giving the authorities access to information about aggregate positions is that they may try to find out which particular institution is behind the action in their markets and may attempt to penalise that institution unfairly. This is unlikely to be a serious problem. In the first place, an institution like the BIS is better able than other international financial institutions to resist such pressures. But that presupposes that the BIS itself knows the name of individual parties: if hedge funds report directly to the BIS then the BIS would know the names of the reporting parties, but if the banks which provide facilities to hedge funds report to the BIS, then they might only report aggregate hedge fund positions held with them, which would mean that the BIS would not know individual funds' names. Moreover, for the reasons set out above, it is not clear how most countries could use this information even if they had it since HLIs' speculative position-taking is typically conducted from offshore centres.

Information on aggregate positions by institutional class could also be reported publicly to other market participants. This has the particular advantage that all players would know the broad trends and vulnerabilities in markets, and hence should be able to make better decisions. This is a general public-good argument.

It could also have three other stabilising effects on markets. The first is that the release of information about aggregate positions may constrain some large players from establishing positions as big as they would otherwise have done. This would be especially likely in currency markets. Given that the macro-hedge-fund sector tends to be the one that does most of the plays in currency markets, and given that the macro-hedge-fund sector has tended to be dominated by a half dozen large players, the release of large aggregate positions by hedge funds would tend to be an indicator of substantial activity by a few key funds. Macro hedge funds generally dislike attention, and would likely be inclined to establish smaller positions as a result.

The second stabilising impact is that periodic public release of aggregate positions removes the powerful advantage hedge funds have in timing the release of information to the market about the direction or size of their positions. A classic large-player speculative strategy is to establish the bulk of positions quietly in a market and then engage in some well-publicised trading to spark trading which can shift prices in a profitable direction and provide the necessary liquidity for the large player to reverse his position without causing price movement detrimental to the profitability of his position. The public release of data on aggregate positions to the market on a regular basis tends to deny large players the informational advantage that the academic literature suggests can be a crucial element in generating herding.

The third stabilising effect from releasing data on aggregate positions by institutional class is that it may encourage contrary position-taking. If market participants assess that the market is unsustainably overbought (oversold), they may establish short (long) positions, which would tend to stabilise the market. This is not a necessary outcome: other players may think that the large positions by hedge funds suggest a trend and so mimic their positions.

This is difficult to evaluate. On the one hand, the fact that during the east Asian financial crisis the market tended to sell when there was news of selling by hedge funds suggests that herding could be a problem. But, on the other hand, this was in conditions when HLIs had, to some degree, control of the timing of the release of information to the market, which was certainly in conditions when the market was primed for a fall. Moreover, the information on positions would be, as suggested above, monthly data released with a monthly lag. The effect of this sort of information on herding and momentum trading in a market would likely be less than the effect of the release of information about *current* hedge fund buying or selling in the market. The latter is live information highly relevant to current pricing and momentum, feedback and copycat effects.

One possible disadvantage of releasing aggregate positions by institutional class is that banks and securities firms may lose the informational advantage they have in analysing and selling data on aggregate positions and flows which they collect from the trade that they do for hedge funds and other financial institutions. There is concern that public disclosure may cause a private loss and generate a reduction in the collection and analysis of information.

This concern seems exaggerated.[14] In the first place, the periodicity of the aggregate positions data and the positions and flows data collected by

---

[14] It is also not good economics in the sense that the public provision of information to a wide set of market participants may be more efficient than the collection by a relatively small group of institutions who sell the information at high cost to a relatively small group of clients. If it is costly for individuals to collect information by themselves, then providing that information to them and others at low cost should be a net benefit to them and to other players. The institutions which collect the information can shift scarce resources to more productive areas, and new entrants can add depth to the market.

banks and others is different – the aggregate positions would be monthly data whereas financial institutions monitor their data on flows and positions on a daily basis to inform daily trading – making it hard to believe that public information would usurp the market value of high-frequency private information. In fact, it may complement private monitoring of markets since it would provide an occasional and independent aggregate benchmark by which individual banks and others can assess the comprehensiveness, accuracy and share of their market assessment.

More generally, some market participants think that the current arrangement by which banks and securities firms aggregate, use and sell information based on flows that pass through their books raises an ethical dilemma: banks and securities firms may be using information obtained from clients in a way that does not serve their clients' best interests. These financial institutions, for example, aggregate stocks and flows data from the brokerage services that they provide to hedge funds and others, in order to obtain a picture of aggregate positions and price trends in a market. Using this information, they may reach the conclusion that a market is oversold or overbought and ripe for correction, and so they may buy or sell in the market. The ethical dilemma is that they are using information provided by their client to take a position contrary to that of their client.

Margining requirements

The position-taking by the large macro hedge funds in east Asian (and some other) financial markets in 1997 and 1998 was not subject to margining requirements by their credit providers. That is, the large macro hedge funds were not required to use any of their own capital in establishing positions in the region; effectively, their positions were infinitely leveraged. In fact, these hedge funds were only required to put up capital once their positions had moved beyond a certain loss threshold. The practice of not requiring a margin for particular hedge funds continued into 1999.

One proposal is that supervisors of banks ensure that all borrowers be required to use some of their own capital in establishing positions. The practice of zero margining and loss thresholds arose because of the market power of these hedge funds. It is not desirable, however, that borrowers can effectively obtain credit without putting up any of their own money. If all hedge funds – and, indeed, all would-be users of these facilities – are subject to some margining requirement, then there is at least some external constraint on the size of positions that can be established in a market.

Codes of conduct

One proposal directed at reducing attempted manipulative behaviour in financial markets is to introduce a code of conduct for all market participants. Yam (1999), for example, has argued for a comprehensive voluntary code of conduct for all market participants. He suggests that such a code should include the adoption of enhanced reporting and disclosure standards, internal mechanisms to prevent the creation of false markets, front-running and insider trading, and strict rules proscribing research reports being written for the purpose of benefiting the firm's trading interests.

The advantages of a code are twofold. It is a clear demonstration that financial institutions are committed to sound practices in financial markets. The vast bulk of market participants do not see market disruption as a viable way for conducting business. The other main advantage of a code of conduct is that it provides market participants with a benchmark by which they can structure discussions between themselves and with the authorities on acceptable practices in financial markets. Generally, market participants need to maintain good working relations with other market participants and the authorities, and this tends to provide a sound discipline on manipulative activities. But it is not itself sufficient, especially in periods when the one-time payoffs from such action may be large relative to the costs.

In response to the report of the FSF Working Group on HLIs (2000), the Federal Reserve Bank of New York, the Hong Kong Monetary Authority, the Bank of England, the Monetary Authority of Singapore and the South African Reserve Bank sponsored a meeting of key market participants in June 2000 to devise a voluntary market-based code of conduct in the foreign-exchange market. Sixteen commercial and investment banks issued a code of foreign exchange trading principles on 22 February 2001. This includes declining customer transactions which may disrupt the market, being careful not to exploit customers' interests when the bank trades on its own account, having strong internal guidelines for handling rumours, avoiding manipulative trading practices, and prohibiting deliberate exploitation of electronic dealing systems to generate artificial price behaviour.

While such a voluntary code may work, it has two potential pitfalls. First, it is not specific enough to provide substantive direction to market participants about what is unacceptable behaviour in a market. Second, to be effective, a code has to be enforceable and have penalties for breach. This means that a purely voluntary code without sanctions is likely to prove ineffective, since participants lack a strong incentive to abide by it.

It is probably more effective to make suspension or expulsion from the accrediting body the penalty for breach of the code. It may also be appropriate for jurisdictions to introduce a system of licensing for foreign-exchange dealers. In this case, the penalty for unacceptable behaviour by a trader would be suspension or loss of licence by the trader or a penalty on the institution. Such a code of conduct would require international agreement and enforcement for it to be effective.

Regulating electronic broking in foreign-exchange markets

Foreign-exchange trading currently occurs primarily in broker and interbank markets – increasingly in the former rather than the latter. Trade also occurs in off-market transactions, but this is less frequent and is discouraged by the ACI Code of Conduct. Most broker trade in major currencies is now conducted through electronic trading systems: these provide narrower bid–ask spreads and so are more attractive to customers.

Given the development and diffusion of electronic broking systems and advances in information technology, this market may come to more closely resemble an exchange-traded market, making it possible to regulate some aspects of foreign-exchange trading that were not previously possible. The foreign-exchange market is increasingly becoming like a virtual exchange-traded market.

Different gradations of regulation may be possible. For example, it should be possible to develop regulations with respect to manipulation and acting in good faith, as exist on exchanges. It may also be possible to impose position limits on individual participants in individual currency markets, where the limit might be, say, some proportion of average customer turnover. To prevent price ramping in a market, it may also be possible to impose market-specific limits on selling or buying for particular intervals of time (such as an hour) by individual traders on their own or on a client's behalf, which would have the effect of limiting the intensity or total volume of selling or buying within specified blocks of time. These would obviously have to be set sufficiently high so that liquidity was not adversely affected.

There are three main caveats to regulating electronic broking. The first is that it needs broad international support and implementation, especially from the US Government, if it is to succeed. The second is that it would be ineffective if regulation were so onerous that customers and traders shifted to alternative trading systems, either to the interbank market or engaged in off-market transactions. For this reason, regulation could only be introduced when electronic broking was firmly established as the primary trading mechanism, and regulation would need to be as unobtrusive and simple as possible.

The third caveat is that, at this point in time, regulating electronic broking would seem to be a radical step. Probably the most radical part of this proposal for the foreign-exchange market is that it may at times require traders to reveal the names of their clients to the regulating authority. This would almost certainly be the case if traders faced a limit on the positions they could establish for individual clients. Client confidentiality is a basic principle of foreign-exchange markets, and precludes traders revealing the names of clients to supervisory authorities. But it is important to keep in mind that this is only a feature of the structure of the market as it currently stands. In exchange-traded markets, for example, investors face position limits and traders have to name their customers to the regulating authority. This is the accepted custom. The key in this case is to ensure that legislative safeguards and penalties are sufficiently strong so that commercial confidentiality is preserved by the regulating authorities.

Direct or indirect regulation

To have effect, these proposals would need to be implemented by the authorities in the world's major financial centres, like New York, London and Tokyo. They can be implemented directly by regulating HLIs themselves, or indirectly by expanding the regulation of institutions which are the conduit by which HLIs access financial markets.

There are three arguments against direct regulation of HLIs. The first is that it is costly. The costs to the HLIs could include regulatory and licensing fees, external auditor fees, regulatory reporting costs, systems upgrades, and additional staff to write reports and interact with officials. The costs to regulators – and ultimately the tax-payer – could include an increase in staff at domestic and international institutions to process, analyse and disseminate the information, and costs of publication of results.

The fact that there are costs involved in regulation is not sufficient to conclude that regulation is undesirable: it all turns on a probabilistic judgment of whether the benefits outweigh the costs. Moreover, the costs listed in the previous paragraph are probably overstated. Much, if not all, of the information that would be reported to the authorities is already constructed by HLIs as a standard part of their internal risk management – and, if not, should be. Moreover, systems and technology are regularly updated, which would reduce the direct compliance costs. This means the actual reporting costs are probably low.

The second argument against direct regulation, mostly made by the United States, is that it would create moral hazard: regulated firms may think that the government would be more likely to intervene and so would either reduce their incentive to control risk or assume more risk than otherwise. This argument is not widely accepted. Governments regulate many aspects of economic behaviour without giving the impression that they will guarantee the objects of regulation. Actions, not words, create moral hazard, and the simple remedy against moral hazard is showing that individual institutions will not be prevented from failing.

The argument that regulation of HLIs would lead to moral hazard is also irrelevant because it is arguable that governments have shown that they will intervene to ensure that systemically important yet unregulated institutions are not exposed to full market pressure if such institutions make mistakes. By its intervention in organising the bail-out of LTCM and by cutting interest rates in the aftermath of the crisis in US financial markets at the end of 1998, for example, the Federal Reserve has shown that it is willing to underwrite excessive risk-taking by the US financial system as a whole. The Fed's intervention may have been justified by the pressures on markets at the time, but it is arguable that the moral hazard its actions may have created is much more serious than any increased risk-taking by HLIs just because they are regulated.

The third argument against direct regulation, made by both G-7 and many non-G-7 nations, is that it may be ineffective: financial institutions and markets are highly fungible and have shown over and again that they can avoid controls costly to them. While most hedge fund managers are based in the United States, most hedge funds are offshore entities and, as it currently stands, the only way they are regulated is if they use onshore exchanges. Comprehensive direct regulation would not reach offshore entities and may force onshore hedge funds offshore. Without the power to influence offshore jurisdictions, the introduction of comprehensive regulation would likely be ineffective. Even if onshore hedge funds were regulated, loopholes may exist which would allow new unregulated onshore entities to emerge. This has been the consistent pattern in the post-war history of the regulation of financial institutions. This implies that the more effective way to influence the activities of hedge funds may be through indirect means.

This is the most serious objection to direct regulation. But it is not an absolute. In the first place, international pressure on unregulated offshore financial centres has increased in the past few years, shown, for example, by the report of the FSF Working Group on Offshore Centres (2000). This suggests that substantial shifts of funds offshore would provoke some international policy response. Moreover, the US government has made clear that it will consider direct regulation if market initiatives to properly manage counterparty risks are not properly implemented (President's Working Group on Financial Markets 1999). That said, direct regulation initiated by the United States would likely be as minimal as possible to reduce avoidance effects.

Most countries engaged in the international debate have expressed a clear preference for indirect regulation. The indirect route to influencing the market activities of hedge funds and other speculators is through the institutions that they use to access financial markets and obtain credit, namely the banks and securities firms. These financial institutions are already regulated and supervised, so the issue is one of extending the coverage of existing regulation, rather than creating a new system of regulations. This has indeed been the approach taken by the United States, United Kingdom and other countries in the policy initiatives taken to reduce the systemic risks posed by HLIs.

Consider the way indirect regulation could be used to enforce disclosure of aggregate positions by institutional class in, for example, the foreign-exchange market. Banks provide the swap and forward facilities that enable hedge funds to establish positions in a currency, which means that each bank knows the positions held by hedge funds and others with it. The bank then reports the aggregate figures for each asset class by institution type on its books to a central authority, and this central authority collates and publishes the total figure on aggregate positions by market by institutional class.

Banks have an incentive to comply with this type of reporting because they value their relationships with supervisors. Because banks are providing generic information rather than names to the authorities, they are not revealing possibly client-sensitive information and so do not have an incentive to lie or to not report. Banks in fact have a powerful incentive to tell the truth because, like in any other system of voluntary reporting, they are subject to audit and to substantial penalties if they are caught out. A market incentive for offshore banks to report can also be created by imposing penalties on onshore banks which deal with non-reporting offshore banks. The key to making this work is for banks in all jurisdictions, especially the United States and Europe, to report: international cooperation is crucial, for without effort to ensure that all banks are reporting, the aggregate figures may be wrong and possibly misleading.

Indirect means could also be used, without direct regulation, to provide a market incentive for hedge funds and other unregulated speculators to report their aggregate positions in markets to a central authority, say the BIS. The key is that banks would be required to impose penalty margins on swap, forward and repurchase facilities provided to non-reporting entities. The penalty in this case would have to be substantial if it were to impact on decision making. This approach makes no distinction between onshore and offshore HLIs: the penalty only applies to non-reporting HLIs, and so both onshore and offshore HLIs have an incentive to report.

Limiting access of non-residents

The issue of direct regulation has so far been considered in terms of the jurisdiction of the financial markets in which hedge funds or at least their managers are based, namely the United States and, to a lesser extent, the United Kingdom. The cooperation of the authorities in these countries is crucial to the success of internationally coordinated policy action.

But national governments can also directly influence the activity of HLIs in their financial markets. In this case, the issue is whether governments should impose controls on the capital account to limit speculative activity. The policy option adopted by many countries in east Asia – including Indonesia, Korea, Malaysia, Singapore, Taiwan and Thailand – in the aftermath of the financial crisis has been to limit offshore speculation in their foreign-exchange markets by limiting the access of non-residents to swap facilities.

As explained in Chapter 2, the basic way to establish a short position in a foreign-exchange market is to borrow the currency in the swap market and then sell it in the spot market, leaving the seller with an obligation to repay the amount at some time in the future. One way to limit this sort of speculation is to raise interest rates because this raises the cost of funding the short position. This was not particularly effective in the east Asian crisis because most speculators are familiar with this strategy and obtained long-term funding – say six months to a year – at lower rates in advance. It was also not a particularly credible action since it is hard for policy-makers to keep interest rates very high for very long without seriously damaging the economy and banking system. A sustained rise in interest rates also makes a fall in the exchange rate more likely, and so a speculator who can hold out against the rise in funding costs is more likely to succeed in his bet.

Rather than resist future speculative attacks by raising interest rates, many emerging economies in the region have opted to limit access to domestic-currency swap-funding facilities, and so head off a build up in currency short positions in the first place. This strategy only works if there is not a substantial offshore market in the currency, for otherwise there is a global market for the currency that speculators can use to fund their short positions. The Malaysian authorities, for example, tried to limit swap funding to non-residents in August 1997 but this did not stop speculative activity because a large offshore market existed next door in Singapore. For this reason, Malaysia revoked the convertibilty of ringgit located offshore in September 1998, which effectively destroyed the offshore ringgit market. This indicates a crucial lesson: swap limits can only work to limit offshore speculation if there is no significant offshore market in the currency.

The strategy of limiting swap access also needs to be strictly enforced by banks if it is to work. South Africa, for example, had swap limits in place for non-residents in 1998 but these were completely ineffective, not just because of the large offshore rand market but also because the laws were widely ignored by local banks (FSF Working Group on HLIs 2000). The South African banks were only allowed to provide swap funding to non-residents who had a legitimate trade or investment purpose, but the banks felt unable to enforce this distinction and were not compelled to do so by the central bank. By way of contrast, the same distinction exists in Malaysia and Singapore but banks in both countries strictly enforce the distinction because they fear the penalties that their respective monetary authorities may impose.

Limiting swap funding by non-residents and restricting offshore markets in the currency can be an effective tool to contain external speculative pressure. The crucial issue is whether such a control is desirable over time. While such limits can probably be effective over time if strictly enforced, as the experience of Singapore shows, there is a substantial structural disadvantage from this policy: it limits the ability of countries to diversify their funding sources by borrowing internationally in their own currency, and it prevents residents from shifting foreign exchange and other risk to parties offshore who want that risk.

Having offshore markets in the domestic currency has proven to be a two-edged sword for mid-sized markets. On the one hand, having a large offshore market can make a currency more vulnerable to speculative attacks. The Australian dollar, for example, is the world's seventh most traded currency, and has been the target of proxy plays by speculators (for example, 'if conditions in Asia are deteriorating, so too must be conditions in Australia') and of proxy hedging (for example, 'if Russia collapses, so too will commodity prices, and so short the Australian dollar to hedge against losses in Russian bonds'). In this respect, being a liquid mid-sized market can make the currency vulnerable to foreign shocks.

But, on the other hand, it means that domestic debtors and financial intermediaries are able to pass their currency risk offshore. This is a major advantage to Australia and New Zealand, which have wide fluctuations in their currencies and substantial external liabilities. While both Australia and New Zealand have relatively large external debt, they have been able to substantially, if not completely, hedge their external liabilities through the large offshore markets that exist in their currencies.

Banks in both countries also have very little foreign-exchange exposure (Reserve Bank of Australia 2000). When banks are unable to pass on foreign-exchange-rate risk, they do one of two things. Either they have to bear that risk themselves, in which case they are more vulnerable to currency shocks and more likely to need bail-outs by the prudential and monetary authorities. Or else they force local firms to bear the risk, in which case the corporate sector is more vulnerable to currency shocks. This has been avoided in Australia and New Zealand.

The two-edged sword indicates that policy-makers face a trade-off. While it is always a matter for the local authorities to decide, so long as the capacity of offshore speculators to create currency shocks is contained, it can be sensible policy to shift risk-bearing from onshore institutions to offshore speculators. But until the international community can address the issues of destabilising speculation, east Asian emerging economies are likely to adopt the risk-averse path of limiting offshore speculators.

Endpiece

The east Asian financial crisis was a complex phenomenon. The trigger of the crisis was the deterioration in the Thai current-account deficit and pressure on a fixed exchange rate, but the severity of the crisis was exacerbated by excessive unhedged short-term borrowing in foreign currencies, weak banking and financial systems, policy errors by national governments and international organisations, excessive risk affinity followed by excessive risk aversion by international investors, and bouts of destabilising speculation by either residents or non-residents or sometimes both. There is no one cause of the crisis.

This book has looked at one dimension of the crisis: aspects of speculation in regional financial markets, with focus on the role of highly leveraged institutions, and macro hedge funds in particular. The argument has been simple. Highly leveraged institutions can be an important stabilising influence in financial markets. They can substantially boost liquidity in financial markets and they can increase efficiency. But it is not right to think that they are purely benign forces in financial markets.

As discussed by the President's Working Group on Financial Markets (1999), the LTCM debacle in the United States in 1998 showed that failure by banks to prudently manage credit to large unregulated market participants, and the failure of some of these institutions to prudently manage market and liquidity risk, can substantially increase systemic risks.

As discussed by the FSF Working Group on HLIs (2000), the financial-market dynamics that occurred in the east Asian financial crisis in 1997 and 1998 showed that the activities of a relatively small number of HLIs could undermine the integrity of financial markets. The crisis showed that players with large concentrated positions could have a disproportionate effect on market prices, not least because other players would mimic the large players or would not take contrary positions. It also showed that HLIs could use unacceptably aggressive tactics in markets to bring about price changes to their advantage.

Just as the crisis was a complex phenomenon, so too must be the policy responses. There is no one-shot solution; no policy is a panacea or guarantee against future crises. There has been substantial progress in improving policy structures and institutions in the crisis economies. There has also been limited progress in improving counterparty risk management of hedge funds by banks. But the issue of ensuring that highly leveraged players do not undermine the integrity of financial markets in the future has not been resolved by the international community. Highly leveraged institutions are key players in financial markets but their effects are not always benign, and it is important to deal with the problems that may arise from their activities so that countries can feel confident that they will receive the benefits of international financial integration.

This chapter has summarised four proposals for public discussion: greater transparency of HLI operations, including public disclosure of aggregate positions by institutional class; imposing margining on all swap and repurchase facilities; the introduction of a code of conduct for financial market participants; and, possibly, the regulation of foreign-exchange transactions conducted through electronic broking.

These are modest proposals and they are not made with any expectation that they will prevent all future crises. It is clear from both recent experience and the academic literature that the threat to financial and economic stability posed by the activities of large speculators is not general – it is only likely to arise when there is some vulnerability or uncertainty in the macro or political economy. This is precisely the time when there is a premium on stabilising forces in an economy, and it is this that these proposals seek to attain.

References

Ackermann, C., R. McEnally and D. Ravenscraft (1999), 'The Performance of Hedge Funds: Risk, Return, and Incentives', *Journal of Finance*, 54(3), 833–74.

Agarwal, V. and N. Y. Naik (1999), 'On Taking the "Alternative" Route: Risks, Rewards, Style and Performance Persistence of Hedge Funds', mimeo, London Business School, February.

Allen, F. and D. Gale (1992), 'Stock Price Manipulation', *Review of Financial Studies*, 5(3), 503–29.

Avery, C. and P. Zemsky (1998), 'Multi-dimensional Uncertainty and Herd Behaviour in Financial Markets', *American Economic Review*, 88(4), 724–48.

Bagnoli, M. and B. L. Lipman (1996), 'Stock Price Manipulation through Takeover Bids', *Rand Journal of Economics*, 27(1), 124–47.

Baily, N. M., D. Farrell and S. Lund (2000), 'The Color of Hot Money', *Foreign Affairs*, 79(2), 99–109.

Bank for International Settlements (BIS) (1999), Central Bank Survey of Foreign Exchange and Derivatives Market Activity, Bank for International Settlements, Basle.

Bank for International Settlements (BIS) (1999), 'A Review of Financial Market Events in Autumn 1998', Report of the Committee of the Global Financial System, Basle, October.

Bannerjee, A. V. (1992), 'A Simple Model of Herd Behaviour', *Quarterly Journal of Economics*, 107(3), 797–817.

Barrell, R., B. Anderton, M. Lansbury and J. Sefton (1999), 'FEERs for the NICs: Exchange Rate Policies and Development Strategies in Taiwan, South Korea, Singapore and Thailand', in Stefan Collignon, Jean Pisani-Ferry and Yung Chul Park (eds.), *Exchange Rate Policies in Emerging Asian Countries*, London: Routledge.

Barth, M. and X. Zhang (1999), 'Foreign Equity Flows and the Asian Financial Crisis', in A. Harwood, R. E. Litan and M. Pomerleano (eds.), *Financial Markets and Development: The Crisis in Emerging Markets*, Brookings Institution Press, Washington, D.C., 179–218.

Becker, G. S. (1991), 'A Note on Restaurant Pricing and Other Examples of Social Influence on Price', *Journal of Political Economy*, 99(5), 1109–16.

Benabou, R. and G. Laroque (1992), 'Using Privileged Information to Manipulate Markets: Insiders, Gurus, and Credibility', *Quarterly Journal of Economics*, 107(3), 921–58.

Bikchandani, S., D. Hirshleifer and I. Welch (1992), 'A Theory of Fads, Fashion, Custom and Cultural Change as Informational Cascades', *Journal of Political Economy*, 100(5), 992–1026.

Blundell-Wignall, A., J. Fahrer and A. Heath (1994), 'Major Influences on the Australian Dollar Exchange Rate', in Adrian Blundell-Wignall (ed.), *The Exchange Rate, International Trade and the Balance of Payments*, Reserve Bank of Australia, Sydney, 30–78.

Bonin, J. and Y. P. Huang (2000), 'Dealing with the Bad Loans of the Chinese Banks', mimeo, Department of Economics, Wesleyan University, Middletown, CT.

Brennan, M. J. (1990), 'Latent Assets', *Journal of Finance*, 45, 709–30.

Brown, S. J, W. N. Goetzman and R. G. Ibbotson (1998), 'Offshore Hedge Funds: Survival and Performance', *Journal of Business*, 72(1), 91–117.

Brown, S. J, W. N. Goetzman and J. Park (1999), 'Hedge Funds and the Asian Currency Crisis', NBER Working Paper No. 6427.

Brunnermeier, M. K. (1998a), 'Prices, Price Processes, Volume and the Information – a Survey of the Market Microstructure Literature', London School of Economics, Financial Markets Group Discussion Paper No. 270.

Brunnermeier, M. K. (1998b), 'Buy on Rumors – Sell on News: a Manipulative Trading Strategy', London School of Economics, Financial Markets Group Discussion Paper No. 309.

Caldwell, T. (1995), 'Introduction: The Model for Superior Performance', in Jess Lederman and Robert A. Klein (eds.), *Hedge Funds: Investment and Portfolio Strategies for the Institutional Investor*, New York: McGraw Hill.

Chadha, B. and A. Jansen (1998), 'The Hedge Fund Industry: Structure, Size and Performance', chapter 3 in Barry Eichengreen, Donald Mathieson, Bankim Chadha, Anne Jansen, Laura Kodres, and Sunil Sharma (eds), *Hedge Funds and Financial Dynamics*, Washington, D.C.: International Monetary Fund, May, 27–41.

Chamley, C. and D. Gale (1994), 'Information Revelation and Strategic Delay in a Model of Investment', *Econometrica*, 62, 1065–85.

Chinn, M. D. (1998), 'Before the Fall: Were East Asian Currencies Overvalued?', NBER Working Paper No. 6491.

Corsetti, G., P. Pesenti and N. Roubini (1998), 'Fundamental Determinants of the Asian Crisis: A Preliminary Empirical Assessment', mimeo.

Corsetti, G., A. Dasgupta, S. Morris and H. S. Shin (2000), 'Does One Soros Make a Difference? A Theory of Currency Crises with Large and Small Traders', mimeo.

Cottier, P. (1997), *Hedge Funds and Managed Futures*, Bank und Finanzwirtschaftliche Forschungen, Band 246, Bern: Verlag Paul Haupt.

Counterparty Risk Management Policy Group (1999), 'Improving Counterparty Risk Management Practices', New York, June.

Counterparty Risk Management Policy Group (2000), 'Sound Practices for Hedge Fund Managers', New York, February.

Cutler, D. M., J. M. Poterba and L. H. Summers (1990a), 'Speculative Dynamics', NBER Working Paper No. 3242.

Cutler, D. M., J. M. Poterba and L. H. Summers (1990b), 'Speculative Dynamics and the Role of Feedback Traders', NBER Working Paper No. 3243.

de Brouwer, G. J. (1999a), *Financial Integration in East Asia*, Cambridge: Cambridge University Press.

de Brouwer, G. J. (1999b), 'Capital Flows to East Asia: the Facts', in David Gruen and Luke Gower (eds.), *Capital Flows and the International Financial System*, Sydney: Reserve Bank of Australia, 76–88.

de Brouwer, G. J. (2001), 'Does a Formal Common Basket Peg for East Asia Make Economic Sense?', chapter 12 in Gordon de Brouwer (ed.), *Financial Markets and Policies in East Asia*, London: Routledge.

De Long, J. B., A. Shleifer, L. B. Summers and R. J. Waldeman (1990a), 'Positive Feedback Investment Strategies and Destabilizing Rational Speculation', *Journal of Finance*, 45(2), 379–95.

De Long, J. B., A. Shleifer, L. B. Summers and R. J. Waldeman (1990b), 'Noise Trader Risk in Financial Markets', *Journal of Political Economy*, 98(4), 703–38.

De Long, J. B., A. Shleifer, L. B. Summers and R. J. Waldeman (1991), 'The Survival of Noise Traders in Financial Markets', *Journal of Business*, 64, 1–19.

Devenow, A. and I. Welch (1996), 'Rational Herding in Financial Economics', *European Economic Review*, 40, 603–15.

Dooley, M. P. and C. Walsh (1999), 'Academic Views on Capital Flows: an Expanding Universe', in David Gruen and Luke Gower (eds.), *Capital Flows and the International Financial System*, Sydney: Reserve Bank of Australia, 89–108.

Dornbusch, R. (1976), 'Expectations and Exchange Rate Dynamics', *Journal of Political Economy*, 84(6), 1161–76.

Dornbusch, R. and Y. C. Park (1999), 'Flexibility or Nominal Anchors?', in Stefan Collignon, Jean Pisani-Ferry and Yung Chul Park (eds.), *Exchange Rate Policies in Emerging Asian Countries*, London: Routledge, 3–34.

Dunbar, N. (2000), *Inventing Money: the Story of Long-Term Capital Management and the Legends Behind It*, New York: John Wilcy and Sons.

Easley, D. and M. O'Hara (1992), 'Time and the Process of Security Price Adjustment', *Journal of Finance*, 47, 577–605.

Edwards, F. R. (1999), 'Hedge Funds and the Collapse of Long-Term Capital Management', *Journal of Economic Perspectives*, 13(2), 189–210.

Edwards, F. R. and J. Liew (1999), 'Hedge Funds versus Managed Futures as Asset Classes', *Journal of Derivatives*, Summer, 45–63.

Eichengreen, B. and D. Mathieson (1998a), 'Overview', chapter 1 in Barry Eichengreen, Donald Mathieson, Bankim Chadha, Anne Jansen, Laura Kodres, and Sunil Sharma, *Hedge Funds and Financial Dynamics*, Washington, D.C.: International Monetary Fund, May, 1.

Eichengreen, B. and D. Mathieson (1998b), 'Hedge Funds and Financial Markets: Implications for Policy', chapter 2 in Barry Eichengreen, Donald Mathieson, Bankim Chadha, Anne Jansen, Laura Kodres, and Sunil Sharma, *Hedge Funds and Financial Dynamics*, Washington, D.C.: International Monetary Fund, May, 2–26.

Eichengreen, B., D. Mathieson, B. Chadha, A. Jansen, L. Kodres and S. Sharma (1998), *Hedge Funds and Financial Market Dynamics*, Washington, D.C.: International Monetary Fund, May.

Financial Stability Forum (FSF) Working Group on Offshore Centres (2000), *Report*, Washington, D.C., March.

Financial Stability Forum Working Group on Highly Leveraged Institutions (2000), Washington, D.C., March.

Flood, R. and P. Garber (1984), 'Collapsing Exchange Rate Regimes: Some Linear Examples', *Journal of Money, Credit, and Banking*, 11, 311–25.

Frankel, J. and K. Froot (1988), 'Explaining the Demand for Dollars: International Rates of Return and the Expectation of Chartists and Fundamentalists', in R. Chambers and P. Paarlberg (eds.), *Agriculture, Macroeconomics, and the Exchange Rate*, Boulder, CO: Westfield Press.

Frankel, J. and N. Roubini (2000), 'The Role of Industrial Country Policies in Emerging Market Crises', paper presented at the NBER Conference on Economic and Financial Crises in Emerging Market Economies, Woodstock, Vermont, October.

Friedman, M. (1953), 'The Case for Flexible Exchange Rates', in Milton Friedman (ed.), *Essays in Positive Economics*, Chicago: University of Chicago Press.

Froot, K. A. and R. H. Thaler (1990), 'Anomalies: Foreign Exchange', *Journal of Economic Perspectives*, 4(3), 179–92.

Froot, K. A., D. S. Scharfstein and J. C. Stein (1992), 'Herd on the Street: Informational Inefficiencies in a Market with Short-Term Speculation', *Journal of Finance*, 47(4), 1461–84.

Fung, W. and D. Hsieh (1997), 'Empirical Characteristics of Dynamic Trading Strategies: the Case of Hedge Funds', *Review of Financial Studies*, 10(2), 275–302.

Fung, W. and D. Hsieh (1999), 'Measuring the Market Impact of Hedge Funds', mimeo, Paradigm Financial Products International and Duke University, October.

Fung, W., D. Hsieh and K. Tsatsaronis (1999), 'Do Hedge Funds Disrupt Emerging Markets?', presented at the Brookings-Wharton Papers on Financial Services Third Annual Conference, 28–29 October.

Furman, J. and J. E. Stiglitz (1998), 'Economic Crises: Evidence and Insights from East Asia', *Brookings Papers on Economic Activity*, 2, 1–135.

G-22 Working Group on Transparency and Accountability (1998), *Report of the Working Group on Transparency and Accountability*, October, available at the *http://www.bis.org* and the websites of the IMF, OECD and World Bank.

Gennotte, G. and H. Leland (1990), 'Market Liquidity, Hedging, and Crashes', *American Economic Review*, 80(5), 999–1021.

Glosten, L. (1989), 'Insider Trading, Liquidity, and the Role of the Monopolist Specialist', *Journal of Business*, 62, 211–35.

Goldman Sachs & Co. and Financial Risk Management (2000), 'Hedge Funds Revisited', *Pension and Endowment Forum*, January.

Graham, J. R. (1999), 'Herding Among Investment Newsletters: Theory and Evidence', *Journal of Finance*, 54(1), 237–68.

Grenville, S. A. (1998), 'Capital Flows and Crises', Reserve Bank of Australia *Bulletin*, December, 16-31.

Grossman, S. J. and J. E. Stiglitz (1980), 'On the Impossibility of Informationally Efficient Markets', *American Economic Review*, 70(3), 393–408.

Group of Hedge Fund Managers (2000), 'Sound Practices for Hedge Fund Managers', published by the group (Caxton Corporation, Kingdon Capital Management, Moore Capital Management, Soros Fund Management and Tudor Investment Corporation) in New York, February.

Gul, F. and R. Lundholm (1995), 'Endogenous Timing and the Clustering of Agents' Decisions', *Journal of Political Economy*, 103, 1039–66.

Hirshleifer, D. (1995), 'The Blind Leading the Blind: Social Influence, Fads, and Informational Cascades', in Mariano Tommasi and Kathryn Ierulli (eds.), *The New Economics of Human Behaviour*, Cambridge: Cambridge University Press, 188–215.

Hirshleifer, D., A. Subrahmanyam and S. Titman (1994), 'Security Analysis and Trading Patterns When Some Investors Receive Information Before Others', *Journal of Finance*, 49(5), 1665–98.

Hong Kong Monetary Authority (HKMA) 1998, 'Strengthening of Currency Board Arrangements in Hong Kong', HKMA *Quarterly Bulletin*, November, 7–11.

Hong Kong Special Administrative Region Government (HKSARG) (1998), *Report on Financial Market Review*, Financial Services Bureau, April.

Hull, J. C. (2000), *Options, Futures, and Other Derivatives*, Upper Saddle River, N.J.: Prentice Hall International, 4th edition.

Investment Company Institute (1997), 'The Organization and Operation of a Mutual Fund', *http://www.ici.org/issues/organization_operatoin.html*.

Investment Company Institute (1998), 'Differences Between Mutual Funds and Hedge Funds', *http://www.ici.org/issues/organization_operatoin.html*.

Investment Company Institute (2000), 'Mutual Fund Factbook', *http://www.ici.org/aboutfunds/factbook00_toc.html*.

Ito, T., E. Ogawa and Y. N. Sasaki (1998), 'How Did the Dollar Peg Fail in Asia?', NBER Working Paper No. 6729.

Jarrow, R. A. (1992), 'Market Manipulation, Bubbles, Corners and Short Squeezes', *Journal of Financial and Quantitative Analysis*, 27(3), 311–36.

Karpoff, J. (1987), 'The Relation between Price Changes and Trading Volume: a Survey', *Journal of Financial and Quantitative Analysis*, 22, 109–26.

Kawai, M. and S. Akiyama (2000), 'Implications of the Currency Crisis for Exchange Rate Arrangements in Emerging East Asia', mimeo, World Bank, Washington, D.C.

Kawai, M. and S. Takagi (2000), 'The Strategy for a Regional Exchange Rate Arrangement in Post-Crisis East Asia: Analysis, Review and Proposal', mimeo, World Bank, Washington, D.C.

Keynes, J. M. (1936), *The General Theory of Employment, Interest and Money*, Macmillan: London.

Kodres, L. (1998a), 'Hedge Fund Investment Strategies', chapter 4 in Barry Eichengreen, Donald Mathieson, Bankim Chadha, Anne Jansen, Laura Kodres, and Sunil Sharma (eds.), *Hedge Funds and Financial Dynamics*, Washington, D.C.: International Monetary Fund, May, 42–54.

Kodres, L. (1998b), 'Effects of Hedge Funds' Strategies on Price Dynamics', chapter 5 in Barry Eichengreen, Donald Mathieson, Bankim Chadha, Anne Jansen, Laura Kodres, and Sunil Sharma (eds.), *Hedge Funds and*

Financial Dynamics, Washington, D.C.: International Monetary Fund, May, 55–61.

Krugman, P. (1979), 'A Model of Balance of Payments Crises', *Journal of Money, Credit, and Banking*, 11(3), 311–25.

— (1993), 'What Do We Need to Know About the International Monetary System?', Department of Economics, Princeton University, Essays in International Finance No. 190.

— (1996), 'Are Currency Crises Self Fulfilling', NBER Macroeconomics Annual.

— (1997), 'Currency Crises', *http://web.mit.edu/krugman/www/crises.html*.

— (1998), What Happened to Asia?', *http://web.mit.edu/krugman/www/DISINTER.html*.

Kumar, P. and D. J. Seppi (1992), 'Futures Manipulation with "Cash Settlement"', *Journal of Finance*, 47(4), 1485–502.

Kyle, A. S. (1985), 'Continuous Auctions and Insider Trading', *Econometrica*, 53, 1315–35.

Martin, G. (2000), 'Making Sense of Hedge Fund Returns: What Matters and What Doesn't', *Derivatives Strategy*.

Meese, R. A. and K. Rogoff (1983), 'Empirical Exchange Rate Models of the Seventies: Do They Fit Out Of Sample?', *Journal of International Economics*, 14(1/2), 3–24.

Moon, W. S. and Y. S. Rhee (2001), 'Foreign Exchange Market Liberalization Policies in Korea: Past Assessment and Future Options', in Lee (ed.), *Globalization in the New Millenium*, London: Routledge.

Moon, W. S., Y. S. Rhee and D. R. Yoon (2000), 'Asian Monetary Cooperation: a Search for Regional Monetary Stability in the Post Euro and the Post Asian Crisis Era', Bank of Korea, *Economic Papers*, 3(1), 157–93.

Moonen, R. T. L. (1999), 'The LTCM Crisis and its Consequences for Banks and Banking Supervision', OECD, *Financial Market Trends*, 73, June, 97–107.

Murase, T. (2000), *Ajia Antei Tsuukaken: Yuroo ni Manabu Yen no Yakuwari (The Asian Zone of Monetary Stability: Lessons from the Euro and Role of the Yen)*, Tokyo: Keiso Shobo.

Nofsinger, J. R. and R. W. Sias (1999), 'Herding and Feedback Trading by Institutional and Individual Investors', *Journal of Finance*, 54(6), 2263–95.

Obstfeld, M. (1994), 'The Logic of Currency Crises', *Cahiers Economiques et Monetaires (Banque de France)*, 43, 189–213.

— (1996), 'Models of Currency Crises with Self-fulfilling Features', *European Economic Review*, 40(3-5), 1037–47.

OECD Committee on Financial Markets (1999), 'Background Note on Hedge Funds, Highly Leveraged Investment Strategies and Financial Markets', Paris, February.

O'Hara, M. (1995; reprinted 1997), *Market Microstructure Theory*, London: Routledge.

Post, M. A. and K. Millar (1998), 'US Emerging Market Equity Funds and the 1997 Crisis in Asian Financial Markets', Investment Company Institute, *Perspective*, 4(2), June (*www.ici.org*).

President's Working Group on Financial Markets (1999), 'Hedge Funds, Leverage, and the Lessons of Long-Term Capital Management', Washington, D.C., April.

Radelet, S. (1999), 'Indonesia: Long Road to Recovery', Harvard University, Harvard Institute for International Development, Development Discussion Paper No. 722.

Radelet, S. and J. Sachs (1998), 'The East Asian Financial Crisis: Diagnosis, Remedies, Prospects', mimeo, Harvard University.

Rankin, R. (1999), 'The Impact of Hedge Funds on Financial Markets: Lessons from the Experience of Australia', in David Gruen and Luke Gower (eds.), *Capital Flows and the International Financial System*, Sydney: Reserve Bank of Australia, 151–63.

Reserve Bank of Australia (RBA) (1999a), 'Hedge Funds, Financial Stability and Market Integrity', paper submitted to the House of Representatives Standing Committee on Economics, Finance and Public Administration's Inquiry into the International Markets Effects on Government Policy, June.

Reserve Bank of Australia (RBA) (1999b), 'The Impact of Hedge Funds on Financial Markets', paper submitted to the House of Representatives Standing Committee on Economics, Finance and Public Administration's Inquiry into the International Markets Effects on Government Policy, June.

Sakakibara, E. (2001), 'Korea-Japan Foreign Exchange Cooperation', chapter 13 in Gordon de Brouwer (ed.), *Financial Markets and Policies in East Asia*, London: Routledge.

Scharfstein, D. S. and J. C. Stein (1990), 'Herd Behaviour and Investment', *American Economic Review*, 80(3), 465–79.

Schneeweis, T. and R. Spurgin (1999), 'Quantitative Analysis of Hedge Fund and Managed Futures Return and Risk Characteristics', in R. Lake (ed.), *Evaluating and Implementing Hedge Fund Strategies*.

Sharma, S. (1998), 'Regulation of Hedge Funds', chapter 6 in Barry Eichengreen, Donald Mathieson, Bankim Chadha, Anne Jansen, Laura Kodres, and Sunil Sharma (eds.), *Hedge Funds and Financial Dynamics*, Washington, D.C.: International Monetary Fund, May, 62–71.

Sharpe, W. F. (1992), 'Asset Allocation: Management Style and Performance Measurement', *Journal of Portfolio Management*, 18(2), 7–19.

Shleifer, A. (2000), *Inefficient Markets: an Introduction to Behavioural Finance*, Oxford: Oxford University Press, Clarendon Lectures in Economics.

Shleifer, A. and L. H. Summers (1990), 'The Noise Trader Approach to Finance', *Journal of Economic Perspectives*, 4(2), 19–33.

Soros, G. (1987), *The Alchemy of Finance*, New York: Simon and Schuster.

Stickel, S. E. and R. E. Verrecchia (1993), 'Evidence that Volume Sustains Price Changes', Wharton School Working Paper.

Stolz, W. (1998), 'Let the Hedge Funds Grow', *Risk*, November.

Summers, L. (1986), 'Does the Stock Market Rationally Reflect Fundamental Values?', *Journal of Finance*, 41(3), 591–601.

Sveriges Riksbank (1999), 'Hedge Funds Troublemakers?', *Quarterly Review*, 1, 18–42.

Tarditi, A. (1996), 'Modelling the Australian Exchange Rate, Long Bond Yield and Inflationary Expectations', Reserve Bank of Australia Research Discussion Paper No. 9608.

Train, J. (1987), *The Money Matters*, New York: Harper and Row.

Traynor, J. L. and R. Ferguson (1985), 'In Defense of Technical Analysis', *Journal of Finance*, 40, 757–75.

Tsang (1998)

Van Hedge (1999), 'Number of Hedge Funds Increases for Tenth Consecutive Year', 21 September, *http://www.vanhedge.com/size.htm*.

Vila, J.-L. (1989), 'Simple Games of Market Manipulation', *Economics Letters*, 29, 21–26.

Vives, X. (1995), 'How Fast Do Rational Agents Learn?', *Review of Financial Studies*, 7, 97–124.

Welch, I. (1992), 'Sequential Sales, Learning, and Cascades', *Journal of Finance*, 47(2), 695–732.

Wermers, R. (1999), 'Mutual Fund Herding and the Impact on Stock Prices', *Journal of Finance*, 54(2), 581–622.

Williamson, J. (1999), 'The Case for a Common Basket Peg for East Asian Currencies', in Stefan Collignon, Jean Pisani-Ferry and Yung Chul Park (eds.), *Exchange Rate Policies in Emerging Asian Countries*, London: Routledge, 327–43.

Yam, J. (1999), 'Capital Flows, Hedge Funds and Market Failure: A Hong Kong Perspective', in David Gruen and Luke Gower (eds.), *Capital Flows and the International Financial System*, Sydney: Reserve Bank of Australia, 164–78.

Yoshino, N., S. Koji and A. Suzuki (2000), 'Basket Peg, Dollar Peg and Floating: a Comparative Analysis of Exchange Rate Regimes', Keio University, mimeo.

Zhang, J. (1997), 'Strategic Delay and the Onset of Investment Cascades', *Rand Journal of Economics*, 28(1).

Zwiebel, J. (1995), 'Corporate Conservatism and Relative Compensation', *Journal of Political Economy*, 103(1), 1–25.

Index